New York for Sale

Urban and Industrial Environments
Series editor: Robert Gottlieb, Henry R. Luce Professor of Urban and Environmental Policy, Occidental College

For a complete list of books published in this series, please see the back of the book.

New York for Sale

Community Planning Confronts Global Real Estate

Tom Angotti

The MIT Press
Cambridge, Massachusetts
London, England

For information about special quantity discounts, please e-mail <special_sales@mitpress.mit.edu>.

This book was set in Sabon by SNP Best-set Typesetter Ltd., Hong Kong

Printed on recycled paper and bound in the United States of America.

Library of Congress Cataloging-in-Publication Data

Angotti, Thomas, 1941–
New York for sale : community planning confronts global real estate / Tom Angotti.
   p. cm. – (Urban and industrial environments)
Includes bibliographical references and index.
ISBN 978-0-262-01247-8 (hardcover : alk. paper)
1. Community development—New York (State)—New York. 2. Marginality, Social—New York (State)—New York. 3. Gentrification—New York (State)—New York 4. Land use—New York (State)—New York. I. Title.

HN80.N5A627   2008
307.1′216097471—dc22

                                                         2008016470

10 9 8 7 6 5 4 3 2 1

For Emma

Contents

Foreword: So What's Community Planning?

Peter Marcuse

So what's so great about community planning? If it's everything Tom Angotti says it is, then why isn't it better recognized, debated, practiced, and fought for? And what is it, anyway? Is it just community-scaled planning—below the level of the city and above that of the neighborhood? Planning has to be at all scales. What's so surprising about that?

To start with what it is: Angotti is very clear in his text and examples that he has a broad definition in mind, and he often uses the phrase *progressive community-based planning* to indicate it. All four words count. Not every community plan is progressive: some are exclusionary, and Angotti gives examples. Planning for a luxury, predictably white, gated community is not progressive, in any sense of that term. There may be debate about the exact meaning of *progressive*, but there isn't much at the extremes of what is and what isn't progressive. Concerns for social justice and equality, a focus on those with greatest needs, and an emphasis on use values over exchange values all come into play. In any case, the mere fact that the word *community* is invoked, without the *progressive*, doesn't define the terrain.

Neither does scale: community planning is not simply one level of planning among others, although it is that too. Many (probably most) problems of communities come from the outside and need action at a broader level—from city to nation to global—to get at the causes. And one can plan at the scale of the community from the top down. One can feed community-level data into a technically oriented city planning department and find a community plan coming back down. That doesn't deserve to be called community planning, and Angotti wouldn't admit it as such. He would insist on the *based* in the concept *community-based*. This is a tricky concept. He doesn't mean, necessarily, community-based as an organic intellectual might, although he would certainly acknowledge the importance of the Gramsci concept. It certainly means more than some minimal level of community participation in which the community simply provides information to an outside planner. It means planning that has its basis in the interests and desires and fears of the community and that allows the planner to identify with the community in her or his work. So a professional planner can be working for a city planning department or a local community board on the same project. Whether the outcome is community-based will depend largely on that planner's relationship with the community in which the planner is based.

And *planning*, the fourth term in the definition, is essential. Not every activist struggle on behalf of an oppressed community is planning. The tools, skills, and experiences that professional planners have or should have can be put to use in the service of communities in need and can be transmitted to their proposed beneficiaries in the process. Angotti has in mind in much of this book the professionally trained planner who hopes to put progressive principles in practice, and his examples of the possibilities are telling.

Indeed, that is why this book should be required reading not only for the veterans of the trenches but also for aspiring students and new entrants into the field—to show the range of possibilities that are open to those with a mind for it. Progressive community-based planning is not at the apex of the earning structure of planning. It is messy, often difficult work that usually involves conflicts with higher-ups at various levels and is rarely rewarded with prizes. That's why so little is written about it in establishment circles and why books like this one are important.

And yet what Angotti describes here stands in a proud tradition in planning and in the history of city development. In New York City alone, the names that spring to mind include Jane Jacobs, Paul Davidoff, Walter Thabit, the Architects Renewal Committee for Harlem, Planners for Equal Opportunity and Planners Network, and countless others. An honor roll of planners concerned with progressive causes might be well worth putting together. As a start, the list might include Chester Hartman, Jackie Leavitt, Ken Reardon, Norman Krumholz, Frances Goldin, Leonie Sandercock, Susan Fainstein, and the Right to the City Activists.

And a final word on what this book does: Planning is not just process (although it is that). It is process in an immediate reality. Progressive community-based planners are not born that way. They become that by seeing what is happening in the world, the city, and the communities around them. To portray community planning as simply another field of technical competence, as many see transportation planning or environmental planning or housing, misses the point. Progressive community-based planning is produced by the issues that confront low-income, often neglected communities in our cities. Angotti has picked out the two front-line issues of this nature in New York City, but relevant everywhere—(1) the extent to which strong real estate interests dominate the planning process in the interests of maximizing real estate values and profits and (2) the resistance to many of the proposals pressed by those interests that result in displacement of established neighborhoods and destruction of communities. These are classic conflicts. This is what progressive community-based planning today is all about, willy-nilly. By putting planning process in this real-world context, Angotti adds the touch and feel and smell of truth to the picture he paints and the proposals he makes.

May this book be widely read and widely taken to heart.

Preface

This book comes out of two decades of my own involvement in neighborhood-based planning in New York City as a professional planner both inside and outside government. I worked with the Red Hook and UNITY (UNderstanding, Imagining and Transforming the Yards) plans in Brooklyn, among many others, and with the Organization of Waterfront Neighborhoods. For six years, I chaired the Pratt Institute Graduate Center for Planning and the Environment and worked with many communities on planning issues. I am a member of the Steering Committee of Planners Network, an organization of progressive urban planners and activists since 1975, and coedit *Progressive Planning Magazine*. I am also a founding member of the New York City Campaign and Task Force on Community-based Planning and write the monthly Land Use column for *Gotham Gazette* (<http://www.gothamgazette.com>). This book is thus a product of engagement in practice, and I wrote it primarily to help inform the practice of community planning. I have tried to be faithful to the truth and the facts I have uncovered but make no claims of total objectivity. I remain an unabashed advocate of community-based planning as an instrument for achieving greater social justice. I do not glorify local community planning and make a clear distinction between the inclusionary, democratic practices linked to global struggles for social equality and the exclusionary, elite practices that serve exclusionary local property interests.

This book is written for community planners, both the experts who have no formal professional training but learned by doing and the professionals and students everywhere who do and study community planning. Its purpose is to develop the theory and practice of community planning, community organizing, and long-range political strategies that improve the quality of life and eliminate inequities in urban neighborhoods. I have put references in an end-of-book notes section and a

selected bibliography to help make the narrative more accessible to those
who are outside academic communities. While this is clearly an insider's
view of New York, I expect that it will be meaningful to planners and
organizers in other cities around the world, especially those with powerful finance and real estate sectors. New Yorkers may be familiar with
the stories told here, but I do not think anyone has put them together
before and interpreted them in the way I have. And few have made the
connections I have made between urban social movements, global real
estate and urban planning.

Several escapes from New York during the more than five years it took
to complete this work helped achieve some detachment, including five
months at the Cornell program in Rome, two months as a Fulbright
senior specialist, and two weeks at the Mesa Refuge in Point Reyes,
California.

Three friends who recently passed away—Linda Davidoff, Ed
Rogowsky, and Walter Thabit—were inspirations and are sorely missed.
Many thanks to Peter Marcuse, James DeFillipis, Eva Hanhardt, and
Tom Gogan for comments on early drafts. Eddie Bautista, Eva Hanhardt,
and Ron Shiffman deserve special mention for their contributions to the
cause of democratic community-based planning and environmental
justice in New York City. I have learned a great deal from them. Caterina
Timpanaro's work on community planning in Italy has been insightful,
and I thank her for her work on researching the illustrations for this
book. Laura Saija's expertise in graphics is responsible for the cover
design and finishing of all the illustrations. Thanks to Andrew Maroko
for compiling two maps. The many grassroots community activists I
have interacted with, too numerous to mention, are the real experts who
have taught us all. I also appreciate the collaboration and support I have
received from Eve Baron, Ethan Cohen, Mario Coyula, Nadia Crisafuli,
Dana Driskell, Ann Forsyth, Frances Goldin, Filippo Gravagno, Rosalind
Greenstein, Jill Hamberg, Chester Hartman, Michael Heiman, Marie
Kennedy, Brian Ketcham, Carolyn Konheim, Norman Krumholz, Jac-
queline Leavitt, Norma Rantisi, Ken Reardon, Marci Reaven, Alejandro
Rofman, Bruce Rosen, Arturo Sánchez, Mitch Silver, Beverly Moss Spatt,
Lorenzo Venturini, and Julie Sze. I have learned from the work of my
Hunter College colleagues Nick Freudenberg, Jill Gross, Lynn McCormick,
Terry Mizrahi, Jan Poppendieck, Laxmi Ramasubramanian, Sigmund
Shipp, and Susan Turner-Meiklejohn. Cecilia Jagu helped with research on
Cooper Square. The Gotham Center Seminar in 2004, which was
organized by Mike Wallace, helped me develop the early chapters, and

the final chapters were drafted in the supportive environment of the Mesa Refuge in California. A grant from the Lincoln Institute of Land Policy assisted with research on Cooper Square. City Council member Leticia James and State Assembly member Valmanette Montgomery provided valuable leadership and funding for work on the Atlantic Yards environmental assessment through the Council of Brooklyn Neighborhoods to the Hunter College Center for Community Planning and Development.

List of Acronyms

AAFE   Asian Americans for Equality
ACORN   Association of Community Organizations for Reform Now
ARCH   Architects Renewal Committee of Harlem
BID   business improvement district
BMT   Brooklyn-Manhattan Transit
CAFE   Community Alliance for the Environment
CBA   community benefits agreement
CBD   central business district
CCRP   Comprehensive Community Revitalization Plan
CDBG   Community Development Block Grant
CDC   community development corporation
CEQR   City Environmental Quality Review
CLT   community land trust
COHRE   Center on Housing Rights and Evictions
CPC   City Planning Commission
CRA   Community Reinvestment Act
CURE   Communities United for Responsible Energy
DAMP   Division of Alternative Management Programs
DCP   Department of City Planning
DOS   Department of Sanitation
DOT   Department of Transportation
DUMBO   Down under the Manhattan and Brooklyn Overpass
EDC   Economic Development Corporation
EDF   Environmental Defense Fund

EFCB	Emergency Finance Control Board
EIS	environmental impact statement
EPA	Environmental Protection Agency
ESDC	Empire State Development Corporation
FAC	Fifth Avenue Committee
FCR	Forest City Ratner
FIRE	finance, insurance, and real estate
GAGS	Groups against Garbage Stations
GIS	geographic information systems
GOLES	Good Ole' Lower East Side
HKNA	Hell's Kitchen Neighborhood Association
HPD	Department of Housing Preservation and Development
IBO	Independent Budget Office
IND	Independent Subway
IRT	Interborough Rapid Transit
JASA	Jewish Association of Services for the Aged
JPC	Joint Planning Council
LCAN	Labor Community Advocacy Network
LMDC	Lower Manhattan Development Corporation
LULU	local unwanted land use
MHA	mutual housing association
MTA	Metropolitan Transporation Authority
NIMBY	not in my back yard
NRDC	Natural Resources Defense Council
NYCEJA	New York City Environmental Justice Alliance
OPEC	Organization of Petroleum Exporting Countries
OWN	Organization of Waterfront Neighborhoods
PAC	project area committee
PANYNJ	Port Authority of New York and New Jersey
PDC	Public Development Corporation
PICCED	Pratt Institute Center for Community and Environmental Development

PILOT	payment in lieu of taxes
PN	Planners Network
REBNY	Real Estate Board of New York
REIT	real estate investment trust
RPA	Regional Plan Association
SBLDC	South Brooklyn Local Development Corporation
SWMP	Solid Waste Management Plan
TA	Transportation Alternatives
TIF	tax increment financing
TIL	Tenant Interim Lease Program
TINA	There is no alternative
UDC	Urban Development Corporation
UHAB	Urban Homesteading Assistance Board
ULURP	Uniform Land Use Review Procedure
UPROSE	United Puerto Ricans of Sunset Park
WE ACT	West Harlem Environmental Action

Chronology of Major Planning Events in New York City

1898   The City of New York is established as a consolidation of Manhattan, Brooklyn, Bronx, Queens, and Staten Island. The United States invades Cuba, the Philippines, and Puerto Rico.

1916   The Zoning Resolution is passed.

1921   New York State passes the first law regulating rents.

1933   The Great Depression begins.

1934   Fiorello LaGuardia becomes mayor and serves until 1945. First Houses in the Lower East Side is the first public housing project.

1949   The federal urban renewal program is authorized.

1961   A new Zoning Resolution is passed. Jane Jacobs publishes *The Death and Life of Great American Cities*. The Cooper Square Alternate Plan, the first community plan in New York City, is completed.

1964   President Lyndon Johnson launches the federal War on Poverty.

1965   Black parents and residents launch a school boycott to advocate for community control of schools.

1966   John Lindsay becomes mayor.

1969   The New York City Master Plan is completed (but never approved).

1968   Workers and students protest globally. Martin Luther King Jr. is assassinated. Students occupy buildings at Columbia University to protest the university's expansion in neighboring Harlem.

1974   Abraham Beame becomes mayor.

1977   The Uniform Land Use Review Procedure (ULURP) takes effect, and 59 community boards are established.

1978   Edward Koch becomes mayor.

1980   Ronald Reagan becomes president and consolidates the rollback of federal antipoverty programs and the hegemony of neoliberalism.

1988   West Harlem Environmental Action (WE ACT) is founded.

1989   Voters approve a change to the city charter that authorizes community plans (under section 197a) and the use of the fairshare principle.

1990   David Dinkins becomes the first African American mayor.

1991   The first People of Color Environmental Leadership Summit is held in Washington, DC.

1992   The plan by Bronx Community Board 3 becomes the first community plan to be officially approved under section 197a of the city charter.

1993   The We Stay!¡Nos Quedamos! plan for Melrose Commons in South Bronx is approved.

1994   Rudolph Giuliani becomes mayor.

2001   The World Trade Center is destroyed on September 11.

2002   Michael Bloomberg becomes mayor.

2003   Plans for Midtown West, Olympics 2012, and Atlantic Yards are announced.

1
Community Planning without Displacement: Strategies for Progressive Planning

Political classes are never convinced merely by arguments at the round table. These groups match power, not wits.
—Oliver C. Cox, *Caste, Class and Race*

Since the rise of the modern metropolis over a century ago, urban social movements have opposed giant public and private redevelopment schemes that threaten to displace residents and businesses. As part of these movements, people organize, say "we won't move" in a collective voice, and try to stop the bulldozers. This scenario occurs in every region of the world, including rich and poor countries.[1] The Habitat International Coalition[2] regularly broadcasts news from its members around the world about their struggles against displacement. For example, in Karachi, Pakistan, residents are now organizing to protest the demolition of thousands of homes to make way for a new freeway. Further south, the Israeli Committee against House Demolitions works with Palestinians to stop demolitions and rebuild some of the 18,000 Palestinian homes destroyed by Israeli bulldozers since 1967.[3]

According to the Center on Housing Rights and Evictions (COHRE),[4] a global nongovernmental organization, "Security of tenure is one of the cornerstones of the right to adequate housing," yet an estimated half of all households in the world have no access to basic housing rights. International housing rights groups normally include in the right to housing the right to a stable, healthy, living environment that is free from threats of displacement. In the United States, however, the 1949 Housing Act established the broad goal of "a decent home and a suitable living environment for every American family" without explicitly making a connection between housing and security of tenure, and federal housing policy has contributed in many ways to insecurity among households, particularly low-income people and communities of color.[5] Forging this link between housing and security of tenure has been a consistent goal of urban housing and community movements. In one of the first major works on displacement, Chester Hartman, Dennis Keating, and Richard LeGates stated that

The term [*displacement*] describes what happens when forces outside the household make living there impossible, or hazardous, or unaffordable. The fact of displacement is a grotesque and spreading feature of life for lower-income people in the United States. It also means a process by which they are engineered out of their traditional neighborhoods, to make way for new occupants deemed more "desirable" because of the color of their skins, the taxes they will pay, or the "life style" they lead.[6]

For the last century, struggles against displacement in New York City have been a central part of one of the largest and most diverse urban social movements in the United States. These struggles include the fights against the eviction of unemployed people in the 1930s, government-sponsored urban renewal programs in the 1950s and 1960s, landlord abandonment in the 1970s, expressway projects such as Westway and the Lower Manhattan Expressway, university and hospital expansion, and large-scale luxury housing projects that displace low-cost housing and encourage gentrification. The community struggles arose along with labor, civil rights, and radical civic and political movements that developed strong bases in New York City. As an indicator of their relative strength and maturity, in the last half century the struggles against displacement in New York have moved beyond protest and individual battles. Now community activists create their own proactive community plans that seek to protect residents and businesses in the long-term future. They have also promoted new citywide plans that address the needs of many neighborhoods that are facing displacement (figure 1.1).

Community Planning and Real Estate in New York City

In 1959, community activist Frances Goldin organized a group of residents and businesses to stop a city-sponsored urban renewal program from evicting people and turning her Lower East Side working-class neighborhood into a middle-class enclave. She sought the help of Walter Thabit, a professional urban planner, and the Cooper Square Committee completed the first community plan in New York City in 1961. Nine years later, it became the first officially adopted community plan in the city.

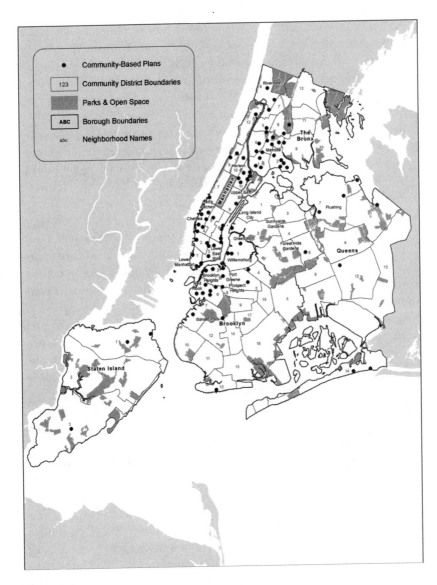

Figure 1.1
Map showing community-based plans in New York City. *Credit:* Municipal Art Society Planning Center

In 1993, Yolanda García, a South Bronx mother, stood up against a city-sponsored urban renewal plan, protesting that it would turn her neighborhood into an exclusive enclave of homeowners. She led a community-planning process and won endorsement by government for a plan that guaranteed no displacement of residents and businesses and reshaped the city's project in other important ways.

In 2003, residents and businesses organized Develop Don't Destroy Brooklyn to prevent being displaced by the largest development project in Brooklyn's history, sponsored by Forest City Ratner, a major real estate firm. They prepared their own plan, which called for development without displacement, and today the struggle against Forest City Ratner continues in the streets and in the courts.

These are only three examples (described in detail in chapters 4 and 7) from a large pool of community-based plans in New York City, many of which emerged out of protest and struggles against displacement and gentrification, sometimes in opposition to government-sponsored plans and other times after winning battles against unwanted megaprojects. Some community plans were subsequently adopted, in whole or in part, by city government. Today there are at least 100 community plans in New York City, a municipality with over 8 million people and fifty-nine officially designated community districts, and many grassroots community planners like Frances Goldin and Yolanda García. Though much of the city's territory is not covered by community plans, the grassroots plans dwarf in number the land-use plans produced by government agencies, and together they represent perhaps one of the largest collections of community-initiated plans in the world. Reflecting wider imbalances in economic and political power in the city, proportionately more of the plans came from low-income, working-class communities with people of color, and many recent ones emerged from the environmental justice movement. The citywide Campaign for Community-Based Planning— which brings together over fifty community-based organizations, community boards, and professionals to advocate for community planning—arose in 2001 after decades of grassroots planning efforts in the city's neighborhoods to press local government to recognize and support community planning.[7]

This book tells some of the many stories of community planning in New York City with the objective of understanding how and why community planning occurs, how it influences (or does not influence) public policy, what the prospects for the future are, and what lessons can be learned. It aims to demonstrate the close relationships between community planning and the political strategies of urban social movements against displacement and gentrification and for environmental justice. The visions for the future in community plans are usually much more than static, abstract ideals or laundry lists of needs and desires, although they sometimes look like that on the surface. Community plans are products of ongoing political processes and usually reflect the contradictory elements in those processes. To community organizers, plans are usually conscious political strategies that seek, within the context of broader struggles for social justice, to change the relations of political power both within neighborhoods and between neighborhoods and outside forces. They are a means for setting priorities and principles that people believe should govern what happens in their communities. Understanding this relationship between political strategy and community planning is essential to the growing ranks of community planners as they seek guidance about how to plan. This includes the community planners like Walter Thabit, who have formal academic and professional training that too often fails to link community organizing and planning; community organizers with no formal training in planning like Yolanda García and Frances Goldin; and students who would aspire to be community planners. The pioneering community planners were especially skillful in linking political strategy with planning strategy, so that both the content of the plan and the process followed to develop it were connected to the struggles against displacement, for social justice, and for a better quality of life.

This book is not intended to be a detailed analysis of New York City's community plans. An entire book could be written about any one of the plans to be covered, either as a history, an ethnography, or a sociological or decision-making study. Instead, it looks broadly at representative community plans and places them in their political and social contexts to help better explain their content and the diverse processes followed in developing them. A broad overview of major historical trends and the economic, social, and political conditions that gave rise to them is combined with selected case studies that illustrate these trends and conditions.[8] This work cannot include the complete stories of any of the neighborhoods discussed herein. There are already many books that analyze individual New York City neighborhoods in detail.[9] And while it starts from an interdisciplinary urban planning approach, this book is not intended as a definitive work on urban planning in New York City or the region. There are several texts that cover part of the territory, but any comprehensive historical and

political analysis of urban planning in New York would be an ency-
clopedic project.[10]

Much of what has been written about urban policy in New York City
focuses on broad issues of political power, the prominent role of hegemonic state institutions, and the role of important private actors.[11] An
ample body of literature also focuses on electoral politics and the protagonist role of prominent elected officials.[12] Many comprehensive historic studies include important social and political analyses of the city's
urban history.[13] While this literature is crucial for an understanding of
urban reality, it is not sufficient for community planners. Too often
the urban policy narratives fail to include individuals and urban social
movements as active agents of social change, thereby contributing to the
impression that they are relatively passive subjects of unchangeable globalization trends.[14] This book instead looks at urban policy from the
bottom up from the vantage point of the mature, progressive community
movements whose struggles for social justice continue to play a powerful
role in shaping the city.[15] The purpose, quite simply, is not only to
understand the world but to learn how to change it.[16] This study therefore begins with a question: *what knowledge and analysis will help
community planners in developing their plans and linking them with
political strategies?*

It may appear self-evident to many that race and class play central
roles in New York City politics, given the city's historic role as a center
for working-class immigrants and its wide ethnic diversity. But very little
has been written about the central role that has been played by race and
class in the city's urban planning and development policies. This book
highlights their significance in the formulation and evolution of land-use,
zoning, and community-planning policies. Furthermore, it attempts to
show that race and class are not just two among many variables but the
central factors needed to understand planning in the city.

One of the most remarkable facts about community planning in New
York City is that it has flourished in the shadows of an immensely powerful private real estate industry. NYC and Company, the city's tourist
agency, claims that New York is "the real estate capital of the world."
Local folklore has it that real estate is to New York what oil is to
Houston. As demonstrated in Robert Fitch's *Assassination of New
York*,[17] the finance, insurance, and real estate (FIRE) sector has increas-
ingly come to dominate the city's land-use and fiscal policies. Powerful
real estate clans and financial corporations (Fitch focuses mostly on the
Rockefellers) control the most valuable land in Manhattan and the new

business and residential districts in the city's four outlying boroughs. They are the largest single source of campaign funding for local elected officials. They backed the construction of the nation's largest subway system and helped create one of the most dynamic metropolises in the world. They are truly a hegemonic economic, social, and political force.

This determined opposition—the most powerful real estate growth machine facing dynamic and sophisticated community movements—is critical to understanding the logic and future of community organizing and planning everywhere. This book aims to unravel this contradiction. It is written for the community organizers and planners in the city's neighborhoods, professionals in city government, and activists in the many organizations and institutions engaged in the process of preventing displacement, controlling development, building viable communities, and combating racial and economic inequalities. But it is also for everyone outside New York who faces similar contradictions and cares about neighborhoods. We all live in a world that is increasingly dominated by global metropolises—centers of global finance and real estate—where real estate and community collide in a complex regional territory divided up into neighborhoods of diverse sizes and shapes.[18]

The purpose here is to unravel the diverse stories of community planning in a way that will inform and support community planners in New York City and every other metropolis. This is not a cookbook with recipes about how to do a community plan. The conditions facing community planners are so distinct that they require flexibility, creativity, and adaptation, and their point of departure should be political strategies that are dynamic and complex. No formula for community planning will suffice.[19]

In this book, *planning* is defined as a conscious human activity that envisions and may ultimately determine the urban future. Since the first human settlements, all urban environments have been the product of planning of one kind or another by both individuals and the state. Under industrial capitalism, planning became an explicit function of the state, and it both reflects and mediates the contradictions of capitalism—contradictions within the capitalist class and between capital and labor. Urban planning has been a means for addressing these contradictions as they are manifest in the realm of urban space.[20] In chapter 2, the dynamics and contradictions of real estate capital in New York City and the ways that they affect urban planning and the role of the state are analyzed. Community planning reflects a new social practice that joins the urban social movements as they confront and engage the state.

A common myth in the urban planning profession is that planning should be a neutral process carried out in the public interest outside the political arena (more about this later).[21] Another myth is that plans are or should be about life within the limited territorial boundaries of neighborhoods and should avoid addressing broader economic and social issues they cannot resolve. As the case studies in this book illustrate, community planning is rarely politically neutral at the local level and often addresses citywide, regional, and global political issues.

Progressive Community Planning

Progressive community planning is defined here as planning that seeks to achieve local and global equality, social inclusion, and environmental justice. Progressive planning in New York City has been part of a long-standing local progressive political tradition based on principles of racial and economic inclusion. It is based largely in low-income, working-class neighborhoods, most of them communities of color. It is preceded by a long history of community, labor, and progressive social movements.[22] The pioneer of this inclusive planning model, the Cooper Square plan in Manhattan's Lower East Side, is described in more detail in chapter 4. For the last two decades, the environmental justice movement has further advanced the progressive approach to community planning, as illustrated in chapter 5. In fact, today environmental justice advocates are the most outspoken proponents of inclusionary community planning in the city. In this book, some of these vanguard neighborhood plans—including Melrose Commons in the Bronx, Greenpoint/Williamsburg in Brooklyn, and West Harlem in Manhattan—disprove the charge that all community planning is by definition exclusionary and driven by not-in-my-backyard (NIMBY) sentiments. In fact, community planning in many cases is more inclusionary than large-scale government or private planning.

Another longstanding trend in community planning attempts to achieve social exclusion through land-use controls. These community plans are devices for consolidating control of the most powerful property interests and often create a façade of consensus to undermine those who challenge these interests. Over the last century, the tradition of suburban zoning and planning in the United States has been built on exclusionary principles.[23] Exclusionary planning practice in New York City has been less apparent because of the city's dynamic growth, ethnic diversity, and relative acceptance of new immigrant populations. Yet chapters 2 and 3 show how zoning and land-use planning in the city have contributed to the segregation of neighborhoods by race and class. In the city's most exclusive neighborhoods, the planning process is not truly open and transparent and is used to obscure negotiations that occur behind closed doors. Chapter 7 shows how real estate megaprojects such as Midtown West, the rebuilding of lower Manhattan after 9/11, and Brooklyn's Atlantic Yards are shrouded in highly controlled processes of planning that may involve some citizen participation but severely limit any public role in decision making. They are examples of planning for the few that may in practice involve many people.

Many plans fall in between the extremes of exclusionary and progressive approaches, and some are ambiguous and self-contradictory. No plan is entirely progressive because all communities include both tendencies, and community plans often bring them into the open for discussion, debate, and compromise. And in all cases, the role of the state is contradictory and reflective of wider struggles related to race, class, and urban space.

Progressive planning implies an awareness of regional and global issues beyond the neighborhood level, and community planners must struggle for such an awareness. Because they usually have to work one neighborhood at a time, they can easily become disconnected from larger territorial and global issues. However, as shown in this book's narratives of community plans, the possibility of isolation and failure in lonely neighborhood struggles incessantly drives community activists and planners to seek broader coalitions and objectives. Solidarities of class, race, and social justice are powerful instruments for relatively powerless communities. And in building solidarity, community planners begin to make the connections between what they are doing and the long history of place-based struggles against displacement in the city. Chapter 3 examines these connections in a way that has not been done before, going back to slave rebellions, tenant organizing, the civil rights movement, the struggles against the federal urban renewal program, and the long string of government reforms that were demanded by grassroots groups that were attempting to decentralize decision making.

This work follows the tradition of participatory action research in which scholars engage in the processes that they seek to describe and analyze, address questions of vital importance to the communities they study, and design their research in a dialogue with the people they work with.[24] In the field of urban planning, this approach implies an engagement by professionals in the complex process of community organizing and political change.[25] It follows a long tradition within the urban planning profession of insurgent theory and practice—moving from advocacy toward new models of progressive planning.

Rational-Comprehensive Planning and the Neoliberal City

New models of progressive planning are needed to address the complex tasks facing both professionally trained community planners and those who have learned by doing. New models will build on the rich legacy of advocacy planning and incorporate lessons from the practice of community planning. To develop these new models, community planners need to recognize the significance of *community land* (defined below) and the roles played by conflict, contradiction, and complexity. This will help resolve the most critical dilemma currently facing community planners—*how to win the struggles against the concentration of noxious land uses without contributing to displacement and gentrification.* Preserving and developing community land are critical to resolving this question.

The orthodox approach to urban planning in the United States is the *rational-comprehensive planning model,* which arose at the beginning of the twentieth century as the nation underwent a dramatic transformation from rural to urban and as metropolitan regions began to dominate the landscape. The ideology of rational-comprehensive planning has its roots in the Enlightenment faith in the ability of humans to determine the shape of their environment through scientific knowledge and practice, which was put into practice by the modern state. It arose in large part as a reaction to the miserable conditions of the cities of early industrial capitalism and the insurgent working-class movements in those cities.[26] Its best-known example was the monumental late nineteenth-century plan for central Paris that displaced vibrant working-class neighborhoods, imposed uniform building heights, and created public parks, wide boulevards, and an enormous sewer system. In the United States, it led to the City Beautiful movement, which created the elite civic center epitomized in the Chicago Columbian Exposition of 1893, Daniel Burnham's 1906 Chicago Plan, and later the federal urban renewal program. It also led to Ebenezer Howard's Garden City idea, which created planned new towns outside older industrial cities in Great Britain and, though it never had much practical success in the United States, lent credence to the practice of low-density suburban sprawl that characterized twentieth-century urban growth in this country.[27]

One of the first and most durable critiques of rational-comprehensive planning came out of New York City's vital social movements. In her classic 1961 book, *The Death and Life of Great American Cities*, Jane Jacobs showed how the orthodox planning approach placed too much power in the hands of professional planners, relied on grand schemes for urban transformation that often made some problems worse, and failed to take into account the multiple ways in which people and neighborhoods develop organically.[28] Jacobs was stimulated to write her book after years of struggling against megaprojects in New York City that came out of the orthodox comprehensive planning tradition. Her nemesis was New York's Robert Moses, the master of urban renewal, giant civic projects, highways, and parks, many of which were built by bulldozing neighborhoods.[29]

Rational-comprehensive planning promised physical solutions to social problems, an example of *physical determinism*. Urban renewal and public housing programs, for example, were supposed to resolve the problems of urban poverty, when in practice they only changed the geography of poverty and displaced millions of poor people. They fed the thirst of real estate investors for centrally located land and further marginalized the neighborhoods of low-income people. One of the theoretical underpinnings of this approach is the orthodox urban planning principle of "highest and best use of land," which relies on quantifiable measures of land value, defined by the real estate market, to suggest to planners what uses are appropriate at any given location.

With respect to the planning process itself, rational-comprehensive planning promises a neat, logically constructed process of plan development engineered by technically trained planners. It often starts with an inventory of existing land uses, community assets and liabilities, and goals and objectives; goes on to examine alternative scenarios; and finally outlines a physical plan or set of strategies. This approach is consistent with the theory of scientific management that heavily influenced the twentieth-century urban reform movements and created the foundations for the growth of regulatory institutions in government, including city planning commissions and departments. The professional planners would be the prime movers, and the plan would be a product of the rationally organized process that they managed.

Rational-comprehensive planning thrived during the era of Keynesian political economy and the expanding, interventionist state. Under assault by structural changes in global capitalism and by community movements, it has receded as a hegemonic theoretical construct. While it has fallen into disuse among planning academics, the rational-comprehensive model still exercises a powerful pull in practice on community planners no less than others.[30]

In the 1970s, *neoliberalism* called into question the underpinnings of traditional rational-comprehensive planning. Neoliberalism calls for deregulation, privatization, market-driven development, decentralization, and the downloading of government functions to weak local governments, nonprofit organizations, and civil society. Neoliberal urban policy was a product of global capitalist restructuring that resulted in the globalization of industrial production, flexible accumulation strategies, and the restructuring of the state. During the 1980s, the administrations of Ronald Reagan in the United States and Margaret Thatcher in the United Kingdom consolidated the neoliberal shift in public policy. The near-bankruptcy of New York City in 1975 was a well-publicized trigger in the dramatic shift away from public spending, public works, and public spaces in all U.S. cities, and in New York it diluted the traditionally powerful role of organized labor and allied social movements. As aptly summarized by Jason Hackworth in *The Neoliberal City: Governance, Ideology, and Development in American Urbanism*,[31] neoliberal urban policy is based on classical notions of individual liberty, an unfettered marketplace, and a noninterventionist state. These traditional eighteenth-century ideas were resurrected as challenges to Keynesian political economy and the modern welfare state. A strong public sector is to be replaced by public-private partnerships or outright privatization. As a result, communities now confront local governments that are both less aggressive in leading land development and more dependent on hegemonic real estate interests and the progrowth civic coalitions they are able to assemble.

According to Hackworth, "The boundaries of urban governance have shifted dramatically in the past thirty years, partially because of structural constraints to governments (municipal or otherwise) in the capitalist world . . . but also because of a related ideological shift toward neoliberal governing practices."[32] Neoliberalism rejects the belief that aggressive state action is required to maintain market demand, correct market imperfections, and prime economic growth. Neoliberal thinking denies that the state is needed to provide for certain "public goods" or "public space." Instead, the public goods that were created under Keynesian regimes should be privatized, including public housing, parks, transportation, and services. The role of the state in the neoliberal city is to stay out of the way of the real estate market, reduce its regulatory powers (including land use and zoning) to a minimum, limit taxation, and divest itself of all but a minimal public infrastructure. Neoliberal ideology "is not a thing as much as a process"[33] and has been applied unevenly in the real urban world.

With the collapse of the socialist camp, neoliberalism became religion, and former British Prime Minister Margaret Thatcher's boast that "there is no alternative" (TINA) was internalized by many, including activists and professionals. But throughout the United States and the world, the new social movements that arose since the 1970s, with both their practice and new theories, have proven that "another world is possible," to use the phrase of the World Social Forum.[34]

A reflection of the contradictory trends within the neoliberal state, grandiose comprehensive planning is experiencing a minor revival in New York City (discussed in chapter 7), and consequently there is a trend toward rehabilitating the discredited master planners of the past. One reason is that public planning disasters that affect the accumulation of capital continue to occur even with the private sector clearly in command.[35] But for the most part, rational-comprehensive planning has ceased to be a defensible theory, and Jane Jacobs's critique has withstood the test of time. New York's official planners rely not so much on any comprehensive theory or strategy but instead on a neoliberal faith in the magic of the real estate marketplace.

As is shown in chapter 2, despite the powerful role of Keynesianism, Robert Moses, and New Deal public works, New York City's land-use policy has from the very start been strongly dominated by liberal economic theory and a powerful real estate sector. The first plans were made by surveyors to facilitate land subdivision. After the consolidation of the city in 1898, government turned away from any comprehensive approach to development of the region and instead limited its role to the narrow tool of zoning, which followed growth instead of leading it. While other cities and towns in the United States produced comprehensive master plans, New York produced only one, and it was never approved. Even the efforts of the heroic Robert Moses to direct and control development appear from the long historical perspective to be both fleeting and inadequate. New York City is an excellent test case for the city that grew in tandem with the needs of the financial, insurance, and real estate sector, and paradoxically it is also the test case for community planning, which has emerged in the large void left open by liberal capitalism.

The Roots of Progressive Community Planning
Since Jane Jacobs's classical critique of rational-comprehensive planning in the United States, multiple theories and practices of community planning have emerged that have roots in urban social movements, beginning

with advocacy planning. A review of this legacy can help inform any search for new progressive approaches to community planning beyond neoliberalism and the rational-comprehensive orthodoxy.

Advocacy planning is the foundation for all progressive planning in the United States today.[36] While its philosophical roots can be traced to the Enlightenment faith in human self-determination and political pluralism, advocacy planning was an innovation of the 1960s. It was a direct consequence of the engagement of urban planners in the civil rights movement, the struggles against the displacement of low-income communities by the federal urban renewal program, and the opportunities for innovation offered by the federal War on Poverty, including the Model Cities program. The theory of advocacy planning was first outlined by Paul Davidoff, an urban planner who helped found the graduate planning program at Hunter College in New York City. Davidoff's theory was informed by the multiple practices of community activists and professionals who sought to redress issues of racial and class oppression. It confronted a planning profession that was narrowly focused on the physical city, rationalized the destruction of "slums" by urban renewal, sided with powerful real estate interests, and was overwhelmingly a club of white males who claimed for themselves a position of technocratic superiority over protesting communities. Advocacy planning was a prescription meant for urban planners, but the theory applies to all professions and disciplines that confront the political and ethical dilemmas bound up in their practice—social work, public health, public administration, and all of the social sciences that deal with urban policy.

Davidoff's seminal 1965 work, "Advocacy and Pluralism in Planning,"[37] made the following main points:

• The planner is not solely a *value-neutral* technician. Instead, values are part of every planning process.

• City planners should not attempt to frame a single plan that represents the "public interest" but should "represent and plead the plans of many interest groups." In other words, planning should be pluralistic and represent diverse interests, especially minority interests.

• So-called citizen participation programs usually react to official plans and programs rather than encourage people to propose their own goals, policies, and future actions. Neighborhood groups and ad hoc associations brought together to protest public actions should create their own plans.

• Planning commissions were set up as supposedly neutral bodies acting in the public interest, but they are responsible to no constituency and

too often irrelevant. There is no escaping the reality that politics is at the very heart of planning and that planning commissions are political.
• Urban planning is fixated on the physical city. Davidoff stated that "the city planning profession's historical concern with the physical environment has warped its ability to see physical structures and land as servants to those who use them." He thought that professionals should be concerned with physical, economic, and social planning. He also said that "the practice of plural planning requires educating planners who would be able to engage as professional advocates in the contentious work of forming social policy."[38]

One of the limitations of the advocacy planning model is that it is based on a legal approach where the advocate planner represents the interests of clients who do not have access to professional help. There is a need to expand this approach now that the civil rights movement has ebbed, black and white divisions are complicated by a new array of ethnic divisions and identities, the War on Poverty was subverted in the Nixon years, and the Reagan revolution undermined critical public-policy instruments for achieving racial equality and equal economic opportunity. The banner of affirmative action, for example, has been covered up by charges of reverse discrimination. Poor people have again been blamed for poverty, and public assistance has been cut back, even as tax cuts and subsidies continued to flow to the rich. And perpetual foreign wars, now an indefinite war against terrorism, have diverted resources needed to solve solvable urban problems.

After the demise of federal urban programs in the 1970s, many professionals dedicated to social justice went to work in public agencies and became quiet advocates from within. Norman Krumholz popularized the term *equity planning* based on his own practice as planning director under Cleveland Mayor Carl Stokes, the first African American mayor of a major U.S. city. Krumholz and John Forester questioned the inaction of professionals in public service when confronted with evidence of social injustice:

The Cleveland experience helps us to move beyond a perplexing paradox, one we will call *the practical paradox of professional style*. The gist of the paradox is quite simple: "neutral" action in a world of severe inequality reproduces that inequality.[39]

This approach borrows from advocacy planning and models of normative policy making and proactive public administration, casting aside those that favor incrementalism and "muddling through" in bureaucracies.[40] It continues to be relevant for community planning because neoliberal ideology penetrates deeply into the ranks of the public sector, which helps legitimize private accumulation strategies that reinforce displacement pressures. Community strategies invariably include mining information and building alliances within government. Such an inside-outside approach to organizing rejects a strictly instrumentalist view of the state in which there are no conflicts or contradictions in government, the state at all levels is presumed equally as powerful or impotent, and there are no humans in government institutions who are capable of conscious political action.

Feminism has had a profound impact on planning by uncovering the many and diverse practices of women who have shaped cities and neighborhoods. Dolores Hayden's *Redesigning the American Dream* and *The Power of Place: Urban Landscapes as Public History* and Leonie Sandercock's *Making the Invisible Visible: A Multicultural Planning History*[41] are but a few examples. Perhaps it is no accident that as women entered the workforce in large numbers, the women's movement brought into focus the importance of place to the reproduction of capital and labor. Women have traditionally played a central role in urban social movements and community planning. This book's stories of community planning show how women, whether or not identified with feminist movements, have helped transform the planning profession. Jane Jacobs is a key figure not only because she is responsible for the classic critique of orthodox urban planning and played a prominent role in New York City's dynamic urban struggles but also because she rejected a patriarchal assault, led by "visionary" male planners, on a domain of great concern to women—her community.[42] What started as an exclusively male urban planning profession emphasizing physical form has now changed to one in which women make up about half of all planning students and social and economic aspects of planning are routinely included in their training.

In the United States, *indigenous planning* occupies a unique space by incorporating diverse approaches, ranging from rational-comprehensive to advocacy and progressive planning, on Indian reservations and in indigenous urban communities.[43] The space for indigenous planning is unique because it has evolved from the struggles of the first nations to gain control of land that was taken from them and placed under a semi-colonial structure dominated by the U.S. government. Community planning can learn several lessons from the theories and practice of land use in indigenous communities.

Finally, the environmental movement produced what is coming to be called *sustainability planning*, which starts with the objective of meeting today's needs without compromising the needs of future generations.[44] Environmentalism emerged both as a protest against the negative consequences of uncontrolled growth and as a trend within capital to moderate growth in line with its needs for global restructuring. Theories of sustainability also brought forward efforts toward more holistic, grassroots approaches that integrate public health and quality-of-life issues in land-use planning.[45] Chapter 5 discusses how the environmental justice movement brings a progressive approach to sustainability by underlining the role of social justice in environmental and land-use planning.

Transformative community planning evolved with the maturation of the civil rights movement beyond advocacy and protest to the question of political empowerment. It reflected a shift of the civil rights movement after the landmark Civil Rights Act of 1964, following Martin Luther King Jr.'s call to go from the struggle to get a seat at the lunch counter to the struggle for the money to pay for lunch. It reflected the move from legal battles, which often put professional advocates in key positions, to broader political struggles for decent jobs and housing and for a role as equals in politics and society. This meant building the capacity of communities to control their own destinies. According to Marie Kennedy,

Genuine community development combines material development with the development of people, increasing a community's capacity for taking control of its own development. This requires building within the community critical thinking and planning abilities so that development projects and planning processes can be replicated by community members in the future.[46]

Kennedy and many others base their transformative approach on Paolo Freire's notions of engaging people in ways that empower them and bring about social change. The Freirian dialogue among people rejects the "banking" approach to development, in which the professional is the supposed repository of technical knowledge about planning and transfers it to "students" who must listen and learn.[47] The theories of transformative planning help explain how new generations of effective community planners emerge without formal training as they "learn by doing" and by engaging in dialogues with the people who can help them to solve their community's problems and bring about radical social change.[48]

The long tradition of *utopian planning* also has a place among progressive approaches because it can help challenge the despair engendered by TINA and dare us to imagine a better world. Utopian thinkers dating back to Plato and his *Republic* imprinted on their ideal communities characteristics present in their own societies, and many of them validated existing inequalities. But the utopian socialists of the nineteenth century imagined new societies based on equality and cooperation instead of competition. Some of them intentionally created new communities based on these principles (none of which lasted very long).[49] There is sometimes a nostalgic strain in utopian thinking, when utopia harkens back to preindustrial villages instead of looking forward to an urban future. There is also a utopian strain in the classical rational-comprehensive theories of urban planning.[50] But unless community planners are able to imagine a better world and incorporate the progressive legacies of the past in that world, there is little hope for planning as a human endeavor.[51]

Marxist critiques of utopian schemes rest on the assertion by Karl Marx and Friedrich Engels that "Men make their own history, but they do not make it just as they please; they do not make it under circumstances chosen by themselves, but under circumstances directly encountered, given and transmitted from the past."[52] Marx's associate, Engels, was one of the first to develop a critique of utopian reformism, capitalist urbanization, and the housing market under capitalism.[53] Marx and Engels introduced the methodology of dialectical and historical materialism, which is valuable for understanding the contradictions in urban development and the ways that the production and reproduction of capital are critical determinants of urban history. They also showed how a scientific approach to understanding the world required going beneath superficial events and human behavior and understanding underlying class relations.

Urban planning in the socialist countries of the twentieth century, which was not always based on the theories of Marx and Engels, offers many important lessons, including successes and failures. If we ignore them and fall prey to blind historic prejudice, we may well be doomed to repeating the mistakes in our search for new alternatives.[54] One of the great achievements of the socialist city was to minimize displacement and social segregation and create a freely accessible public infrastructure. But this also led to a lack of mobility in jobs and housing and economic stagnation. After a brief period of experimentation with utopian ideas, the Soviet Union's Bolshevik revolution sank into an urban policy that discouraged innovation and diversity as a price for growing quantitatively by producing more jobs and housing. Urban planning became a highly centralized practice monopolized by the state and dependent on decisions about the location of production facilities. In some important ways, it mimicked the undemocratic rational-comprehensive model. Nevertheless, there are many rich lessons[55] for those who would dare to imagine an urban future not dictated by invisible free-market forces, not the least of which is the importance of linking socialism and participatory democracy.

Urban scholar David Harvey has asked whether it is possible to construct "a stronger utopianism ... that integrates social process and spatial form." The task, he says, is to define an alternative

> not in terms of some static spatial form or even of some perfected emancipatory process. The task is to pull together a spatiotemporal utopianism—a dialectical utopianism—that is rooted in our present possibilities at the same time as it points towards different trajectories for human uneven geographical developments.[56]

Each of the theories discussed above, from advocacy to Marxism, is as much a critique of mainstream planning as it is a rich mine of ideas for alternative theories and practices, but none of them alone is adequate for progressive planning today. Progressive planning today incorporates all of these concepts and practices, but it must be more than the sum of the parts. This book attempts to show how *progressive planning in New York City is uniquely characterized by its focus on local and global equality, social inclusion, environmental justice, and community land*. It must be more than a collection of critiques because its purpose is to yield new strategies to bring about fundamental change in our economic and political systems. It must involve a holistic, comprehensive approach to planning that joins land, people, and environment, physical and social planning, local and global economics, individual and community, and preservation and development. It is planning for healthy and sustainable cities with many differences but fewer inequalities and with planning at multiple levels for the short-term and long-term that improves our urbanity and our urban places. This is not an unreachable panacea but must be closely tied to strategies for community organizing and empowerment. Given the enormous imbalance in political power between real estate and community, these strategies necessarily include "biding time" in a long-term struggle to gain a better position that may pay off when real estate's hegemony erodes, wanes, or is ended in the ultimate market crash.[57] Further details about how this approach can be applied to New York City are provided in chapter 8.

Elements of Progressive Community Planning

Three key elements of progressive planning are community land; the bundle of processes including conflict, contradiction, and complexity; and the tension between eliminating environmental injustice and preventing gentrification.

Elements of Progressive Planning: Community Land

A central aspect of progressive community planning in New York City must be a strategic approach to land, including the planning, development, and control of land. Unlike rational-comprehensive planning, the starting point is to question who controls land and who benefits from its use. The urban planning professional is trained in ways to conserve, develop, and regulate land. Land use is the urban planner's special domain.

This is perhaps one area in which community planners have fallen short by too often focusing on immediate struggles and pragmatic tactics and too infrequently looking at strategic, long-term issues of land use. This very North American tendency toward pragmatism plays into the orthodox approach to land-use planning that sees urban planning as a mechanism for pragmatic accommodation to market forces. One of the leading texts in land-use planning begins with the statement that "Local land use planning and decision making can be seen as a big-stakes game of serious multiparty competition over an area's future land use pattern."[58] According to this text, the role of the urban planner is to help manage this competition so that the market produces positive outcomes: "The goal of the land planner is not simply to accommodate market demand for development, but to guide the market toward producing good communities."[59]

Community-based planners may share this view and see themselves as incrementalists who are there to "play the game." Often community activists have to spend so much time and energy just getting into the game that they have little energy left to change the rules of the game. As a result, they may see no need to look strategically at the question of land. In part, this has to do with objective limitations in community movements. For example, people struggling against displacement are often tenants who own no land and whose tenure is precarious. Their most urgent concern is to keep a roof over their heads, and they may be less interested in the right to housing or the long-term future of their neighborhood. Nevertheless, progressive community plans almost always go beyond pragmatic accommodations and express, in practice if not in theory, the collective efforts of residents, workers, and businesses to take control of the land on which their housing and neighborhoods lie, and many incorporate broad strategies for the city and region.[60]

One of the main themes of this book, illustrated in the history and practice of community planning in New York City, is the central importance of community land. To gain control over their land, communities do not necessarily need to own the land. *Community land* may be held in various forms of social ownership or regulated in a way that is consistent with community strategies. More concretely, *community land is land taken out of the speculative real estate market and owned by public, nonprofit, or private entities that are responsible for holding the land in public trust, using it for a public purpose, or limiting profits from resale.* It may involve a wide variety of forms of ownership: locally based nonprofits, limited-equity cooperatives, and community land trusts; publicly owned community facilities and open spaces; and private homeowners in a local real estate market that is stable and not in flux. Privately owned land can become community land if its private use is restricted by democratically controlled zoning, land-use regulations, condemnation powers, deed restrictions, easements, and other measures.[61]

Community planning can strengthen community land as a basic element in building a sense of *place* and showing that place matters.[62] By building up the stock of community land, neighborhoods can build places that slow or stop the process of dislocation and *displacement* caused by giant development projects or the gradual process of gentrification. Community land can help stake out public space in the national and global struggles against the uncontrolled speculative marketplace.

However, there is a logical contradiction between community control of land and the principles of progressive planning (outlined above) that criticize physical determinism and emphasize human transformation in the planning process. Local control of land can easily perpetuate or worsen existing relations of oppression and inequality. Therefore, there also needs to be a fundamental paradigm shift in the way land is defined and treated. According to Davidoff, land should be thought of not as simply a physical object but as *a set of social relations. Community land should sustain the human relations and cultures associated with places while progressively eliminating inequalities.* The modern North American tradition of urban land treats land as only the physical *space* used for human activities, as a commodity to be bought and sold on the market, and as an instrument of economic and political power. For those who came to occupy the land, exploit it, and sell it for a profit, it was an object measured in spatial terms and located on a grid by geographic coordinates—a site for producing buildings and reproducing investments. New Yorkers are further alienated from land in yet another sense: most of the city's surface is covered by concrete and asphalt (which required the diverting and covering of many local streams), so that residents and workers have little direct contact with natural soil and water and only visit the buildings that occupy the land. A more humane conception of land has to go beyond the notion of a physical, material space demarcated by a finite number of square feet. It also must be understood to be an integral part of the social and spiritual life of our communities—socially produced *places* that have meaning for all of us.[63] This view is consistent with and responds to the struggles against displacement and for the protection of urban places. When land becomes space alone, its utility to anyone whose name is not on the deed is purely secondary, and there is no expectation that it must serve a broader social purpose.[64]

Perhaps we can learn something from the cultural traditions in the world that deal with land free from the realm of commodity exchange. According to Australian indigenous activist Mudrooroo,

Life came from and through the land and is manifested in the land. The land is not an inanimate thing: it is alive. Land to us Aborigines is not a possession in material terms, as the white man looks upon land, but a responsibility held in sacred trust. We do not say the land belongs to us, but we belong to the land.[65]

As is shown in chapter 7, this idea that land can have a spiritual value emerged among the families of the 9/11 victims. And in other chapters, stories of people threatened with displacement show how land may evoke deep feelings and emotions associated with the everyday lives and activities of people. This approach cannot be understood as purely "subjective" because ideologies and symbols have a material base and are a material force in the world. Sacred places are defined not just by what humans did or did not do on the land but by the myths and cultural values passed on through the generations.

According to Lakota elder Vine Deloria Jr., there are many different kinds of sacred places, and they all come "out of a lot of experience. The idea is not to pretend to own it, not to exploit it, but to respect it."[66] The kind of sacred place that is most difficult for non-Indians to understand teaches and gives to humans, who are in turn obliged to preserve it as a healthy place. "The creed of the Lakotas," says one observer, "requires not a general reverence for land (though that is a near-certain outgrowth of it) but a particular attentiveness to place."[67] In such a framework, the very modern term *land use* seems jolting. If there is an organic tie between land and people, how can it be "used"?

This approach should not romanticize non-Western cultures or suggest they never abused the land but should stretch our imaginations beyond our own culture to find alternatives to modern uses and abuses.[68] If we simply drop all land titles and dismiss property owners, all problems will not be solved. Such simplistic notions miss the main point about the nature of land and its relationship to people.

The following story of Maria Lai and a small town in Italy further demonstrates how an issue of land can be intimately connected to the history, culture and spiritual life of a community. Lai is a well-known sculptress who was asked to design a memorial to war veterans in her home town of Collasai on the island of Sardinia (Italy). Wanting to avoid yet another mundane obelisk or heroic statue, Lai set out to create something with more meaning to the people of Collasai. She held many discussions with people in the town, who identified what they felt best symbolized the town's history. Women, who were not often consulted in civic matters, consistently brought up the myth of the blue ribbon. In this folk tale, a young girl was stranded in a cave on the hillside above the town during a flood. As flood waters rose and entered the cave, a blue ribbon descended from the heavens and pulled her to safety on the hilltop.

The women of the town together with Maria Lai invented the Festival of the Blue Ribbon, a three-day festival that coincided with the annual celebration of the town's patron saint. The women sewed together strips of blue denim, strung them from window to window, covering all the households in town and finally reaching skyward to the hilltop overlooking the town. In the traditional procession, the patron saint was bedecked in blue ribbons. The Festival of the Blue Ribbon is now an annual event in Collasai. Maria Lai brought together the ingredients of a progressive community plan—history, culture, equity, and democratic participation. The story is a parable of community planning and answered the question of how to use the land in the center of the town—the town's public space—not simply by proposing a physical change but by creating new public places that integrate land with the social and spiritual life of the community.[69]

The Commons: Land in the Public Trust

When considering patterns of land ownership, local land-use planning often looks at only two categories, public and private land. In reality, there are many different forms of land tenure throughout the world, but throughout Western history one other main form of land tenure has been prevalent—*the commons*. The ancient Romans had private, public, and common property. In medieval England, villagers kept certain lands to be shared by all. The concept of the commons is used today as a generic term including all land for which a community has responsibility.

According to The Friends of the Commons, it "embraces all the creations of nature and society that we inherit jointly and freely, and hold in trust for future generations."[70]

Over a century ago, conservationists in the United States started creating natural reserves to protect selected land from exploitation by private owners. By using a combination of public ownership, nonprofit land trusts, public easements, environmental laws, deed restrictions, and tax benefits, about a fourth of the land in the United States came to be held in the public trust. Unfortunately, this kind of conservation tends to reinforce the value of land owned by large private owners and often involves huge direct or indirect public subsidies to private concessions. Corporate mining, ranching, and logging interests have found ways to get cheap access to exploit the 20 percent of all U.S. land managed by the U.S. Department of the Interior. But even with these limitations, land that has many of the nation's most valuable natural resources is still subject to public control. The community-planning approach to community land dares to propose that *urban* land be placed in the public trust.

The idea of putting urban land in the public trust is not just a pipe dream. This book's stories of community planning in New York City illustrate the extent to which community land is not only possible but already exists. Over at least the last century, accumulated protest and action by displaced people and tenants have expanded the stock of land that is off-limits to speculation, creating a new *de facto* urban commons. As is noted in chapter 8, most of New York City's land is already restricted in one way or another. The question now is how to bring it under conscious, democratic control and remove the inequalities in access to land.

Elements of Progressive Planning: Conflict, Contradiction, and Complexity

Progressive community planning in one of the world's largest cities has emerged out of a complex and contradictory process and in a political environment that is rich in conflict. It comes from political struggles for social justice, not from any idealistic desire for social harmony. Community planning is anything but a tidy, rational, or linear process, and attempts to force preconceived notions of order on the process invariably succumb to the interests of the most powerful social forces.

Plans and planning are not static *things* but nodes of social and political relations that occur in urban places. Community planning necessarily involves multiple and complex social relations, some of them highly antagonistic. In *Dialectical Urbanism: Social Struggles in the Capitalist City*, Andy Merrifield calls for "an understanding of what gives cities their frightening force and awesome grandeur . . . an understanding of dialectical urbanism, of an urbanism of ambiguity and contradiction and conflict."[71] Such a dialectical approach is necessary to understand the tensions, debates, and asymmetries that are part of planning as they are part of every social process.

The first major set of contradictions is between real estate and communities. Perhaps community movements in New York City would not be as pervasive if real estate were not as powerful as it is and did not pose serious threats to communities. Community planning arises in response to real estate growth and thrives in "the real estate capital of the world." Real estate and community planning are inexorably tied to one another and in conflict with each other just as capital and labor are.

Conflicts between real estate and community are common in global cities like New York because as major nodes for the transaction of global capital, they are repositories of an abundant surplus, some of which is absorbed locally and invested in real estate, which in turn creates pressures on communities. Also, "capitalism is always under the impulsion to accelerate turnover time, to speed up the circulation of capital and consequently to revolutionize the time horizons of development," and "capitalism is under the impulsion to eliminate all spatial barriers."[72]

This dynamic movement of capital places pressure on urban working-class neighborhoods where land values and rents go up and endanger low-cost housing. In *The Housing Question*, Engels showed how local land markets further create opportunities for the circulation of capital:

The expansion of the big modern cities gives the land in certain sections of them, particularly in those which are centrally situated, an artificial and often enormously increasing value; the buildings erected in these areas depress this value, instead of increasing it, because they no longer correspond to the changed circumstances. They are pulled down and replaced by others. . . . The result is that the workers are forced out of the center of the towns towards the outskirts; the workers' dwellings and small dwellings in general become rare and expensive and often altogether unobtainable, for under these circumstances the building industry, which is offered a much better field for speculation by more expensive dwelling houses, builds workers' dwellings only by way of exception.[73]

As a consequence of local resistance and a host of geographical anomalies, the patterns of real estate growth are spatially uneven because investors are forced to leap-frog over areas that pose serious opposition. Thus, uneven spatial development is as central to market-driven real estate development as the drive for speedy capital turnover.

As detailed in chapter 2, from its early days as a Dutch settlement New York City's real estate development was tied to global trade and a dynamic, flexible, and expanding capital market. Until well into the nineteenth century, it thrived on the profits extracted from slavery and Southern agriculture. As the U.S. empire expanded in the twentieth century, more capital accumulated in the city's banks and on Wall Street. The New York region became one of the world's largest centers of global finance, producing an unprecedented surplus for which investors sought speculative outlets. A century ago, the appetite for profit in real property led the city's landlords to create what is now the largest mass transit system in the country, which made possible high central densities, widespread growth throughout the city's five boroughs, and a new metropolitan region that now includes some 20 million people. With the decline of manufacturing in the twentieth century, the myth that real estate is the city's main industry is now deeply imbedded in the city's policy discourse.

The second set of conflicts of concern to community planning is within the finance, insurance, and real estate sector. As is shown in chapter 2, the city's real estate industry is large, complex, and diverse. Wealthy individuals and clans have formed the backbone of the propertied elite, and they have always sought to distance themselves from the thousands of small developers, builders, and agents who are scattered throughout the region's neighborhoods and who may alternatively be both their competitors and allies in a broad political bloc promoting growth. The large rifts between corporate real estate giants and small, local property interests underlie many local political battles and community plans. With the arrival of powerful new real estate investment trusts (REITs) and global real estate brokers, big real estate and global finance have reached a new level of integration, and their conflicts with locally based small-scale property interests have widened. These contradictions also help to explain the uneven spatial development of real estate in the city. They are of strategic importance for community planning, which has often found a natural ally in small-scale local property interests and taken advantage of rifts among the giants.

Underlying this division between globalized and local real estate is a basic underlying economic tension between the relatively fixed nature of real estate investment and the dynamic needs of flexible capitalism.

David Harvey has pointed to capital's need to address this tension with a "spatial fix," which requires pouring capital into urban infrastructure and housing to both absorb surplus capital and create conditions for the reproduction of capital and labor.[74] The spatial fix is also related to a giant contradiction within New York City's real estate and financial elite—between the expanding and dynamic global market that creates excess capital for real estate investment and the need of the local economy to provide affordable housing for people who work for them in the city. Most sectors of the local economy need affordable housing because without it labor costs would soar. Labor and working-class communities also need affordable housing so that they can have access to local jobs. New York City's real estate giants have therefore sought a sort of social contract with labor and community by supporting programs that provide affordable housing for low-income workers. As a consequence, New York has the largest stock of public, cooperative, and municipally owned housing for low-income people in the nation. Because of the dynamic nature of the local real estate market, however, affordable housing is constantly constrained and under siege. Real estate interests must limit affordable housing so that it does not threaten the most active and dynamic sectors of the market, and (as is shown in chapter 2) they benefit handsomely from the public subsidies for affordable housing. On the other hand, workers organized in unions, housing advocacy groups, and neighborhood-based organizations try to maximize affordable housing. Community planning is one arena in which this contradiction gets played out.

The more general contradiction confronting capitalism everywhere is that as capital accumulates so does labor and that labor needs to be housed to be of any value to capital. Displaced from their jobs and homes by invading U.S. capital, millions of people from less affluent countries around the world migrate to the urban centers of capital in the United States and Europe to fill low-paying industrial and service jobs. If real estate could rule solely according to its own profit-making logic, the new urban immigrants would have no place to live. The city would be one homogeneous luxury enclave if developers simply produced only the most profitable housing for people with the largest disposable incomes. But since real estate is wedded to other sectors of global and local capital that are constantly expanding, displacing more people and drawing them into its urban centers, the urban real estate establishment must find a way to produce and preserve housing for the new immigrants. Thus, cities like New York have a diverse mix of housing for the very wealthy, very poor, and many in between—a true reflection of the global capitalist economy.

The upscale growth and gentrification that drive the city's real estate market have never reduced poverty or poor housing, contrary to the claims of the trickle-down theory of economics and advocates of perpetual growth. Instead, gentrification and poverty are intimately linked and dependent on one another. To care for the Park Avenue coops selling for $5 million, there must be a pool of poorly paid cleaning people, drivers, cooks, and nannies, some of whom are not able to find a place to sleep and therefore join the homeless population. That is why even the biggest real estate magnates believe there is a place for affordable working-class housing (but not in their backyards) and programs to care for the homeless. Indeed, the globalized real estate industry dominates the development of both market-rate and affordable housing (see chapter 2).

The third important contradiction is within communities. Community organizing and planning require both conflict and harmony—not for the sake of conflict but because conflict is a preexisting condition and normal. If there is no conflict, there is no stimulus for communities to organize or do planning. As shown in the case studies throughout this book, democratic community planning arises most often not because someone thought it would be nice to have a plan but because people organize to protest the conditions under which they live. According to Manning Marable,

It is from the site of community that many of us wage struggles in the living space around the reality of day-to-day existence: access to decent and affordable housing, public health services, crime and personal safety, the quality of the environment, public transportation, the education of our children.[75]

The early work of Frances Fox Piven illustrates how successful community action arises from protest and struggle.[76] Conflict *within* communities also drives community planning. Communities are not homogeneous entities in which everyone has the same needs, problems, and priorities. Community plans can reach some consensus on key issues, but by ignoring difference and diversity community plans will surely perpetuate inequalities and imbalances in political power and fail to transform both individuals and communities. Fetishizing consensus is but one part of a larger methodological problem—seeing reality as a static set of ideas or values and not a set of social contradictions.[77]

In his critique of the New Urbanism, a recent trend among architects and planners, David Harvey states that "community has often been a barrier to, rather than facilitator of, social change." This happens when the myth of community is used "as an antidote to threats of social disorder, class war and revolutionary violence."[78] If community planners use "the community" as a palliative and tranquilizer, they will surely fail to confront the most serious community issues. They may very well be using it to protect their own roles as power brokers. Planners should ask themselves what groups they are referring to whenever they talk about "the community."

The orthodox approach to urban planning in the United States tends to worship consensus through planning. "Best practices" in planning are always those that have a happy ending in which a community agrees on a common program. In reality, consensus too often serves those in power because it requires those who are not in power to accept the dominant ideology and political agenda, posited in seemingly neutral terms as a product of consensual agreement in the public interest. Consensus-driven planning, often accompanied by "visioning" and "strategic planning," works well in relatively homogeneous, exclusive white communities where the objective is protection from outside development pressures.[79] But it also plays a powerful role in low-income communities where it is often promoted by influential foundations, nonprofits, and public agencies. From the point of view of social justice, consensus-driven planning can be counterproductive when it legitimizes the most powerful factions within communities instead of empowering those who have been historically marginalized, as Marie Kennedy proposed.[80]

The win-win scenario of consensus planning is a myth from an imaginary world where there is no conflict or contradiction, everybody benefits, and nobody ever loses. Such a static paradise is impossible. "Participatory planning" is another myth that can obscure real differences, and while it has been a widely accepted practice in the United States, it is now increasingly gaining ground throughout the world. In practice, participation can mean nothing more than sitting silently at a public hearing or attending scores of meetings that have no significant role in making decisions that matter. Participation can be confused with real democracy—the power of people to collectively control the decisions that affect their economic and environmental futures.[81] Progressive community planning must be inspired by new visions of participatory democracy and not the traditional approach of representative democracy, in which stakeholders represent other people in a planning game.

Elements of Progressive Planning: Environmental Justice versus Gentrification

The most difficult dilemma facing community planners today is how to join the struggle against the concentration of noxious land uses in low-income communities of color without encouraging displacement and gentrification. Community-based social movements, particularly the environmental justice movement,[82] have fought against the concentration of noxious land uses in their neighborhoods only to find themselves confronting the threat of displacement by gentrification—that is, the more or less gradual land-value and rent increases that force tenants and owners to move.[83] Unlike the urban renewal bulldozer, its effect is gradual and highly uneven and may vary drastically from one block to another. There is no simple or definitive solution to this contradiction, especially in a loosely regulated real estate market.

Environmental justice advocates confront gentrification when they focus on removing locally unwanted land uses (LULUs)—waste-transfer stations, bus depots, highways, waste-treatment plants—that are concentrated in low-income communities of color. If LULUs are removed and distributed more equitably and the threats they pose to public health and the environment are reduced, the threat of displacement by gentrification emerges. Activists who struggled for decades to make their neighborhoods better places to live and work find themselves unable to stay in their communities as land values and rents skyrocket.

In the worst years of neighborhood abandonment during the 1960s and 1970s, New York City's engineers and planners looked on areas like the South Bronx as likely places to locate and expand facilities that nobody wanted in their backyards. They either consciously targeted the struggling neighborhoods, citing low land costs, or simply neglected to intervene by using their regulatory powers to ensure that no neighborhood had more than its fair share of such facilities. The neighborhoods most affected were low-income communities of color that were already facing epidemics of asthma and respiratory disease that were linked to existing and new polluting facilities. Whether there was conscious racial discrimination on the part of the planners is secondary. The effect of their actions and inactions was to reinforce structural racism, which is based not on individual or institutional behavior but on "interinstitutional arrangements."[84] Out of the grassroots resistance against these facilities emerged the environmental justice movement.[85] As told in the stories in chapter 5, environmental justice activists have led the search for sustainable strategies to eliminate the disparate effects of LULUs and prevent displacement by gentrification.

The struggles against gentrification are intimately tied to struggles to protect public space and the commons from neoliberal urban policies. For example, activists who took over Tompkins Square Park in Manhattan's Lower East Side in 1993 argued that the expulsion of poor people from the neighborhood's premiere public space was tied to gentrification. While gentrification pressures have always been a feature of market-driven land development, they became more pronounced since the onset of neoliberal urban policy in the 1970s. They represent the single most important challenge facing community planners in the twenty-first century.

In the search for a new progressive community planning that addresses gentrification, the construction of a theory and practice of community land is critical. This requires moving beyond struggles for individual parcels of land toward a strategic conception of community land incorporating local, regional, and global scales. It also requires that planners develop a sophisticated understanding of how community and real estate interact and conflict, the contradictions within each, and the complex ways in which communities, cities, and regions change at local, regional, and global levels. The most immediate task for progressive community planning is to develop a deeper understanding of how community land can help prevent displacement and gentrification while at the same time addressing the concentration of noxious land uses. This is one of the central objectives of this work.

How the Book Is Organized

Part I of the book (chapters 2 and 3) provides background and history on planning in New York City. The two chapters in part I are there for several reasons. First, though community planners may confront and cooperate with developers and property owners individually and collectively, we tend to know very little about real estate. How can such a powerful real estate market be addressed without knowledge of how it works and its internal contradictions? Second, we tend to know very little about our own roots. How can we hope to develop community planning in the future if we do not know where we came from? This part of the book is presented in the spirit of Howard Zinn's history of the United States, which looks not at the powerful people in history but

at history from the point of view of the people out of power.[86] It seeks
to demonstrate the active agency of organized community movements in
transforming the way planning is done in the city. The chapters in part
I are not a definitive history. Their purpose is to look at the city's history
and search for the underlying currents of class and race that have evolved
and relate to community planning today.

Chapter 2 is a brief sketch of the political economy of New York City
real estate. Those who are bound up with neighborhood struggles can
lose sight of the big picture, fail to understand the contradictions and
divisions within real estate, and even worse, begin to mimic real estate
practice by getting caught up in the game and making deals that undermine inclusive, democratic planning. Because community plans are inevitably local, planners can also lose sight of the global context. New York
City's real estate from the time of the earliest European settlement was
bound up with global trade and finance and expansion of the U.S.
empire. But the global-local relationship needs to be put in proper
perspective, since neoliberal ideology tends to pose globalization as inevitable and immune to resistance.

Chapter 3 is about the roots of community planning. In a society that
values the present and future and ignores the past, community planners
tend to know very little about where we came from, which invariably
prevents us from understanding where we are going. The pragmatic
American tradition values the successful project or plan—the "best practice" or idealized model—but fails when it comes to projecting a sustainable long-term future. Many community planners do not see themselves
as part of the legacy of slave revolts, tenant organizing, and the struggles
against urban renewal, and many fail to grasp the significance of the
environmental justice movement. This may always be true for planners
whose job is to protect privileged enclaves and prop up real estate values,
but it is not good enough for progressive community planners.

Part II (chapters 4, 5, 6, and 7) tells the stories behind New York City's
community plans in four chapters about two pioneering plans that were
forged in protests against official urban renewal plans, the struggles for
environmental justice that form the backdrop for many community
plans, officially adopted community plans, and plans dominated by
powerful real estate interests.

Chapter 4 is about two seminal plans that emerged out of struggles
against neighborhood displacement. The 1961 Cooper Square Alternate
Plan was the first community plan in the city. It was prepared in response
to a Robert Moses–sponsored urban renewal plan that would have

leveled an eleven-block area and built middle-income housing. Behind the slogan "We won't move," the Cooper Square Committee fought against both the city and real estate abandonment to preserve low-cost housing for low-income tenants. This story is significant because Cooper Square set up one of the city's first community land trusts, an important and underutilized mechanism for securing community control of land. Thirty-two years after the Cooper Square Alternate Plan, residents and business owners in the Melrose section of the South Bronx, under the slogan "We Stay! ¡Nos Quedamos!," defeated an official urban renewal proposal that would have created a suburban-style enclave for home-owners on abandoned city-owned land. Their alternative plan eventually became the official instrument for redevelopment policy in the neighborhood.

Chapter 5 tells stories of the struggles for environmental justice that led to community plans. These include the waterfront battles, incinerator battles, sludge battles, and garbage battles. The first citywide community plan, written by the Organization of Waterfront Neighborhoods, challenged the city's Solid Waste Management Plan and eventually led to changes in the city's waste policy.

Chapter 6 tells the stories of the community-based plans submitted for official approval under City Charter section 197a, known as "197a plans." These and other community plans often challenge the city's land-use and zoning practices and face serious obstacles when it comes to implementation.

Chapter 7 tells stories of planning "for the few," in which community involvement in decision making was severely restricted. Indeed, the community-planning process was dominated by powerful real estate inter-ests. These cases are in the hot property markets of Manhattan—lower Manhattan and Midtown West—and in downtown Brooklyn, where the most powerful real estate interests rule. The cases demonstrate how the space for progressive community planning diminishes as we get closer to the center of global and local economic power. The largest bottom line promotes social exclusion and physically separate enclave development, not inclusive and diverse communities. Progressive planning must be concerned with understanding and exposing the practices of exclusionary planning if it is to promote an inclusionary and socially just alternative. However, planning at the periphery of the most powerful real estate interests offers the best opportunities for strategic advances.

Part III (chapter 8) puts forth proposals for advancing progressive community planning in New York City. This part is designed especially for New Yorkers who care about progressive planning, but it also includes suggestions for global strategies that may be relevant in other cities. Like other dialectics, these proposals will develop and change as they are discussed and debated by community planners in New York and in other global cities who are also struggling against great odds for a new progressive approach to our urban future.

I

Understanding Real Estate and Community

2

The Real Estate Capital of the World

And the skyscrapers of Manhattan, Detroit, Chicago, London, Paris, Berlin—
what will they say when the hoarse and roaring years of their origin have sunk
to a soft whispering?
—Carl Sandburg, *The People, Yes*

There is no greater disaster than greed.
—Lao Tzu

Paradoxically, community planning in New York City would not be as
developed as it is today without the city's powerful real estate market.
Both the power and contradictions of real estate have created space for
community planning. To formulate strategies for community planning,
we must understand the complex and contradictory economic and political roles of the real estate sector. This primer on real estate looks at the
city's real estate clans and the role of the finance, insurance, and real
estate (FIRE) sector and shows how the real estate market is related to
both location and dislocation, feeds on disasters, and divides urban space
by class and race. We note the growing concentration of downtown real
estate and its ongoing merger with finance capital, particularly in the
form of real estate investment trusts (REITs).

This chapter also highlights the relationships among local, national,
and global economic and political trends. Community organizers and
planners need to understand these connections in addressing questions
of local strategy. When should they oppose and when ally with real
estate? Can contradictions within real estate become strategic assets? To
what extent is real estate a local neighbor, and to what extent is it global
and therefore less identifiable and tangible? When is it both?

Finally, city-planning and land-use regulation and reform have
responded to the contradictions and conflicts within real estate and more
recently between real estate and community. To explain these issues, this

chapter provides a brief review of the history of urban planning in the context of real estate development—from the first Dutch settlement to the establishment of zoning in the early twentieth century to the urban renewal program, fiscal crisis, and housing abandonment in the post–World War II period. This is neither a chronological history nor an exhaustive one but simply provides a framework for readers unfamiliar with the context for contemporary community planning. It is complemented by the history of community planning outlined in chapter 3. These two chapters describe how the earliest land-use reforms were instituted by elites who never challenged big real estate and how the terrain for current land-use battles is increasingly dominated by struggles between community and real estate for the control of land. Despite the powerful influence of neoliberal ideology that calls for a reduction in the role of government, a parallel and continuing interest of the real estate industry maintains an interventionist role for local government in land use and housing, thereby protecting the local political equilibrium and its own political hegemony.

The Political Economy of New York City Real Estate

New York City is a perennially desirable piece of property and is in a league with Hong Kong, Tokyo, and Singapore. Its land is worth several hundred billion dollars, more than the annual gross national product of Canada. If you wanted to buy the metropolitan region, you would need trillions.

Some have dreamed of having a huge slice of it. In the nineteenth century, John Jacob Astor "became the wealthiest man in the United States" by investing in New York City real estate. Astor bought land cheap in the panic of 1837, foreclosed on mortgages, and increased his fur-trading fortune when the market went up.[1] Speculators have been falling all over each other trying to reproduce the Astor miracle ever since.

New York real estate today is a medley of established family firms, new corporate giants, and thousands of small players. The names of the real estate clans that built up little empires in the twentieth century are on the cornerstones of Manhattan's biggest buildings—Durst, Helmsley-Spear, LeFrak, Levitt, Milstein, Rose, Starrett, Tishman-Speyer, Trump, and Zeckendorf. But corporate real estate giants that have access to hefty financing sources for megaprojects in many cities are playing an increasingly important role in New York—Vornado Realty Trust, Forest City Ratner, and The Related Group, for example.

The clans and corporations that are the backbone of real estate would face serious political obstacles without a much larger army of allies that support growth. This includes tens of thousands of small and medium-sized landlords in the five boroughs who own everything from five-unit walk-up apartment buildings to multistory elevator buildings. There are brokers who mostly trade residential and commercial property but do not necessarily build it. They include thousands of small, neighborhood dealers, though many are now being pushed out by corporate giants like Cushman & Wakefield, The Corcoran Group, Century 21, and Coldwell Banker. In commercial real estate, Greiner & Maltz, Grubb & Ellis, and Newmark stand out. Many builders and contractors are small and local, but increasingly they are being pushed out by national firms able to take on large-scale projects and consolidate small ones.[2] Then there are the construction trades (whose hard-hat unions can be counted on to demonstrate in favor of every big project regardless of its impact on the environment and neighborhoods). And finally, there are civic groups that are dominated by homeowners who stand to benefit from new development. Together, they make up the growth machine.

REBNY and the Growth Machine[3]

New York City's growth machine is a bloc of economic and institutional interests that favor new construction and public works. It is led by the Real Estate Board of New York (REBNY) and the New York City Partnership, a group of corporate executives mostly from the financial sector, which was founded by David Rockefeller.[4] Real estate drives the growth machine, government oils and repairs it, the building trades make the parts, and global and local capital deliver the fuel. The machine works to create growth and sustain growth. Growth is always presumed to be good, even in a Manhattan that is already densely packed with buildings and has little breathing room. Indeed, REBNY's strategic neighborhoods are Manhattan's two main central business districts, Midtown and lower Manhattan. In response to 9/11, it declared that the downtown should "grow as a powerful engine of the city's, region's and nation's economies" (see chapter 7).

The 5,600 members of REBNY are the bulwark of the landed elite and steer the growth machine. Their survival, individually and as a group, depends on a continuing rise in property values, starting from the center in Manhattan and rippling outward. Since taxes should rise along with property values, REBNY has persuaded the city to institute substantial tax abatements by reasoning that the tax cuts are "incentives" needed to ensure new development. These include twelve- to fifteen-year tax abatements on the rehabilitation of vacant units under the Department of Housing Preservation and Development's (HPD) tax-exemption and -abatement J51 program and twenty-year tax abatements on new construction in many areas of the city under HPD's 421a partial tax-exemption program. REBNY is a leading member of Taxpayers for an Affordable New York. Much of the new development in New York is subsidized by tax benefits, proving that in real estate it is possible to have your windfall and keep it.

One contradiction of the growth machine is that its blind infatuation with growth undermines the residents' quality of life, which in turn suppresses growth. The myth of growth is so powerful that the city's slow rate of new construction over the last half century is still considered to be an aberration to be overcome and not the natural result of the high cost of land in a city that is grossly overdeveloped, its limited population growth, a declining quality of life, and opposition from neighborhoods.

The growth machine depends on the perpetuation of the myth that growth primed by real estate brings money into neighborhoods. In many cases, it actually takes money out of neighborhoods. For example, new global retail and grocery chains from Harlem in northern Manhattan to Red Hook in south Brooklyn were promoted as engines of economic development, yet these businesses take out more money than they invest. The local jobs they provide are notoriously low-paying and dead-end and usually result in high turnover rates. But even when the new businesses pay for local neighborhood improvements, these are often token public relations gimmicks or the beneficiaries are outsiders. For example, the new IKEA furniture store in Brooklyn's Red Hook will invest in local street improvements, but the changes will benefit mainly the 85 percent of customers who will come from outside the neighborhood by car.

The ties that bind real estate, finance, and the growth machine together are almost self-evident. Not so obvious are the conflicts and contradictions within this bloc. While real estate would not function without this alliance of big and small players (banks, insurance companies, contractors, brokers, construction unions, and civic groups), money and power are concentrated in the hands of a few large players. For example, the top five commercial banks in the New York area account for 95 percent of all financial assets.[5] And as shown elsewhere in this chapter, large real estate investors such as real estate investment trusts (REITs) are joining banks, insurance companies, and brokerage firms with global reaches to make real estate the last major industry to come under the rule of monopoly capital. This means that all of the minor players are losing power in a relative sense and represent potential allies for communities.

The Real Estate Clans

Despite this trend of increasingly impersonal corporate dominance, New York City's real estate world is still filled with colorful local characters who represent powerful clans. Finance is preeminently global, and real estate is preeminently local, but global always meets local in the real spaces of the real city made up of real people, who often make property development a family affair.

Donald Trump is Mr. New York City real estate to the rest of the world. Rich, coiffed, and sociable, if not truly a socialite, he invests the same bizarre flair in his buildings as he does in his own persona. His kitsch erections are scattered around Manhattan, bearing names like Trump Tower and Trump City. He founded Trump University and *Trump Magazine*. His empire extends to Atlantic City and other places around the world where ostentation has become an organic part of commercial culture. Trump has become the iconic persona of the merger between media and real estate. In the staid Manhattan culture of traditional real estate heavies, Trump is the bad boy from his father's original Brooklyn-based real estate clan who brings glitz to sedate Fifth Avenue properties. He, not his architect, is embodied in the signature Trump building. To the world outside the spreadsheets of downtown deals, he is the star of the show. He used his notoriety to flirt with a bid for the U.S. presidency, in which he stated that his loyalty to family and firm were bound up with loyalty to the nation.[6]

Leona Helmsley, on the other hand, earned a reputation as a wicked witch for her harsh treatment of staff at the hotel and real estate firm she operated with her husband, Harry. Perhaps her worst crime was telling the truth when she said, "Only the little people pay taxes." Helmsley was convicted for tax evasion and sent to prison. As with the Martha Stewart case in 2004, it is hard to imagine any of the male captains in the industry getting battered so heavily in public. Of the top fifty corporate executives in New York City, only one is a woman, according to *Crain's New York Business*.

Some clans, like the Dursts, are in the forefront of new trends in green building and sustainable architecture. Others, like the Roses, have both green and gray branches. And there are many lesser clans in the outer boroughs, including companies specializing in building low-cost and affordable housing. In any case, the colorful personalities and quirky exceptions may soon be history as impersonal corporations take bigger bites out of the Big Apple.

The City on FIRE

Real estate's political influence in New York City far exceeds its actual economic role in creating wealth and employment. In fact, the real estate industry mostly redistributes wealth that has been created in the region and throughout the world by manufacturing and services. Finance, insurance, and real estate combined (the FIRE sector) generate about 20 percent of all income in the city, but they employ only 13 percent of all workers. Neighborhood mom-and-pop stores employ more people than real estate does.

The FIRE sector does contribute more than its share of city revenues, however. Over one-fourth of the city budget comes from property taxes, personal income taxes, and corporate taxes from these sectors. The relative importance of FIRE income is due to the rapid decline in state and federal aid, growth in speculative income and the informal non-taxpaying sector, and the impoverishment of workers in the low-paid service sectors. As a result, the city's budget is more and more like a lottery, subject to the wild swings of the stock market and real estate booms. This unstable situation is now used as an excuse for cutting back on service expenditures—except, of course, when it comes to new real estate deals like Midtown West that are favored by the mayor (for more on Midtown West, see chapter 7).

Real Estate 101: *Dislocation, Dislocation, Dislocation*

As Susan Fainstein notes in her book on New York and London, "Although government agencies play an important role in affecting the physical environment, the main progenitor of changes in physical form within London and New York is the private real estate development industry."[7] Growth in the FIRE sector has a ripple effect far beyond its geographical center in Manhattan's midtown and financial districts. It creates excess capital that gets invested, in part, in local real estate throughout the city and region.

In Real Estate 101, we learn that the three universal principles of real estate for people who own property are location, location, location. What we don't learn is the three equally important principles for people who don't own property or are threatened with displacement—*dis*location, *dis*location, *dis*location. We also are told little about the relation between location and dislocation. Central locations are generally highest in land value,[8] and as land values in central areas go up, rents go up.[9] As shown in chapter 1, this creates a ripple effect that forces people out and creates opportunities for redevelopment. This is the central dynamic underlying what is now called *gentrification*, a product of the normal operation of the real estate market as it pushes out poor people and people of color and brings in people who can pay higher rents.[10]

The more New York's economy follows the dictates of real estate, the more it experiences the agonies of dislocation. With the landing of the first Europeans in America, a perpetual cycle of displacement, settlement, and displacement began. This is a country of chronically displaced people—indigenous Indians, English Pilgrims, African slaves, European immigrants, and now immigrants from every country in the world. The arrival of immigrants on the east coast of the American continent did not end displacement. For the first two hundred years after the English settlement at Jamestown, displaced Europeans were drawn into the continent's vast unsettled territory. They went west to search for new land, gold, freedom, and, above all, work. The frontier was an ever-expanding imperative. It shaped what they did but also penetrated American culture and ideology and influenced the way Americans would think about cities, land, and public places in the following centuries.[11]

America's dynamic new capitalist economy, unfettered by feudal remnants and fortified by the enslavement of Africans, had one great advantage over Europe. Its capital and labor were highly mobile. *Flexible accumulation* did not start with the globalization of the late twentieth century but was there from the beginning. Capital from the industrial north, principally New York City, was invested in the rural south, and profits from the plantation economy and slavery immensely enriched New York–based capital. Capital also migrated to the west. And when there was no more frontier, U.S. capital broke out of its isolationist shell to find new land, resources, and opportunities for expansion abroad.

Paradoxically, the last hundred years of relatively permanent urban settlement in the United States allowed for greater mobility of capital and labor around the world. New York City became more like a tornado than a mushroom, a whirlwind of explosive activity. As capital became more flexible and limber, it chased profits in and out of town, dashing across the globe in less than a second through new fiber-optic vessels, leaping over language and cultural barriers. Labor, politically weak and poorly organized, had little choice but to follow. Full-time, lifetime employment at the same place became a myth; today almost half of the labor force in the U.S. does part-time or temporary work. Labor has to keep its bags packed: the average household moves once every five years.

Even when capital touches down in places like New York, it never ceases being mobile. Businesses come and go (over half of all new businesses fail within five years). Residents come and go. New York's neighborhoods are revolving doors for tenants and retailers. Fast men and women use fast cash and dine on fast food (and drive fast cars, except in Midtown, where even capitalist mobility cannot defy the laws of physics). New York City deserves its reputation as the fastest-paced city in the world, a distinction that ought to be tied to the speed of capital exchange and not to the behavioral characteristics of the people who live and work there.

Life in the fast lane reinforces the value and power of central locations and therefore the role of the real estate market. This pattern reflects a central contradiction of modern capitalism and continues to hold despite (and because of) the communications revolution.[12] Most Internet servers are located in central cities. Like the telephone before it, the Internet reinforces concentration. Global air travel increases the importance of central hubs. Flexible, decentralized production increases the importance of the large global cities. New York's land market will therefore continue to follow the three rules of real estate—*dis*location, *dis*location, *dis*location.

Chasing Disasters

In the twentieth century, New York City's real estate industry flourished in tandem with three great disasters—the Great Depression, the post–World War II federal urban renewal program, and the vast neighborhood abandonment of the 1960s and 1970s. (Chapter 7 shows how real estate benefited from the 9/11 disaster.) While at times real estate may seem to be an example of what Naomi Klein calls "disaster capitalism,"[13] it seems to thrive in both good times and bad. In bear markets, it works for investors who are looking for stability and safe havens to balance portfolios. In bull markets, it welcomes the adventurers who are looking for quick profits. But even as the city's many disasters subsided, real estate became a vehicle for expanded control and influence of the FIRE sector in the local economy.

For example, in the Great Depression, when rents and property values dipped, the boldest adventurers (those who had not lost their shirts in the stockmarket crash) bought up everything in sight and waited around for the windfall. The Rockefeller family made a bold speculative move in Midtown Manhattan that engraved the family name on what would become a city landmark—Rockefeller Center. This pioneer in branding would not have been such a stunning success for the Rockefeller clan if it had not been for the generous public support it received. The Rockefellers struck a deal with Columbia University, which owned the property: Columbia would retain ownership of the land while the Rockefellers bought development rights. Columbia was exempt from real estate taxes because it is an educational institution. Thus, the Rockefellers ended up paying a reduced, negotiated payment in lieu of taxes. While Rockefeller Center was being built, shantytowns for homeless workers spread throughout the city, on vacant lots and in parks, not far from the new construction site.

In the Depression, federal public works and welfare programs helped stabilize the local real estate market and lift sagging land values. Public investments in infrastructure and housing created new private opportunities in surrounding neighborhoods that developers cashed in on after World War II. With strong backing from both the New Deal left and elite reformers, public housing was born. In 1936, the city renovated a group of tenements on Manhattan's East 3rd Street and Avenue A on the Lower East Side, now known as First Houses. This was to be an anomaly among public housing: most public housing built after this was the result of new construction, often on sites where older housing had been acquired and demolished. The 1937 Housing Act provided federal funds for these projects, but by and large this Depression-era housing functioned as much if not more as a mechanism to provide jobs in the construction trades and a spur, though a feeble one, to languishing real estate.[14] Not far from First Houses, a much larger private project completed after the war on land provided by government, Stuyvesant Town and Peter Cooper Village, soon overshadowed the public effort, at least until the 1950s surge in public housing development.

The post–World War II federal urban renewal program provided substantial federal funds to local authorities so they could acquire land and buildings in areas with depressed market value—very often low-income communities of color. As discussed later in this chapter, the urban renewal program often contributed to neighborhood decline and abandonment and opened the door for subsequent upscale redevelopment. The very threat of the use of eminent domain powers to acquire land can further depress land values and contribute to the displacement of housing and people. Also discussed below is how real estate investors chased the disaster of neighborhood abandonment. The tens of thousands of vacant lots and buildings in New York became opportunities for real estate speculators, who bought them for discount prices at city auctions.[15] However, as shown in chapter 3, until community-based organizations and government invested money, time, and ingenuity in these neighborhoods, speculators were unable to realize any significant gains.

How Real Estate Divides: The Landscape of Inequality

The excessive concentration of real estate wealth in New York has produced a system of land use with gaping inequalities. Ashfort Warburg, a Manhattan broker, recently offered, in a *New York Times* ad, an 11,000-square-foot mansion on "one of the most beautiful streets in New York" for $12 million. This was a bargain compared to the top price for Manhattan homes, now over $20 million. If you don't want to bother finding a mortgage, you can rent a five-bedroom apartment in an East Side townhouse for only $23,000 per month, over twenty times the gross monthly minimum wage and affordable only to those making over eight times the area median income.[16] Manhattan's Upper East Side is arguably the wealthiest neighborhood in the world. The median household income there is about four times the rate for the city. And in a country where homeownership is (falsely) equated with wealth, about 70 percent of all households on the Upper East Side are renters (though many households own property elsewhere and can afford to bypass the benefits of homeownership). Although government holds out homeownership as the key to the accumulation of wealth, those who already have accumulated wealth by investing in financial markets have no such illusions.

There is at least one elite enclave in the other four boroughs, too—Brooklyn Heights in Brooklyn, Riverdale in the Bronx, Forest Hills Gardens in Queens, and Todt Hill in Staten Island. We can contrast the lavish multimillion-dollar condos on Manhattan's Upper East Side to the cramped tenements in the Lower East Side, the home to generations of working-class immigrants. Compare the charming Brooklyn Heights brownstones to the crumbling walk-ups in East New York, which are surrounded by vacant city-owned lots where unscrupulous contractors dump cars and construction waste. Compare Riverdale's suburban-style mansions with the rough apartments surrounded by trucks and waste-transfer stations in Hunts Point.

Most New Yorkers cannot afford even a fraction of the rents in the city's upscale neighborhoods (figure 2.1). About one-third of all households in the city are paying more than 50 percent of their gross incomes for housing (which means 60 percent or more of take-home pay). According to a stream of fairly consistent press reports over the last several years, every day an average of 35,000 people sleep on New York's streets or in homeless shelters because they cannot afford or find even the cheapest accommodations. Over a million city residents (12.5 percent) eat in soup kitchens or rely on some form of food assistance, and fully 20 percent fall below the government's (rather low) poverty level. With a vacancy rate that has not gone above 5 percent for generations, the city has one of the tightest housing markets in the country. But those who have the cash and credit feel the crunch the least. The vacancy rate for high-rent, newer apartments is at least double the average.

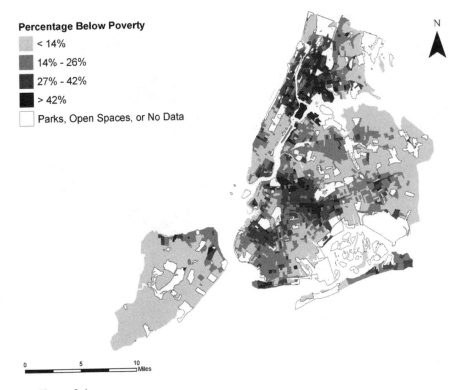

Figure 2.1
Map showing below-poverty-level neighborhoods in New York City (percentage). *Credit:* Andrew Maroko

These stark facts contradict several myths that have been advanced by real estate advocates: (1) new apartment development will trickle down to the poor, who will move up into better housing when more units become available; (2) the market's invisible hand (the law of supply and demand) will solve the housing problem; (3) rent controls are blocking the development of much needed housing;[17] and (4) building and zoning regulations block new construction.[18]

On the map of segregated ethnic enclaves in New York City, there are very few melting pots (figure 2.2). This is one of the most segregated and unequal metropolises in the world, a fact related to its role as a global city. The segregation is significant at two levels—within the five boroughs and within the metropolitan region.[19] Forty years after the federal Civil Rights Act and almost as long since the federal Fair Housing Act, residential segregation has changed little. Within the five boroughs, the

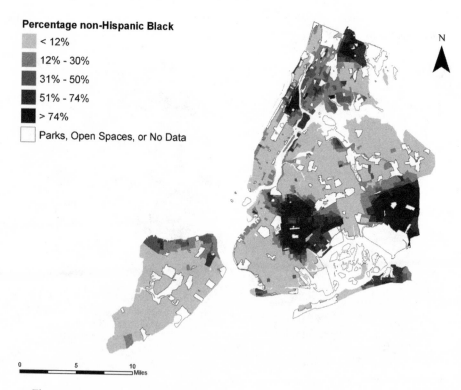

Percentage non-Hispanic Black

- < 12%
- 12% - 30%
- 31% - 50%
- 51% - 74%
- > 74%
- Parks, Open Spaces, or No Data

N

0   5   10
                    Miles

Figure 2.2
Map showing non-Hispanic black neighborhoods in New York City (percentage). *Credit:* Andrew Maroko

majority of African Americans live in northern Manhattan and central Brooklyn, areas that also have high proportions of people living in poverty. Incomes in African American neighborhoods are 55 percent of incomes in white neighborhoods.[20] Racial separation by itself might not be of any great concern, but it also correlates strongly with class apartheid. Within the city, poverty is concentrated in northern Manhattan, the South Bronx, central Brooklyn, and several pockets in Queens and Staten Island, areas that are all disproportionately made up of people of color. Other high-poverty areas are disproportionately made up of Latinos and new immigrants. Even among Asian, Latino, African, and Caribbean ethnicities, where there is some sharing of neighborhood space, identities and allegiances with countries of origin remain more powerful than any emerging regional identity. In addition, transnational relations remain strong among many new immigrants.[21]

Equally dramatic is racial segregation in the New York metropolitan region: 63 percent of African Americans in the New York region live in New York City.[22] Most blacks and other minorities outside New York City are in the inner suburbs immediately adjacent to the five boroughs—places like New Rochelle, Yonkers, Newark, and Bridgeport. Thus the gradual integration of the suburbs is really more of an expansion outward of segregated ghettos to inner-ring suburbs than it is a racial mixing.

Racial separation is not just a matter of individual discrimination—an attitude problem, as it is often portrayed. It is institutional and structural, and the principal institution through which it operates is the real estate industry. The sale and rental of property is color-coded. While there have been a few notorious cases in which realtors and rental agents (and even public housing management) used codes on application forms to identify the race of the applicants, for the most part discrimination operates through a myriad of subtle, informal ways that discourage people of color from even searching in certain neighborhoods. This *racial steering* turns people of color away from white neighborhoods, and white home seekers steer themselves away from historically integrated and black neighborhoods.

Blockbusting is the flip side of racial steering. This practice occurs in primarily white or middle-class neighborhoods that are of interest to speculators for redevelopment. Realtors exploit racial stereotypes and spread the word that people of color are moving in, which will lead property values to go down. White homeowners sell at below-market rates, and realtors turn around and sell to people of color at above-market rates. This happens throughout the outer boroughs, which are becoming increasingly multiethnic at the same time that they are increasingly segregated.

The exceptions to the city's racial apartheid seem to be passing phenomena. For example, Harlem and Bedford-Stuyvesant (Brooklyn), neighborhoods that have had significant black populations since the late nineteenth century, are gentrifying into more of a racial mix. But the integration of Harlem is just the latest phase in the uptown expansion of the high-income, white Upper East Side. While Harlem is losing some blacks, the Upper East Side remains overwhelmingly white, and its racial composition has not changed over the last fifty years. Blacks make up a mere 3 percent of this elite enclave, compared to 25 percent citywide.

The Postindustrial City: Myth and Reality

The global trends of deindustrialization and flexible production accelerated in the decades after World War II, and local real estate helped move manufacturers out.[23] The number of manufacturing firms and jobs in New York City declined steadily. Since the late 1950s, jobs in the industrial sectors plunged from 1.7 million to 800,000. Manufacturing suffered the greatest proportional losses.[24] Today there are less than 200,000 manufacturing jobs in the five boroughs. A portion of manufacturing migrated to New York City's suburbs, braking the region's overall decline. In the immediate postwar period, suburban industrial parks attracted assembly-line industries that searched for cheap land to expand horizontally and ready access to the interstate highway system. (New York City's feeble attempts to create industrial parks produced few results.) Bedroom suburbs drew off the city's more experienced labor force. All of this was subsidized by the federal government through the home mortgage and interstate highway programs. To top off the process, container shipping was introduced in the 1960s, and most of the Port of New York was moved to New Jersey, leaving vacant large sections of the city's waterfront and nearby industrial districts.

As a result of all these trends, New York City lost proportionately more manufacturing jobs than any other major industrial center in the United States. But while these multiple forces pulled manufacturing out of the city, real estate speculation helped by giving a big push.

Today, a major goal of REBNY is to rezone industrial and waterfront sites from manufacturing so that they can be developed for commercial and residential purposes. As shown in its recent studies of New York

City industry and the waterfront, the city's planning department is eager to oblige.[25] In his $3 billion housing plan, Mayor Michael Bloomberg targeted the waterfront as a strategic location and supported rezoning to promote housing development. This is likely to result in the privatization of the city's last remaining potential public spaces. Although the waterfront zoning instituted in 1993 requires that developers build public esplanades on the waterfront, these may well serve as backyards for the residents of their luxury towers and not for the public. The model is Battery Park City in lower Manhattan, a planned, state-sponsored luxury enclave with an attractive waterfront esplanade that only local residents and Wall Street brokers can get to with ease.

Even though it has lost many industrial jobs, New York City is still one of the largest manufacturing centers on the East Coast. New York retained the jobs it did since it was what scholar Joshua Freeman calls "a non-Fordist city in the age of Ford."[26] New York never had large assembly-line factories but instead had small, flexible businesses, many of which are linked together in chains of suppliers and producers. New York's industries also benefited from strong unions, now principally in the service sectors, that fought to raise wage levels and lower the cost of living with liberal social expenditures. The real estate and financial industries, which are in large measure responsible for the decline of industry, have created the false impression that they, not services, have filled the gap left by manufacturing and that they are the indispensable sector of the city's economy. Real estate investors care less about what goods are produced or consumed in the city than they care about how much capital is traded or parked there. To Wall Street investors, the capital they trade also comes from industries that were moved out of the city to places with cheaper land and labor.[27]

Globalizing Cultures and the Branding of New York

As capital's system of industrial production becomes increasingly globalized, New York City, always a major center of culture and consumption, is now producing culture for export. All services, art, music, culture, and ideas—indeed, everything both tangible and ethereal—are commodified and transformed into investment capital that can be traded in financial markets. Mayor Michael Bloomberg and his 2012 Olympics plan epitomize this approach (see chapter 7 for further discussion).[28]

The city's official marketing enterprise, New York City, Inc., promotes globalized New York as a world city of many harmonious ethnicities. Ethnic enclaves like Harlem, a product of the nation's profound racial apartheid, are now marketed as chic destinations for international travelers who arrive by air-conditioned coach to eavesdrop at jazz clubs and night spots. Chinatown is sold as a restaurant district, though Manhattan's Chinatown is only one of at least three viable and diverse Asian neighborhoods with dynamic livelihoods that transcend the restaurant trade. Little Italy is truly little and has very little of Italy in it, as the Italian neighborhood surrounding this commercial strip disappeared long ago. All of these ethnic neighborhoods, according to the official propaganda, add up to the global city that even Disney could not build. The rosy imagery of the glossy brochures fails to point out the segregation and discrimination that produce these neighborhoods and reproduce them in different locations when they are displaced.

Beyond the fuzzy notion of a happy melting pot of immigrant countries, the real focus of the city promoters and the destinations for most tourists are the monuments to global capital in the Manhattan central business districts—the Stock Exchange, Empire State Building, and Times Square. When all is said and done, the central business district is capital's favorite neighborhood and the one it shows off to tourists. The neon-lit Times Square is the ultimate destination for glitz, where signs that might otherwise be considered visual pollution are not simply allowed but planned for and encouraged. The transformation of this seedy central district into a globalized cultural district in the last several decades is a dark saga of intrigue and competition between local real estate magnates, elected officials, and elite civic groups,[29] but the result is emblematic of the rule of the FIRE sector.

REITS: Global Finance Unites with Local Real Estate
Mayor Michael Bloomberg's personal business interests and residence are on the East Side of Manhattan, where his new corporate headquarters stand. The developer of his new headquarters building is Vornado Realty Trust, which is also heavily invested in Midtown West, called the last frontier of Manhattan real estate (see chapter 7). Vornado is the largest REIT in the nation and the largest commercial real estate owner in New York City. The company owns large chunks of property around Penn Plaza and throughout Midtown, including twenty-one office buildings totaling 15 million square feet of space. It is the codeveloper of the proposed new Penn Station.

REITs represent the takeover of local real estate by publicly traded investment firms—a globally oriented finance capital. REITs bring together investors from all over the country and world, including big institutional investors. REITs may specialize in real estate equity, mortgages, or both. They are moving in faster than the powerful Hong Kong, Tokyo, and European investors who bought up pieces of Manhattan real estate during recent slumps in values. According to the National Association of Real Estate Investment Trusts, there are 180 publicly owned REITs in the United States with assets totaling $375 billion. According to Daniel Rose, patrician of one of the city's leading real estate clans:

> If [J. P.] Morgan himself would be bewildered by the more complex financial derivatives, he would have understood clearly that a capital-intensive industry like real estate sooner or later would attract publicly traded vehicles for both debt and equity; but even he would be impressed that the market for commercial mortgage-backed securities has now reached $300 billion and is growing and that the market for Real Estate Investment Trust shares stands today at $150 billion. Morgan might not have anticipated that control of the nation's capital would shift, as it now has, away from commercial banks and life insurance companies and to pension funds and mutual funds; but he would have understood the drive toward industry consolidation in a globalized economy under conditions where the development of regional malls, say, or of investment grade hotels is generally beyond the reach of local speculative developers, and where the economies of scale can be substantial. . . .
>
> Only a few years ago, New York structures were built, financed, owned, managed and occupied by New Yorkers, just as those in Chicago or London, San Francisco, or Paris were controlled locally. In today's globalized world, capital, ideas, and people flow freely across state and national borders.[30]

Perhaps it is no coincidence that Bloomberg, Inc., the giant financial information exchange founded by Michael Bloomberg, should feel comfortable in partnership with Vornado CEO Steven Roth, developer for Bloomberg's new headquarters on the Upper East Side of Manhattan. Almost half of Bloomberg's customers are outside the United States. Both he and Roth are globalists leading whatever is local about New York City into the twenty-first-century financial marketplace. And if this trend of REIT expansion is added to the well-established dominance of global traders in municipal bonds, we begin to understand how much the city's budget and fiscal policies are dependent on the needs of global financial markets.[31]

Low-Income Housing for Profit

One of the more perverse contradictions in today's real estate market is the use of public subsidies for low-income housing to back real estate speculation. In part, this points to a trend in which the contradiction between market-rate and affordable housing referred to in chapter 1 is becoming internalized within finance capital. Until the 1980s, the federal government subsidized public authorities and private developers to build low-income housing. Today, as the public sphere is privatized, the largest source of development funding is the Low-Income Housing Tax Credit program, which allows investors to claim tax deductions when they join a syndicate that sponsors low-income housing. One of New York City's largest new real estate firms, The Related Company, develops both low-income housing and high-value downtown commercial property. Its property is worth $11.5 billion, and 90 percent of its apartments are subsidized housing, largely financed through an affiliate investment company, CharterMac. Profits from subsidized housing help prop up high-risk commercial ventures in New York City, like the new Time Warner Center and Madison Square Garden. Related is a partner with Vornado in the latter project and Related's CEO Stephen Ross is a major player in Manhattan real estate. The *Wall Street Journal* puts it rather succinctly:

This massive low-income housing operation throws off a river of cash for Related that runs fairly steadily through real-estate boom and bust. It helps Mr. Ross bankroll some of the nation's ritziest—and riskiest—commercial developments.[32]

The Related/Vornado partnership on Manhattan's West Side is likely to transform that area into the next major downtown nucleus. Vornado already has over 6 million square feet of space in the area, and the rebuilding of Madison Square Garden and Penn Station with Related would result in another 5.5 million square feet. The $7 billion deal is touted as a growth engine for Manhattan real estate.[33] Related's Stephen Ross told a conference on REITs at the plush Waldorf Astoria Hotel: "We are about making money here on a grand scale."[34]

New York City zoning policies give private developers incentives for financing low- and moderate-income housing. Affordable housing advocates fought for mandatory inclusionary zoning rules that give developers 20 percent more floor area if they ensure that 20 percent of the units are permanently affordable housing. However, the new inclusionary rules are strictly voluntary and are likely to be inadequate.[35] The benefits to real estate likely outweigh benefits to low-income tenants. Programs like this that link the fate of low-income and market-rate housing can pave the way for gentrification and displacement because new construction that is 80 percent market-rate is bound to raise property values and rents, spurring the displacement of existing affordable housing.

The Diverse Ways of Globalized Real Estate

According to Saskia Sassen, New York City is one of about forty global cities that function as central nodes of finance capital and political power in an expanding global network of cities. But she also states that global capital and political power have diverse, concrete expressions at the local level.[36] Global capital touches down in distinct geographical environments, intersects with, is shaped by, and helps shape local capital and labor. Thus New York City retains a share of the developing world within it, just as its leading institutions keep the third world at bay. As William Sites notes in *Remaking New York: Primitive Globalization and the Politics of Urban Community*:

Strong-globalist accounts may blur important distinctions between globalization and capitalism, overdraw the novelty and extent of international interdependence, fail to recognize embeddedness, or downplay the inability of any single national or regional system to demonstrate economic supremacy. More useful approaches suggest, instead, that national and subnational environments operate both as enduring structures that mediate the local impacts of global processes and as dynamic arenas where political actors reconfigure the economic and social subarrangements of international developments.[37]

The globalization of New York City's real estate is by no means complete, and in some ways it is even less globalized than other U.S. cities. While McDonalds, Starbucks, and the Gap are all over the place, there is not a single Wal-Mart in New York City—and Wal-Mart is the largest corporation in the world. New York is a notorious latecomer in mall and big-box retail development. It is not just that developers have trouble shoe-horning megaprojects into such a densely developed city or that nonunion retail chains face stiff opposition from organized labor. Neighborhood retailers and residents have also created a political environment in which big-box retailing has had to struggle to enter the market. In 1996, the City Planning Department proposed to revise the city's zoning code to make it easier for big-box retailers to locate in manufacturing districts. After concerted protest from neighborhoods and local retailers, the proposal was defeated.[38]

However, the corporate invasion of local real estate in New York does not necessarily have to take the form of the usual suburban-style big-box retailer. Vornado's track record before it stormed New York was with suburban malls, and it cleverly shifted its investment strategy to meet New York City's unique density and regulatory environment, something that the clunky Wal-Mart has had trouble doing. Real estate giant The Related Company recently pulled off the kind of coup that Wal-Mart could not with its deal to evict local merchants and turn over the Bronx Terminal Market to corporate retailers. Related could do this because it was not a complete newcomer to local politics and CEO Stephen Ross was a friend of the mayor.

New York Real Estate's Global Roots

New York City's marriage with globalization is not recent but was forged at the time of its founding. This historic fact is especially significant because it suggests just how deeply rooted are the ties between local real estate and global finance.

Peter Stuyvesant, the first political leader of the city, was director of the Dutch West India Company, which at that time was one of the most powerful global trading monopolies. The development of property in Manhattan was made possible by the economic surplus that was earned from trade conducted by the Dutch West India Company and therefore was made available to Dutch settlers. The settlers chose to live within walking distance of the waterfront, which was the nexus for global trade, and the wealthiest of them built estates conveniently distant enough to separate themselves from the growing urban crowd. Land in lower Manhattan was bought and sold by the small class of elites that had access to the surplus capital generated by the Dutch West India Company, the main instrument of global economic power in the Americas.

The Global Empire
In the nineteenth century, the expansion of New Amsterdam northward paralleled the land grabs in western America by European settlers. Cornelius Vanderbilt and the railroad barons, many of them urban property owners as well, showed how public infrastructure could facilitate the capture of land in the American West. Manhattan also saw private rail lines grow under public franchises and subsidies similar to the rail lines that pierced the western territories. As the United States expanded under Manifest Destiny and speculative land development, Manhattan's propertied elite also set out to conquer its local territory.

By the end of the nineteenth century, 70 percent of the U.S. population lived in rural areas, mostly in small towns and on farms. Unlike Europe, where cities were central to the formation of nations and the decisive end of feudalism, accumulation of capital in the United States, unfettered by a feudal past, was linked to the conquest of frontiers beyond the thirteen colonies. The western territories were taken from Indian tribes and settled by whites. The U.S. government offered land to European settlers (under the Homestead Act) and made land speculators rich by subsidizing the nation's transportation infrastructure (railroads and highways). And as the nineteenth century drew to a close, the frontier was expanding rapidly beyond North America. This would parallel and in some ways affect the way urban land developed at home and the role that the state played in that development.

Around the end of the nineteenth century, the United States and its relationship to the world changed drastically. U.S. corporations sought to secure raw materials and low-cost labor not only in the recently acquired North American territories but abroad as well. As land developers ran out of territory and slavery was no longer a desirable option for modern industrial capital, both the U.S. regime of accumulation and the regime of urbanization changed dramatically. Industrial complexes in northern cities expanded, company towns grew, and large cities like New York and Chicago underwent a qualitative change as they were transformed into large, complex metropolitan regions.

The year 1898 was a turning point for both the United States and New York City. In that year, major territorial additions were made to the evolving U.S. empire with the invasions of the Philippines, Cuba, and Puerto Rico. Under President William McKinley and his successor, Teddy Roosevelt, the United States consolidated its political control over the Western Hemisphere. This was a major advance in the globalization of U.S. economic, political, and military power. The United States went from an agrarian frontier nation to a major industrial and military power that competed with the colonial powers of Europe, an example of what Carl Polanyi called "the Great Transformation."[39] This was the turning point in the growth of the modern metropolis, a qualitatively new form of human settlement that was much larger and more complex than the industrial cities it left behind.[40] The use of land in the metropolis was defined by a complex internal division of territory that was parallel to capital's new international division of labor. The service sectors grew apace along with the expansion of industry (contrary to the mythology of industrial cities, most people employed therein were in the service sectors).[41]

This great transformation of cities into modern metropolitan areas set the stage for neighborhood and community movements and community planning. Earlier cities going back to the first human settlements had neighborhoods, but the modern metropolis created for the first time multiple large residential and mixed-use districts, each of them often as big as entire cities and towns. Usually, these neighborhoods did not have their own formal institutions of governance, and this created space for the growth of community-based organizations, ethnic and religious groups, and social movements.

The New York Empire

In the nineteenth century, New York City was the financial center of an emerging global empire in the Americas. The city's financial barons had profited richly from the southern plantation economy, westward expansion into Indian territories, and sweatshops in northeastern cities. They traded the commodities produced throughout the American hinterland and invested the surplus in new speculative ventures. Part of that investment stayed in Manhattan's own backyard, where the local real estate empire was born.

In 1898, the local empire achieved formal political status: the City of New York was created as a consolidation of the territories of Manhattan, Brooklyn, Queens, the Bronx, and Staten Island. The imperial reign of Manhattan-centered real estate began. The new empire was based on the hegemony of the largest and most aggressive landowners. In 1896, the Real Estate Board of Brokers was founded by twenty-seven developers, land owners, and brokers. Their objective was to "facilitate transactions in real estate, such as buying, selling, leasing, mortgaging and insuring of property." This landed aristocracy wished to distinguish themselves from two-bit speculators and homeowners and claim a monopoly on access to government. They said they would "bring together the 'better element' among real estate brokers and agents for the promotion of their own and their clients' interests."[42] Just as trusts and syndicates were mastering the new global economy, New York City's landowning elites pushed aside any upstarts and joined arms to conquer the vast undeveloped territories of the new urban domain beyond Manhattan.

The government of the City of New York in 1898 had a territorial jurisdiction that today would be considered a regional government. If ever there was an opportunity for regional planning in the United States, this was it. The vast majority of the new city's territory was sparsely populated, including substantial farmland throughout the outer boroughs. Most of the urban population was clustered in lower Manhattan. There was a single government that could have developed a comprehensive plan for the city that might preserve parkland and farms, concentrated new development around rail lines, and integrated industry, housing, and retail development. At about the same time, across the

Atlantic the Swedish crown was setting in motion a comprehensive planning process for Stockholm that would do all of the above. In New York, however, only one government institution had a demonstrated capacity to plan for the future of the metropolis. This was the Central Park Commission, whose Andrew Haskell Green had gained respect among the propertied elites for his bold vision of the city's future embodied in the creation of Central Park.

Strongly influenced by real estate developers, however, the new central government rejected comprehensive planning for the entire city. The ability of government to even contemplate such an undertaking was limited because the city's main governing body, the Board of Estimate, was a fragmented institution made up of citywide elected officers and the president of each of the five boroughs. Conveniently for real estate developers, the borough presidents were tied to local political machines that protected and favored real estate development, but the Manhattan-based developers wielded disproportionate influence in the powerful citywide offices of mayor and controller. Contrary to the rhetoric of the Progressive reformers, Tammany Hall, the base of the Democratic Party, was not a single machine but a complex coalition of neighborhood-based machines that were the link between the city's increasingly diverse and segregated immigrant communities and real estate developers. The main opportunity for access to political power in the neighborhoods was through these machines. By default, the fractured city government allowed the more powerful fraction of the real estate industry to take the initiative in developing the five boroughs. This resulted in an overdeveloped central core, sprawl in the outer boroughs, subway lines that did not connect with one another, poorly served portions of the outer boroughs, a dearth of open space, and lack of public places. Farmland was completely wiped out by uncontrolled real estate speculation, eliminating any possibility of integrating food production and consumption (which occurred in many European cities and is now a cornerstone of twenty-first-century sustainable urban development). In sum, urban expansion in the new region was driven by the subdivision of land for speculative development, as it had been from the start in Manhattan.

The city's 722-mile public subway system, today the largest in the United States and one of the largest in the world, started as a scheme by private investors to spur real estate development outside lower Manhattan. William Steinway built his famous piano factory in Astoria, Queens, and began a career in real estate when he bought land to build housing for his workers and to subdivide for sale. Steinway understood the need to connect his new bedroom suburbs with Manhattan and headed a municipal commission that proposed the first subway lines in 1892. This stimulated a rash of speculation along the proposed routes, and the speculators became big subway boosters and rich. Steinway's initiative went down with the stock market crash of 1893 but was later implemented by others. The Chamber of Commerce of the State of New York, with strong backing from the Real Estate Exchange, pushed through a state law that would make for privately built and operated subways under municipal franchise. The first subway lines of the Interborough Rapid Transit (IRT) made possible residential development in Manhattan's Upper West Side, Harlem, and the Bronx. In the next two decades, new IRT and BMT (Brooklyn-Manhattan Transit, another private company) lines linked Manhattan's business districts with the far corners of Brooklyn, the Bronx, and Queens. Some elevated lines were torn down, creating new above-ground real estate opportunities.[43]

While new rapid transportation technology made possible rapid development of Manhattan's hinterland, another technological innovation—the elevator—made it likely that the subway and elevated lines would all converge in Manhattan. The elevator was essential to high-rise construction, which would help property owners capture steep land value increases around subway stations. These increases were the greatest in Manhattan, where all mass transit lines converged, a convenient geography for Manhattan property owners, the core of the city's landed aristocracy. Unlike many other metropolitan regions in the world, New York has only one rail line (the G line) that links neighborhoods outside the core, and that line has poor and infrequent service. Auto use is significantly higher outside the Manhattan core. One geological condition favored Manhattan-centric development, and without it the current skyline might not have been possible: the island's solid bedrock can support seemingly unlimited vertical growth.

Through the early decades of the twentieth century, subway expansion coupled a building boom in Manhattan with an explosion of new development in the outer boroughs. Fed by dramatic economic growth in the 1920s, streetcars also served new areas that opened up to land subdivision. But the boom turned to bust with the Great Depression in the 1930s, when real estate losses were catastrophic. The New Deal came to the rescue by financing extensive public works, including yet another set of subway lines, the Independent Subway (IND), and consolidating public control of the three subway systems. Mayor Fiorello LaGuardia, elected with strong labor support, was a New Deal ally who fought against an entrenched neighborhood-based political machine that at times proved an obstacle to large-scale development. Robert Moses, the architect of many of the new public works, bypassed many of the ailing real estate developers, but in the long run the expensive public infrastructure projects of the New Deal would buttress the value of real estate for both the Manhattan-based oligarchy and outer borough upstarts. (See the following section of this chapter on the roles played by the urban reform movement, Robert Moses, and land-use policy.) In sum, *publicly financed fixed infrastructure helped to mobilize capital and in the long run was a boon to the most mobile of capital.* In the tradition of Keynesian political economy, the state provided the conditions for the accumulation of private capital and, to use David Harvey's term, capital achieved its "spatial fix."[44]

Land-Use Planning and Zoning for Real Estate Development

When Peter Stuyvesant took charge of developing the town of New Amsterdam in the seventeenth century, he encountered what he thought was a chaotic settlement. He ordered that all property be surveyed and streets be laid out. This was the first example of city planning (if you can call it that) in New York City and set the pattern for future land-use controls. From the start, planning was in the hands of land surveyors who worked for powerful landowners. Stuyvesant did not project an image for a future metropolis but simply tried to organize rationally the property relations that already existed. This also systematized racial segregation as an institution linked with private property. Stuyvesant himself owned forty slaves, more than anyone else in town, and in the first instance of "Negro removal" in the city's history took over several "Negro Lots" that were previously set aside for former slaves.[45]

Throughout the city's history, the most powerful property owners managed to thwart serious efforts in comprehensive land-use planning and the establishment of any large public places that would be kept off the market. The 1811 grid plan and 1916 zoning law followed the land market and did not try to lead it. They allowed for orderly growth stimulated by private land subdivision. The grid plan and zoning were not, in fact, plans that would consciously project a future urban landscape with significant public places. They codified existing physical development, liberally allowed new land subdivision, and could be changed to accommodate even greater growth with changing market demand. They followed modernist principles of rational growth and orderly development, codified the existing spatial patterns of social inequality, and avoided any explicit planning for social and cultural development.[46]

In Manhattan's grid plan, avenues running north and south were intersected by streets going east and west, forming relatively uniform blocks that could be easily subdivided and sold off. The typical lot was 100 feet deep, with a frontage ranging from 10 to 25 feet. In the decades before the plan, land surveyors were already cutting up Manhattan's farmland into building lots. The 1811 plan sought to harmonize these grids and establish the new grid as the standard for the rest of the island. Since the plan left no room for public places such as squares or major parks, the city's streets and sidewalks became the main public places and until today the main transitional space between private and public activity.

But isn't Central Park a major, planned public space? Actually, Central Park was built on 700 acres of land that had limited development potential at that time because of serious drainage and topographical problems. Wealthy property owners in the area favored the project because it would increase the value of their houses and give them a large backyard. Labor was feeling the brunt of an economic depression and saw construction jobs in the new scheme. And the city administration under William Tweed (who was indicted and convicted a decade after the park was built) saw a good opportunity to sell influence. In the way of the new park were the farms and settlements of poor people, who were evicted without mercy.[47] The design for Central Park by Frederick Law Olmstead and Calvert Vaux followed in part the modern English tradition of landscape architecture in which parks were to be quiet preserves designed for "civilized" elites, not noisy playgrounds for an urban working class that nevertheless might be invited there.[48]

Central Park became a model for urban open space in the city and throughout the world. But its success obscured the other great need in the densely developed city—a need for many small neighborhood green spaces that are accessible on a daily basis to people of all ages, incomes, and abilities. Central Park made public open space a grand enclave and left the rest of the land in the city open to subdivision for real estate development. And it set the precedent of using parks to reinforce land values at their peripheries.

Zoning Instead of Planning

In the early twentieth century, land-use regulation exploded with the new urban region and the expansion of the interventionist state. Since creation of the city's 1916 Zoning Resolution, zoning has been the principal tool of land-use regulation, served the largest and most powerful property owners, and helped mediate and preempt disputes within the real estate sector. Increasingly, however, as is shown in the following chapters, organized neighborhoods have managed to shape zoning and land-use controls to reflect some of their collective interests.

Commercial property owners in downtown Manhattan backed passage of the 1916 Zoning Resolution, which they saw as a tool to protect their property values. Upscale shops on Fifth Avenue were located near the bustling garment manufacturing district, where factories paid low rents. Low-rent buildings kept rents in the whole area down and limited redevelopment ambitions. Also, the elite customers of the fancy shops did not like running into the working-class women who were going to and from their jobs or sitting outside on their lunch breaks. So from the start, zoning was designed to promote the interests of downtown commercial property owners, isolate industry, and separate the working class from the "better" classes.

From the start, zoning and planning focused on Manhattan, where the stakes in land were the highest. Until the Zoning Resolution was revised in 1961, most parts of the other boroughs outside Manhattan were zoned as "unrestricted." This meant that industry, housing, and commerce could be mixed. So the land outside Manhattan was a relatively wide-open frontier in a market-dominated free-for-all where many smaller developers could establish themselves among the large speculators. Unrestricted zoning allowed for the evolution and further development of classical mixed-use neighborhoods such as Greenpoint, Williamsburg, and Red Hook in Brooklyn.

The pattern of tight regulation in the core and relatively minimal regulation in the periphery corresponded with the classical pattern of imperial city planning that has prevailed throughout history. Ancient Greece, for example, imposed a strict grid pattern on the core of its colonial cities as a way of consolidating its economic and political control. Spain's Law of the Indies dictated the layout of cities in its Latin American colonies, but the law never extended to the masses of poor people who lived far from the central plaza. New York City's Zoning Resolution was made to protect the interests of Manhattan real estate, leaving the rest of the city to the vagaries of a less imperial and somewhat less profitable marketplace.

Zoning in the outer boroughs permitted a range of low- to midrise housing development on relatively cheap land. Most were fairly

uninspiring commercial ventures, but there were some notable exceptions. For example, in 1927 the Amalgamated Clothing Workers Union
built its first low-cost apartments in the Bronx.[49] As time went by and
low-cost land in Manhattan became scarce, high-rise clusters developed
in areas of the outer boroughs served by mass transit. In the post–World
War II period, federally subsidized public housing, city- and state-
subsidized middle-income housing, and union-sponsored cooperative
housing complemented private high-rise development in areas like the
south Bronx, central Brooklyn, and central Queens.

New York City's zoning regulations failed to comprehensively plan
for future development on a regional scale. More visionary reformers,
taking inspiration from Ebenezer Howard and the Garden Cities movement in England, created the First Regional Plan and what is known
today as the Regional Plan Association (RPA). But this was a private,
nonprofit organization with some notable prestige and no formal authority to implement any of its proposals (the RPA is discussed further
below).

Urban Reforms against the Working Class

In the early twentieth century, a national urban reform movement arose
in the United States, and New York City was a leader in implementing
its program. Under the sponsorship of the Progressives, reformers sought
changes, including housing and zoning codes, that would address the
miserable living conditions in the "slums" to eliminate the breeding
grounds for both disease and radical political ideas.[50] Their political
program opposed party machines that served neighborhood-based immigrant groups, claiming they were corrupt and exploitative. The program
called for nonpartisan elections, at-large representatives, professional
city managers, Taylorist-type economic efficiency, and merit-based civil
service regulations. Robert Moses (1888–1981) was the reform movement's most accomplished representative.

The urban reformers believed that politically neutral technocrats and
civil servants like Moses should replace neighborhood-based politicians
and institutions, who were presumed to be corrupt. Moses was an upper-
middle-class professional known for his commitment to engineering,
efficiency, and development. He cleared working-class neighborhoods,
built highways and parks for the new middle class, and created downtown development opportunities. The class origins of Moses and the
reformers were related to the class bias of their policies:

Analysis of the social class backgrounds of reformers reveals, especially in the cities, a uniformly upper-class bias. Studies of the origins of reform movements show that business and upper-class elements normally championed reform, while lower- and working-class groups usually opposed it. For example, the New York City Bureau of Municipal Research, founded in 1906, was initially financed by Andrew Carnegie and John D. Rockefeller. The U.S. Chamber of Commerce provided office space and paid the executive secretary of the City Managers Association for several years. Civil clubs and voters' leagues generally contained names from elite social directories. Professional people involved in reform tended to be the most prestigious members of their professions, and many of them had upper-class origins.[51]

The backdrop for the urban reform movement was the growth of a large immigrant working class and radical labor and community organizations in the late nineteenth and early twentieth centuries. Already the industrial and financial center of U.S. capital at the end of the nineteenth century, New York City attracted labor in record numbers from among the poor workers and peasants of Europe. The revolutions of 1848 in Europe, the Paris Commune of 1871, and growing socialist movements had aroused working-class aspirations and middle-class fears of social unrest. Many European immigrants—Germans and Irish and the working-class Jews, Scandinavians, and Eastern Europeans who followed them—brought with them radical socialist and anarchist ideas and the ethnic, religious, political, and mutual aid associations that became central institutions in city neighborhoods. They joined the voices of the International Workers of the World, the Socialist Party, and in the 1920s the Communist Party (the last two were headquartered in New York City). The successful Bolshevik revolution in 1917 inspired hope in many New Yorkers that the imperial rule of capital could be overthrown. Rural and urban landlords were under assault in the Soviet Union, and private property no longer ruled without obstruction. Could it happen in New York?

The empire fought back on its domestic front to ensure that it would not happen. The Red Scare and Palmer raids were key elements of anti-immigrant, antilabor, and anticommunist hysteria whipped up by conservative citizen groups, the press, and government. The nativist panic targeted New York City, already the nation's emblematic center for working-class immigrants.[52]

While the urban middle classes felt threatened by radical organizing among immigrants, the more enlightened among them focused on the difficult living conditions faced by immigrants. They were afraid not so much of poverty itself but the concentration of poverty, which they thought ignited radical political tinder. Also, if the "slums" were to grow, they could negatively affect property values in the wealthier neighborhoods, and diseases like tuberculosis and cholera could migrate.

The urban reformers advocated charity as well as government regulation. The photographs of Jacob Riis document extreme urban poverty and were used to attract sympathy for the reform agenda and philanthropy from the wealthy. They are also a testimony to the class bias of this famous reformer. In Riis's photos, workers are passive and quiet, their sad eyes seemingly begging for pity and salvation. The dark hovels inspire middle-class moral outrage and call out for building codes that bring light and air. The very title of Riis's book, *How the Other Half Lives*, speaks in the voice of the privileged half. Mixed in with Riis's condemnations of urban landlords are views of immigrants (especially Italians) and blacks that range from patronizing to outright racist:

Poverty, abuse, and injustice alike the negro accepts with imperturbable cheerfulness. His philosophy is of the kind that has no room for repining. Whether he lives in an Eighth Ward barrack or in a tenement with a brown-stone front and pretensions to the title of "flat," he looks at the sunny side of life and enjoys it. He loves fine clothes and good living a good deal more than he does a bank account. The proverbial rainy day it would be rank ingratitude, from his point of view, to look for when the sun shines unclouded in a clear sky. His home surroundings, except when he is utterly depraved, reflect his blithesome temper.[53]

Scores of settlement houses in areas of concentrated poverty were created by social reformers, some of them inspired by religious commitments to charity. They were more paternalistic than participatory and would do for poor people what they thought was good for them. Clustered in the Lower East Side, the neighborhood with the highest concentration of new immigrants, were the University Settlement, Grand Street, the Educational Alliance, Henry Street, the Hamilton-Madison House, the Union Settlement, and the Hudson Guild. They provided social services and educational programs years before government got in the business. They were run with the help of volunteers drawn mostly from the middle class.

Settlement house work was not all paternalistic and in some ways supported progressive social movements. Staff and volunteers were often among the first to survey and document living conditions and social needs in working-class neighborhoods. By creating human services, they helped to slow displacement and protect neighborhoods and thus were precursors to neighborhood movements. They also opened their doors to other community organizations and sometimes hosted radical political activities even if they did not promote them. They became social and cultural centers that reinforced a sense of solidarity, sometimes even mixing loyalty to local community with loyalty to class.[54] Although they relied on private philanthropy, they also helped lay the groundwork for public entitlement programs, such as social security and home relief.

The largest and most powerful Manhattan-based real estate developers backed the urban reform movement and the system of land-use controls that would limit the role of small-scale, upstart real estate enterprises. Tenement legislation did away with the worst abuses by small-scale speculative developers. The crowning achievement of reformers was the New Tenement Law of 1902, which called for more light and air in new apartment buildings and gave an advantage to the larger, established developers who could more easily meet the new codes.

The urban reform movement was influenced by the British Garden Cities idea,[55] which called for the creation of neat model communities at the edges of cities as an alternative to dense central working-class neighborhoods (see chapter 1). In New York City, it led to a few new residential developments in the outer boroughs like Sunnyside, Fresh Meadows, and Forest Hills, Queens, but these enclaves were soon surrounded by conventional speculative development projects and rarely emulated. Forest Hills is an exclusive, low-density upper-income enclave that offers little as a model for affordable housing development in the city and region. In the United States, suburban subdivisions, not planned Garden Cities or New Towns like those found throughout Europe, are the norm.[56]

Corporate Vision of the Region: The Regional Plan Association

Yet another product of the urban reform movement, the Regional Plan Association (RPA) was founded in the 1920s and produced three plans for the metropolitan region—in 1929, 1968, and 1996. The approach of the RPA has been to rationalize the concentration of growth in the region's central business districts, with Manhattan as the most powerful center. The RPA has sought to rationalize suburban growth, incorporating conservationist principles and ideas from the Garden Cities tradition. In its plans, it has sought to balance production and consumption activities, mass transit and the private automobile, concentration and dispersal, downtown corporate goals and suburban real estate interests. The RPA's focus on regional transit echoes the urban reform movement's emphasis on efficiency and productivity. Since there is no single governmental entity responsible for planning and managing this evolving region, the RPA's voice, though only an advisory one, is often listened to if not always acted on, if for no other reason than the prominence of its corporate backers.[57] While the RPA's sponsors are a Who's Who of the financial, insurance, and real estate sector and the RPA approach to strategic planning follows the corporate model and serves the interests of the wealthy and powerful, they are not simply instruments of real estate and finance.[58] They are forever tied up in the contradictions of the real estate–driven model of metropolitan growth to which their corporate sponsors are wed. This reproduces irrational suburban sprawl, the destruction of the environment, overconcentration in the center, and declining public health and quality of life, all elements that RPA strives to mitigate.

Although the RPA's founding leaders were all white men, the organization took on issues of social equity and race, however imperfectly, in their last two plans.[59] But even as community planning sprang up under their noses, the RPA has continued to keep its eyes on the issues that matter most to its corporate sponsors—downtown development, the quality of life in suburbia, regional mass transit, protection of open spaces at the suburban fringes, and utilization of the vast reserve army of labor in New York City and its inner suburbs. It has tried to engage the hundreds of large municipal governments in the region in some sort of regional dialogue that goes beyond RPA-sponsored conferences, but in a region where exclusionary suburban land-use practices rely on the perpetuation of fragmented local government powers, there is no political space for this. And New York City, the largest of all the municipal governments, has been an unenthusiastic partner of RPA because its political leaders fear that a central city and suburban alliance would mean suburban dominance.[60] RPA has even less experience working with the city's hundreds of neighborhoods, which could be natural allies in promoting regional planning. In the end, the RPA has been either unwilling or unable to challenge the supremacy of real estate development as the driving force in the region and therefore has been unable to really address the problems that have gone along with it—displacement, segregation, suburban sprawl, and the loss of public open space. The RPA has begun to forge alliances with community-based organizations throughout the region in the interests of linking local and regional planning, but these are fairly modest.[61]

The RPA's Second Regional Plan, released in 1968, a landmark year of urban struggles against displacement (see chapter 3), rationalized downtown growth as a development strategy. Compelled to acknowledge the plight of central city neighborhoods since they were exploding in rage, RPA supported mainstream efforts to redevelop them. Since the RPA had no power to implement anything, its plan mostly gave an air of legitimacy to real estate growth and the displacement caused by the federal urban renewal program. The Third Regional Plan in 1996 reaffirmed RPA's rational-comprehensive approach to the region, calling for growth that balances economy, equity, and environment.[62]

The RPA faces a perplexing contradiction between its noble planning principles and its dedication to real estate–induced growth. This hinders its ability to be an effective advocate for and ally of communities, which it is at times. While the regional perspective is often lacking in the community movements, the community perspective is lacking among the regional planners. For example, RPA's qualified support for a giant real estate venture, the Atlantic Yards project in Brooklyn (discussed further in chapter 7), overlooked strong community opposition and focused on the purported efficiencies of building over a transit hub.

Postwar Expansion: Suburban Sprawl and Central City Renewal

New York City's growth spurt after World War II was closely tied to its central role as a center of global capitalism. The United States emerged as a powerful victor after the war, with new global spheres of influence, an expanded economic surplus, and a strong industrial base. The city replaced war-battered London as the global financial center. As a result, substantial surplus capital was available for real estate investment. As the home of the new United Nations, New York City became the center of the emerging dynasty that would displace Europe as the main protagonist and power broker in global politics.

In the postwar decades, cities in the United States would be redesignated as *central cities*, suburbs would become the habitat for the majority of the nation, and the nation's historical antiurban bias (rooted in its rural, frontier origins)[63] would now be directed at the central cities, which increasingly were occupied by African Americans and new immigrants from Latin America, Africa, and Asia. After the war, the federal government launched what a visitor from the moon might have called a massive national urban plan, even as the government was deriding central planning in the Soviet Union. If the definition of *planning* is a conscious human activity that shapes the urban environment (see chapter 1), then the postwar national policies that shaped urban development were consciously aimed at changing the nation's urban landscape. Postwar urban policy was in effect a *comprehensive plan* for low-density suburban development, and it was consistent with the endemic antiurbanism that the nation inherited from the nineteenth century.[64] What was first named the Defense Highway System in the 1930s later became the Federal Interstate Highway System, the largest public works project ever implemented in the United States and the central element in national urban policy. Another pillar of national policy was the system of federal mortgage guarantees offered by the Federal Housing Administration and Veterans Administration. Unlike New Deal planning, however, the beneficiaries of national policy were the auto, oil, and tire monopolies, construction industries, and the mostly white homeowners who followed their jobs as they were moved to the suburbs. The new freeways also made commuting to central cities easier and replaced rail and trolley systems. (New York City lost its extensive street car network, which served most neighborhoods in the five boroughs, but preserved its Manhattan-centered subway and suburban rail system.)

The national policies that decentralized industry and workers were consistent with the designs of military strategists who believed in the myth that dispersal of the population and industrial infrastructure would minimize losses in the case of nuclear attack.[65] The fear of attack by foreign powers was accompanied by the racial fears that lead to white flight from central cities. Industries in cities like New York became disposable. New York had many small and medium-sized industries, little developable land for large-footprint low-rise industrial buildings, and despite the best efforts of Robert Moses and his successors, second-rate connections to the interstate highway system.

The low-density sprawl resulting from implementation of the interstate highway system and federal housing policies coincided with exclusionary local planning practices in the suburbs. Small municipal governments were spread throughout a fragmented territory, which allowed the new suburbanites to gain control over their community's land, adopt exclusionary land-use and zoning policies to protect their property values, and thus become the foundation for narrow, conservative community planning in the United States. Ironically, though these small governments were the prime beneficiaries of national policy, they became fervent advocates for local decision making and community participation as opposed to federal intervention.

The nation's patterns of racial and class segregation were no accident. They continued historic trends from the periods of slavery and Jim Crow and postwar national policies. Federal regulations explicitly forbade loans to homeowners in black neighborhoods. Zoning, conveniently left in the hands of mostly white local government elites, prevented people with limited incomes from moving into suburbs.[66] Just as important were the actions that government failed to take, like cracking down on discriminatory practices in real estate, lending, and insurance or taking away the power of local government to exclude people on the basis of class and race.[67] And in central cities, the federal urban renewal program came to be known as "Negro removal" because of the disproportionately large numbers of blacks among those it displaced.

Making Urban Renewal Work in New York City

The national plan for central cities was as grand as the plan for the suburbs. The cities were to be ringed and penetrated by the new interstate highway network. The federal urban renewal program would help local developers by assembling and clearing land where poor people lived and promoting high-rise commercial and upscale residential development. Title I of the 1949 federal Housing Act and subsequent housing bills gave local authorities funds for the acquisition and clearance of urban land. Public housing would house those who were displaced by urban renewal and other low-income tenants. Housing advocates among the reformers fought hard for the public housing program, but conservatives in Congress made sure that funding would be limited and that austere design rules would prevent the Housing Act from becoming a model for new development (arguing that if working people knew they could get decent public housing, the private market would be threatened).[68]

Real estate corporations were often contracted to do the planning and site development for urban renewal areas, and small local developers often lacked the administrative and political savvy needed to get the contracts. In New York, the model for urban renewal was set early by the insurance industry—real estate's strategic partner—with giant new projects like those launched by the Metropolitan Life Insurance Company in Long Island City and the Lower East Side, the latter including Stuyvesant Town and Peter Cooper Village in 1947.

New York City's storied New Deal liberalism gradually began to erode in the post–World War II economic boom,[69] but Robert Moses retained his skill for securing the funds from Washington. Moses had already done his own planning for major renewal projects, so he immediately knew what to do with Washington's largesse. But Moses was fundamentally the instrument for executing national policies in New York City. He was not the sole author of these policies, and there were many others like him throughout the nation. Because this was one of the most densely populated and liberal cities and had active social and labor movements, the job of stuffing the highways, new office buildings, and civic centers in and throwing the working class out was daunting and required a ruthlessness that Moses was able to provide (one of his favorite phrases was, "You can't make an omelette without breaking eggs"). Without the feisty Moses, the people living in strategic neighborhoods like East Tremont in the Bronx (which was in the way of the new Cross-Bronx Expressway) might very well have won their battles to stay. Contrary to the impression created by Robert Caro's biography of Moses,[70] Robert Moses did not reshape New York, but New York was reshaped by global and local economic forces that required a character like Moses to carry out the plan. The real estate industry appreciated the role played by Robert Moses in urban renewal programs:

[Thus] William Zeckendorf, the nation's biggest Title I developer, noted that whereas most cities required a strong mayor or a cohesive business elite to overcome community mobilization against urban renewal, New York City only "had Bob Moses [who] all by himself [was] worth two-dozen blue-ribbon citizens' commissions."[71]

The 1961 Zoning Resolution and the 1969 Master Plan

The building boom in the 1950s added millions of square feet of office space to lower and Midtown Manhattan. Manhattan led an international trend in large-scale functional office building and the establishment of exclusive central business districts. The Empire State Building, once the tallest skyscraper in the world, was surrounded by vertical rectangles of comparable and greater height. Manhattan was the first to brand itself with its skyline—and not just single iconic buildings—long before construction of the World Trade Center in the 1970s.

As property values soared, the building boom in Manhattan's two central business districts (CBDs), Midtown and Downtown, created development pressures on many nearby low-rent neighborhoods such as Chelsea, Hell's Kitchen, and Greenwich Village. At the same time, the movement of industrial jobs to the suburbs and beyond was tearing apart other neighborhoods, leaving vacant buildings and land in its wake. The military decommissioned the Brooklyn Navy Yard, Brooklyn Army Terminal, and other facilities. With them went thousands of industrial jobs, and acres of land remained vacant and inaccessible for decades because real estate developers could not afford the high mitigation costs for building on contaminated land.

With the commercial and luxury markets saturated, investors sought subsidies that would allow them to tap into the growing middle-income portion of the housing market—those who could not afford market-rate luxury housing, did not qualify for or could not get into public housing, could not afford the suburbs, and worked for modest wages in Manhattan. With generous subsidies in the form of bond financing, low-interest loans, and tax incentives, middle-income housing development, principally through state and city Mitchell-Lama programs, would become profitable.[72] In the postwar era, the real estate oligarchy made below-market housing a stable element in its policy agenda and growth machine and won significant public subsidies to help finance it.

The city's dynamic postwar building boom led the city's planners to propose a complete overhaul of the Zoning Resolution, consolidating Manhattan's modern high-rise skyline, opening up new frontiers for residential and industrial real estate development in the outer boroughs, and generally facilitating millions of square feet of new real estate growth.

The 1961 Zoning Resolution eliminated the vast unrestricted districts outside Manhattan where small-scale developers could once romp and opened up new opportunities for the larger real estate firms. Planners who prepared the 1961 zoning revision were overly optimistic about industrial expansion, and many mixed-use neighborhoods were rezoned exclusively for industry—which would later invite noxious uses and lead to environmental justice campaigns (see chapter 5).

The new code incorporated selected principles of Le Corbusier's modernism by giving Manhattan developers floor-area bonuses in exchange for public space at ground level.[73] Gone were the last farms in the city. Everything was asphalt and concrete except the reformers' neatly planned parks. The potential for regional planning opened up by the 1898 consolidation and New York's "regional government" was long gone. Speculative residential development now spilled out far beyond the five boroughs and out of reach of city control, as workers followed industry to the suburbs. But the grand planning vision underlying the 1961 zoning was not regional. It was really not much more than a new license for the next wave of real estate development driven by downtown expansion.

In 1969, following a mandate established in the city's 1963 charter and years of study, the Department of City Planning (DCP) completed the city's first, last, and only master plan—a huge document that described the city neighborhood by neighborhood and set out general land-use policies to guide future decision making. Though the plan was more descriptive than prescriptive, it projected growth led by downtown development and opened the door for new rounds of urban renewal, neglecting to provide concrete measures to address the needs of working-class neighborhoods. Commissioner Beverly Moss Spatt was the lone planning commissioner to take the plan seriously enough to roundly criticize it:

Hidden behind a very deep concern with the problems confronting the City is a strong desire to avoid commitment to specific programs to solve the problems. . . . By choosing liberal generalities as opposed to specific goals and programs the planners prepared a document that is not a plan, not even a policy guide.[74]

She denounced the plan as an invention concocted without the participation of the city's residents:

I am persuaded to object to the present plan because of the failure of the Commission to involve the Public and the Planning Department staff and the members of the Planning Commission in far greater participation in drafting this document. . . . This Plan represents mostly the works of the Commission Chairman and a few selected people.

Spatt was an early supporter of decentralized planning and saw no reason why the city could not plan with neighborhoods and at the same time promote citywide and regional planning. She wanted to see planning units located within community districts that would coordinate with centralized agencies.[75] "Community people knew better than the commissioners," she said in a recent interview.[76] In her many dissenting votes at the Commission, Spatt went on record opposing zoning and tax incentives to market-rate real estate developers. She also publicly criticized the lack of appointments of blacks and Puerto Ricans to the Commission.

The master plan elicited groans from the real estate industry because it might have limited growth in some areas of the city. The City Planning Commission let the master plan die without a struggle, although Spatt's advocacy of community planning continued and reemerged in a different form within the coming decades. The city's planning agency, the Department of City Planning, dropped all pretexts at planning, both comprehensive and community-based. Instead, since the 1970s the DCP has focused its efforts on the care and maintenance of zoning regulations. Flaunting a basic principle of city planning, the city's professionals rezone without a plan of any kind and instead claim that zoning is the plan. Chapters 6 and 7 discuss some unfortunate consequences of this approach for community planning in the city.

In 1965, the Landmarks Preservation Commission was created following the mostly elite protest against the destruction of historic Manhattan buildings in the postwar real estate development boom. Good-government groups were appalled at the demolition of Pennsylvania Station and rallied to save Grand Central Station. While most of the designated landmarks today are in wealthy neighborhoods and tend to be concentrated in Manhattan, the preservation community today has grown and diversified. Community organizers and planners are now using preservation tools, proposing landmark districts in working-class neighborhoods, and seeking the designation of cultural sites of importance, such as the Audobon Ballroom in Harlem, where Malcolm X was assassinated.

The Permanent Fiscal Crisis and Deregulation

The tectonic shift in global capital that occurred in the 1970s opened up the era of New York City's sustained fiscal crisis. The 1970s saw the collapse of the Bretton-Woods economic regime dominated by the United States, the birth of trilateralism, and the rise of the Organization of Petroleum Exporting Countries (OPEC). A new international division of labor produced an accelerated flight of industry from Rustbelt to Sunbelt, the growth of a global assembly line, and the rise of newly industrialized countries in Asia and Latin America. The impact of this new round of globalization and flexible accumulation on New York City was critical if not devastating. Disinvestment in industry and urban infrastructure followed the outmigration of capital. In a local economy that thrived on excess capital from global profits, New York was clearly in trouble. As capital flows to older industrial central cities diminished, industry continued to move out, and labor followed. The postwar boom in the city's real estate market receded, landlords pulled out of entire neighborhoods, and housing abandonment was widespread (see next section). Homeowners got hit by blockbusting,[77] landlords torched their own buildings, banks and insurance companies redlined,[78] and neighborhoods collapsed.

The city's economic woes were further complicated by the rightward political shift in the nation as Richard Nixon assumed the presidency. In recently released tapes of White House conversations, Nixon denounces "Jews and Catholics and Blacks and Puerto Ricans" and says "Maybe New York shouldn't survive. Maybe it should go through a cycle of destruction."[79] Nixon purposely withdrew federal funds from central cities and terminated the War on Poverty that had barely begun. For city neighborhoods, the only silver lining was the end of the federal urban renewal program—though mostly it was done as part of a general government downsizing and supported by libertarians who hated urban renewal because it violated the sanctity of private property. Nixon and Congress agreed to institute revenue sharing with local governments in place of categorical grants, which set the stage for future cuts in federal assistance to local governments. The war in Vietnam further drained federal coffers.

In 1975, facing a massive debt load and shrinking revenues, New York City was at the brink of default. As screamed by tabloid headlines, President Gerald Ford essentially told the city to "drop dead." Mayor Abe Beame and his predecessor John Lindsay took the political hit, but the fiscal crisis was about much more than too much borrowing to pay for city services. The city would not have faced a fiscal crisis if the postwar liberal alliance between government and labor, inherited from the New Deal, had not eroded and the neoliberal era had not begun.

The New York City fiscal crisis was a kickoff in the game of postindustrial globalization (see chapter 1). It signaled the onset of neoliberalism and the devolution of federal powers to the states that would reach its apex with the Reagan revolution and new federalism of the 1980s. This was the devolution that countered the revolutions of the 1960s. In the decades to follow, city services were cut, and the local tax burden increased. But those who were most able to weather the storm, the groups within the financial sector, got a handsome bailout. The state created the Emergency Finance Control Board (EFCB), which was headed by financier Felix Rohatyn. The EFCB's chief mission was to protect the bondholders, which they did by instituting service cutbacks, deferred maintenance of the city's infrastructure, union concessions, and other measures that hurt working people and the neighborhoods where they lived. Maintenance of the city's bond ratings shapes decision making on services and infrastructure, giving the financial sector a virtual veto on general city policies. Permanent city workers were laid off and hired back at a fraction of their old salaries and with no job security under the federal Comprehensive Employment Training Act. Under the EFCB's tutelage. the city handed out enormous tax breaks to downtown corporations and developers citing the myth that these breaks kept businesses and their money from leaving town.[80] Most of the tax abatements for new construction and rehabilitation that were instituted in the 1970s are still available today, when the market is strong enough to survive without them. Under the EFCB, New York City became yet another indebted government like South Africa and Bolivia. The city is still carrying the debt load from the 1970s, even as Mayor Michael Bloomberg prepares to lead the city into more debt to finance new projects.

The fiscal crisis came at a time when city government faced challenges no less daunting than it faced in the Great Depression. This time, however, the federal government was pulling out. As central cities became increasingly nonwhite and as Congress became increasingly dominated by a suburban majority, the racial significance of the fiscal crisis was not lost on neighborhood activists. Roger Starr, the city's chief housing administrator, advocated "planned shrinkage," the orderly withdrawal of city services from communities of color that were deemed unworthy of being saved. At the national level, Nixon's chief urban adviser, Daniel Patrick Moynihan (later a U.S. Senator for New York) advised his boss to adopt a policy of "benign neglect" of central cities. Moynihan also distinguished himself for a controversial study that attributed the poverty in black communities to problems of the black family. Officials blamed the victims, the ghetto, welfare, and, above all, poor people of color.

The real estate industry continued to blame rent control for every urban problem, including the fiscal crisis, and put forth the idea that the city could build its way out of the crisis.[81] New state legislation in 1974 marked the beginning of the end for strict rent controls and the phasing in of rent stabilization, which allowed for gradual rental increases. One of rent stabilization's unforeseen consequences, however, was that it extended the life of tenant organizing and rent strikes, now a virtually permanent fixture in community life.[82]

The idea of a permanent fiscal crisis was engendered by a structural shift in the model of capitalist accumulation and the rise of the neoliberal state (see chapter 1). Government could no longer be relied on to provide direct services as it had done since the New Deal. Contracting out projects and services was hyped as the antidote to a bloated bureaucracy and government inefficiency.[83] The construction of any new public infrastructure would need to be tied to private real estate development. The most dramatic effect of this policy has been in parks and open space. Corporate and private sponsorship of local parks through conservancies and partnerships like the Central Park Conservancy has helped fill some of the gaps left by cuts in the Parks Department's operating budget, but it has also favored the parks in wealthier neighborhoods. New parks are now developed with commercial enterprises that generate revenue to be used for maintenance. This is the model followed in the Hudson River

Greenway and Brooklyn Bridge Park, where commercial interests that have their hands on the purse strings have a powerful role in shaping the public space to their advantage. In one recent example, the city proposed to allow twenty Manhattan private schools control over public open space on Randalls Island in exchange for their investment in the space.[84] The city's waterfront zoning, adopted in 1993, reflects this public-private approach because the development of new public open space on the waterfront now depends almost entirely on upland private development.[85]

Capital and Communities on the Move: The Abandonment of Neighborhoods

People from all over the world visited New York City during the 1970s and were puzzled by the abandoned neighborhoods with block after block of vacant buildings, empty garbage-strewn lots, and abandoned housing units—hundreds of thousands of units that were clustered mostly in neighborhoods occupied by working-class people and people of color. Many of these visitors knew firsthand about the extensive damage done to cities by war and natural disasters, but they never expected to find such devastation in a rich country that had not experienced war on its own territory for over a century. They saw widespread poverty, crime, and drugs. The press and politicians pointed their fingers at tenants and a few nefarious slumlords. Community-based organizations accused the banks, insurance companies, landlords, and city agencies. But rarely did anyone venture an analysis that looked at the systemic nature of the crisis. Only by looking at the underlying contradictions of real estate and community, capital and labor, and class and race can we really explain how a city that escaped the bombing during the war came to look like Berlin and Dresden after the Allied air raids. Certainly everyone involved played a role in the crisis, but by only looking for someone to blame we will never understand what really happened.

The key question is why all of these institutions collapsed only in certain neighborhoods and all about the same time. Part of the answer lies in the movement of capital, both local and global.[86] As is shown above, dynamic capitalism endlessly uproots labor; the faster that capital moves, the faster labor is forced to move. Capital fled northeastern central cities for the suburbs, the Sunbelt, developing-world duty-free zones, and other havens free from labor laws, unions, and environmental regulation. In its endless pursuit of profits, capital commodified everything, including entire neighborhoods and cities, and some of them lost value in the fierce competition. In the tornado of the capital market, local land and the people living on it can get torn apart.[87]

The other main part of the answer lies in the nation's long history of slavery and racism. Had the neighborhoods of the South Bronx and central Brooklyn been occupied by people of European descent, it is hard to imagine such massive neglect by government. Indeed, there are no examples in New York or any other U.S. city of neglect on this scale. Three decades later, half of the city of New Orleans faced the same fate as the South Bronx: its black population was abandoned by government at all levels.[88]

This short political-economic sketch of the historic roots of real estate development in New York City has touched on the most significant trends for community planning in the city. Starting in the 1980s, the real estate market picked up again, and previously abandoned neighborhoods experienced new growth and gentrification. The story of the last two decades is bound up with the stories of community planning and environmental justice that are presented in the following chapters.

The next chapter turns to the roots of community planning. Community plans usually react to real estate development trends, particularly at the peaks of their boom and bust cycles. Community plans are offered as alternatives to public and private development schemes, and as the role of the public sector is diminished, these plans increasingly pose direct challenges to private developers. As local small-scale real estate is increasingly displaced outward from the commercial core of the city, planning in the core tends to come under the direct purview of the hegemonic sectors of real estate, particularly the corporate clans and REITs. At the same time, new opportunities arise at the periphery for alliances of the displaced to protect and develop community land. As more community residents and businesses are thrust into the battle, they do so as part of a long history of struggle against displacement and for community land.

3

From Dislocation to Resistance: The Roots of Community Planning

Negro slaves in America represented the worst and lowest conditions among modern laborers. One estimate is that the maintenance of a slave in the South cost the master about $19 a year, which means that they were among the poorest paid laborers in the modern world. They represented in a very real sense the ultimate degradation of man. Indeed, the system was so reactionary, so utterly inconsistent with modern progress, that we simply cannot grasp it today. No matter how degraded the factory hand, he is not real estate.
—Frederick Douglass, *Black Reconstruction in America, 1860–1880*

The practice of community planning might appear to be a fairly lonely and hopeless undertaking in a city that has a powerful real estate industry that dominates land-use policy. But that would be the case only if we neglected the long history and accumulated experience of community movements in New York City. That history points to a growing ability of neighborhood residents and businesses to wrest control over the way that land is used from the marketplace and its major players. That history can be traced back to the beginnings of European settlement, through the tenant and working-class organizing of the early twentieth century, the struggles against urban renewal, abandonment, and gentrification, to the recent advocacy movements for progressive land-use reforms and community planning.

The Precursors of Community Planning

The seeds of contemporary community planning, which began in the 1960s, may be found in four signal moments of New York City history— slave rebellions; late nineteenth-century populism and Henry George's campaigns for mayor; the rise of labor, left, and tenant movements; and the organizing for jobs and housing during the Great Depression.

Slave Rebellions

The excess capital that was generated by global trade and investment and that made its way into local New York real estate was in part possible because of slave labor. Contrary to popular opinion among whites in the twentieth century, blacks from the southern United States were not just the latest wave of immigrants to New York following the Europeans. Blacks lived in Manhattan from the start. The large population of slaves in Manhattan could not own property. They *were* property and among the most valuable property—the human commodities that made New York a center for world trade. Blacks were bought and sold at the foot of Wall Street for less than the price of a 20 by 100 square foot lot. But even freed slaves rarely had access to enough capital to buy land, and those who did buy land usually settled outside of Manhattan where prices were lower.

Because they were mostly renters, blacks were among the most vulnerable to displacement. They were pushed out of lower Manhattan and migrated in stages uptown and to the towns outside Manhattan. As they left, their communities and even their burial grounds were purged from sight.[1] In the eighteenth century, they moved north of Wall Street and settled around what is now the Lower East Side and Little Italy. According to James Waldon Johnson,

By 1890 the centre of the coloured population had shifted to the upper Twenties and lower Thirties west of Sixth Avenue. Ten years later another considerable shift northward had been made to West Fifty-third Street and to San Juan Hill (West Sixty-first, Sixty-second, and Sixty-third streets).[2]

The largest internal migration of blacks in Manhattan led to a black Harlem by the early early century. "Harlem offered the coloured people the first chance in their entire history in New York to live in modern apartment houses."[3] Harlem also became a magnet for blacks displaced from the post-Reconstruction South.

Blacks were consistent victims of displacement, first from their homes in Africa and then in America. Slaves and free blacks had less control over where they lived and their living conditions than European working-class immigrants had. They were banned from many public places. Until 1854, for example, blacks were not allowed on whites-only streetcars in New York City.

Thus, it should be no surprise that black rebellions were among the first and the most militant in the city's history. Race riots started not in the 1960s but at least 250 years earlier. In 1712, there was a major slave insurrection. In 1741, a series of fires, including one that destroyed the fort at Battery Park, was attributed to rebellious blacks and led to the lynching of eighteen blacks. A contributing factor to black rage was their continuing exclusion from parts of the city and constant displacement to the periphery.

Blacks were also targets of white rage. There were the infamous Draft Riots of 1863 and another major white riot in 1900, "a brutish orgy, which, if it was not incited by the police, was, to say the least, abetted by them."[4] White riots also contributed to black displacement: those who could afford to do so migrated to black enclaves in the outer boroughs, mostly in what is now Brooklyn, and outside the city, hoping to avoid white rage. In one of the first examples of government instigated urban renewal, blacks, Italians, and others were moved to build a park and widen streets at Mulberry Bend in the Five Points neighborhood.[5]

Successive waves of poor immigrants from Europe fared not much better than blacks, but after a few generations European whites could always drift uptown and then into the suburbs, an option not available to most blacks. Until the post–World War II civil rights movement, federal mortgage regulations prevented lending in neighborhoods with black people.[6]

Henry George Campaigns for Mayor

In the latter half of the nineteenth century, a rare voice rose against the rule of the private land market. In a period of populist discontent with powerful capitalist cartels and notorious robber barons throughout the United States, Henry George gave voice to popular resentment against the rule of real estate in New York City. Rampant speculation was displacing residents and eating up undeveloped land, disrupting lives, and leaving very little public space. An elite reformer with labor support, George proposed his theory of land-value recapture as an alternative to the real estate market.[7] He saw land speculation and unearned gains from real estate as the fundamental basis of poverty and inequality. He proposed taxing speculative land-value increases as a way of recapturing these gains so they could be used for public purposes. Then as now, the bulk of urban land taxes in New York City are levied on assessed building value, not land value. While the two are clearly related, this tends to underplay the significance of the land portion, which is ultimately the most critical in determining the relative value of land ("location, location, location"). George's philosophy would have led to heavy taxes on the land portion, thereby reducing the significance of the geographies of centrality. However, he and his movement were never able to counter the political power of real estate, and his proposals to tax the profits from land were never adopted in any major way in the United States.[8]

In 1886, George ran unsuccessfully for mayor against Tammany Hall, the Democratic Party's establishment. He ran again in 1897 but died four days before the election. George's principles continue to resurface in contemporary land-reform efforts such as conservation and rural land trusts, low-income housing trusts, and regulations that exact improvements from developers. Henry George was the grandfather of *community land*, though the connection is more philosophical than political since community movements of the twentieth century for the most part knew little of and failed to embrace this legacy. His death in 1897, only a year before the consolidation of the five boroughs into New York City, saved him from witnessing the victory of Manhattan real estate over the region. Perhaps George was ahead of his time. The major elements that would have made his agenda feasible were the vibrant community movements that did not emerge until decades after his death.

Labor, Left, and Tenant Movements

As New York City's elites bathed in the benefits that accrued to them with the nation's newfound imperial expansion in the twentieth century, the distance between rich and poor grew. Mountains of surplus wrung from labor, both foreign and domestic, were crammed into the tiny island of Manhattan and then strewn along the newly built transit lines into four of the five boroughs. As capital's surplus expanded around the rapidly expanding metropolis, labor was forced to move. But this time labor began to fight back.

Beginning in the early part of the twentieth century, tenants facing evictions and displacement started organizing and made a collective statement that "we won't move."[9] New immigrants from southern and eastern Europe formed unions and joined left-wing parties, protested U.S. involvement in World War I, and organized against their bosses and landlords. Unions built solidarity to fight for job security, better wages, and working conditions, and tenant organizing, set up on the union model, built solidarity to fight for security of tenure, lower rents, and better living conditions.

In 1904, the city's first rent strike broke out in the Lower East Side. Rent strikes became the main tactic to protect tenants against rent gouging and evictions. Rent strikes were organized building by individual building, and communitywide institutions to preserve neighborhoods

were a rarity. However, many immigrant groups set up mutual aid societies that provided services to communities of shared ethnic origins. These
were precursors to some of the cooperative community development
approaches that reinforced community cohesion in the latter part of the
century.

In the early decades of the twentieth century, tenants who advocated
legislation to control rents and evictions got support from the Socialist
Party. However, the party and union leadership, mostly male, generally
proved to be inconsistent allies of struggles occurring outside the domain
of the workplace and under the leadership of women. Women were the
majority of the union rank and file, particularly among garment workers,
and played a central role in tenant organizing, but they were rarely in
the top echelon of union leadership. Left political parties also faced challenges at workplaces and threats to their survival that pulled them away
from community organizing. During the Red Scare after World War I,
the New York State legislature expelled all Socialist lawmakers and, to
dampen working-class protest, passed the 1920 rent laws, which limited
rents and evictions. Those laws were upheld by the U.S. Supreme Court
in 1921, expired in 1929, but were renewed in 1942 as wartime price
controls.[10]

Rent controls were an historic victory for working-class communities.
They also have helped the city's largest employers keep labor costs down
by preserving a substantial proportion of low-cost housing in and near
the city's center. The benefits of rent control to tenants extend far beyond
the protection of individual tenants and buildings. By preventing evictions, they have helped stabilize low-income and working-class neighborhoods. This has turned into a powerful form of social control over the
use of land, even though economists and many tenant activists think of
it mainly as a form of price control without taking into account the
consequences for place-based communities. Rent control's role in land
regulation became evident particularly after World War II, when downtown real estate speculation and urban renewal dramatically increased
displacement pressures and rent control helped protect many working-
class tenants. Renewal of the city's rent regulations every three years
then became a central element of community struggles and remains so
today. Slightly more than half the city's rental housing now comes
under rent regulations, which were extended in 2003 until 2009, though
under conditions that threaten to reduce drastically the proportion of
rental units covered. In 2003, real estate interests managed to allow
the deregulation of all units renting over $2,000 per month, a threshold

that is likely to eliminate controls on many apartments as housing prices inevitably rise over the next few years. Therefore, community activists will increasingly need to turn to other strategies to save their neighborhoods while at the same time fighting to revive stronger rent controls.

In addition to tenant organizing, many working-class immigrants in the early twentieth century sought to stake out cooperative ownership over land by creating new institutions free from the real estate market. European workers who brought with them socialist ideas and cooperative traditions established their own autonomous institutions for community development. About the turn of the century, Finnish dock workers in Sunset Park (Brooklyn) built limited-equity cooperative apartments. In the 1920s, East European Jews built coops, such as the Workers Cooperative Colony, in the Bronx. The Amalgamated Clothing Workers of America supported new worker housing, replete with community facilities, in the Lower East Side of Manhattan and the Bronx.[11] These were early threads of working-class efforts at proactive community development and were overshadowed by the volume of private development, philanthropy, and, in the New Deal, government-sponsored development. They would prefigure the upsurge in community development corporations that came many decades later (these are discussed later in this chapter).

The Great Depression: Organizing for Jobs and Housing

At the threshold of the Great Depression, New York City's Emergency Rent Laws expired, but by the early 1930s, the entire rental market was near collapse. Landlords suffered huge losses in property value, many couldn't sell, and out-of-work tenants couldn't pay rent. Landlords tried to evict delinquent tenants, and tenants withheld rent from delinquent landlords. Infused with the new Depression-era sense of solidarity and New Deal promises and facing homelessness, tenants again fought back.

Unemployed councils, many organized or supported by the Communist Party USA, actively fought evictions and organized rent strikes. They put together squads that followed city marshals when they threw families and their possessions out onto the street and carried furniture back into apartments. The Citywide Tenants Council, a Popular Front organization in which the Communist Party played an important role, was an advocate for organized tenants and housing reforms. Their strongest base was in black Harlem and the working-class immigrant stronghold in the Lower East Side.[12]

New York's mayor during the Depression, Fiorello LaGuardia, was elected on a fusion ticket with support from labor and new immigrant communities.[13] LaGuardia played a contradictory political role with a strong dose of populism. Although he was a firm supporter of labor and the New Deal, he also allied himself with elite reformers, as mentioned in the previous chapter. Robert Moses helped LaGuardia build New Deal projects that created jobs and public places, including parks and a new subway system. Since there were no massive displacement pressures from real estate during the Depression, the new public works didn't have substantial negative impacts on neighborhoods. But LaGuardia also helped the reformers undermine the neighborhood-based structure of the Democratic Party.

One of the contradictory elements in LaGuardia's legacy that is not always recognized by community movements is his contribution to the demystification of technocratic planning and bureaucrats. At times, he ridiculed the technocrats and scorned their elitist attitudes. While his style was later emulated by Mayors Ed Koch and Rudolph Giuliani, LaGuardia's public fits had a component of social and economic justice, unlike his imitators. For example, LaGuardia reacted to the 1943 Harlem riots by immediately meeting with community leaders and holding the police at bay—which led to the eventual resignation of his police chief. Rudolph Giuliani rarely met with black leaders and on numerous occasions outraged them by allowing police officers to engulf demonstrations in black neighborhoods with overwhelming and intimidating force.[14]

The Great Depression's real estate slump continued into World War II, and rent controls enacted in 1942 eased pressures on tenants. Popular Front politics led to a no-strike pledge by unions and a de facto hold on tenant mobilization as attention focused on support for the war. But plenty of latent neighborhood activism and war-related volunteerism cut across class and racial lines. For example, volunteers created 400,000 victory gardens on 6,000 acres of land, and neighborhood-based Consumer Interest Committees helped to monitor price controls.[15] The victory gardens prefigured the thousands of community gardens that sprang up on abandoned vacant lots during and after the city's fiscal crisis in the 1970s.

Urban Renewal, Negro Removal, and the Struggles against Displacement

The most important foundation for today's community movements was undoubtedly the struggle against displacement at the hands of federal and city urban renewal programs. The roots of current struggles against eminent domain abuse in Brooklyn's Atlantic Yards and Queens' Willets Point (see chapter 6) and the genesis of alternative community plans can be found in the long string of urban renewal battles going back at least half a century.

Long before the bounty bestowed by the federal urban renewal program, Robert Moses had aggressively used the city's powers of eminent domain. For example, in the early 1940s Moses cleared an eighteen-block area in the Lower East Side and turned it over to the Metropolitan Life Insurance Company to build the Stuyvesant Town complex with 8,755 apartments. Development began in 1943 and was completed in 1949. The public announcement of the project, which would be available to middle-income people and whites only, stimulated protest, mostly among African Americans and the left, and may have contributed to the rage behind the Harlem riots in 1943.

While there was apparently little or no resistance by the more than 12,000 people who were displaced by Stuyvesant Town, opposition grew quickly in subsequent projects. Indeed, in the struggles that followed, New York City's community movements emerged full-blown in opposition to displacement in general and urban renewal in particular. Class and racial differences within the community movement emerged as well.

Organized labor played a contradictory role in the issue of displacement. While some unions denounced urban renewal, others benefited from it. In 1955, with the support of organized labor, the state of New York launched the Mitchell-Lama housing program, which provided low-interest loans to limited-profit developers who produced urban housing for workers with modest incomes. Many of the Mitchell-Lama sponsors were unions. The United Housing Foundation, backed by union trust funds, became the largest nonprofit housing developer when it backed the construction of Coop City in the Bronx, a project with 15,375 units of limited-equity coops in thirty-five high-rise buildings. Many Coop City tenants, mostly white workers, left neighborhoods in Manhattan and the South Bronx that were being leveled by urban renewal programs. In an ironic twist, perhaps the largest rent strike ever took place in Coop City during the 1970s. Tenants struck for two years, protesting unexpected cost increases that were indirectly related to the city's fiscal crisis, flawed construction, and an insensitive management. Some also took issue with the segregation of blacks within Coop City. The protestors won control over management, but in subsequent internal battles the deeper financial problems took their toll, and like many other Mitchell-Lama projects, tenants are now sharply divided over whether to privatize the complex, eliminate limits on equity gains, and allow individual tenants to sell their units at market rate.[16] The crisis of Coop City prefigured the coming dilemmas that communities faced when they had responsibility for owning and managing land in a city dominated by the rules of real estate and finance and divided by race and class. It also signaled the beginning of the end of union sponsorship of large-scale housing development in New York City.

The legislation and logic of urban renewal required that city planners first designate the existing communities to be "slums" to be cleared and redeveloped. Federal law allowed local planning agencies to define *slums* and *blighted areas* subjectively, and since most professional planners were middle-class whites, they readily transferred their own racial fears and class anxieties to the piece of paper they were given to rate building conditions. *Excellent, good, fair,* or *poor* were usually the only options. This simplistic grading system mocked the scientific management promised by the municipal reform movement, which mostly supported urban renewal as a promising tool to revitalize the city.

One dramatic example of the professional planner's bias was dug up by Bill Price, a community activist in Manhattan's West Side. The plan for the West Side Urban Renewal Area includes a photograph with a group of people outside a restaurant advertising *cuchifritos,* a popular Puerto Rican dish. The photo was identified by the planners as the "squalid face of blight."[17] This was probably not how the restaurant owners and customers perceived their environment. When the people unfortunate enough to live and work in urban renewal areas were themselves condemned as blighted and told to leave, they received minimal relocation benefits, and these were usually administered by the city's chosen real estate developer.

As the postwar building boom consumed Midtown and threatened to move into the genteel Silk Stocking district on the East Side, city planners shifted development incentives to the West Side of Manhattan. The New York Coliseum, Lincoln Center, and the West Side Urban Renewal Area opened up new frontiers for real estate by eliminating the working-class neighborhoods that were in the way, especially large chunks of Hell's Kitchen (part of which is now known as Clinton). In the meantime, there was a backlash by white residents against the construction of new low-income housing in urban renewal areas. A homeowner's group on the West Side played into racial fears and prejudice when it adopted the "tipping point" theory—a notion that once the numbers of people of color reached a certain point, the neighborhood would lose all its white population. The courts declined to uphold the tipping point as a policy to restrict the amount of low-income housing in the neighborhood. But the issue illustrated the extent to which the class and racial divides influenced the urban renewal process and the policy debates about it.

Urban renewal became known as "Negro removal" because blacks were disproportionately among the displaced (though Puerto Ricans in Manhattan's West Side were also heavily affected). This explains why the struggles against urban renewal were not just about local neighborhood issues and were understood to be a central part of the national civil rights movement. While activists desegregated southern lunch counters and schools, they stopped the urban renewal bulldozers in northern cities. The struggles for access to public places and the struggles against the displacement of neighborhoods were seen as two sides of the same coin.

Throughout the United States, the mounting opposition to urban renewal was led by neighborhood residents and businesses that were forced to move and had no involvement in planning for redevelopment. But it also came from property owners who saw urban renewal as a scheme for robbing one owner to give their land to another, a violation of the right to own property guaranteed in the U.S. Constitution's fifth amendment. Nevertheless, the 1954 U.S. Supreme Court ruling upholding the use of eminent domain gave the green light to slum-clearance projects all over the city and nation.[18] But opposition to urban renewal continued to grow. Bending to local pressures, Congress passed the 1954 Housing Act, which allowed local authorities to rehabilitate housing in renewal areas instead of tearing it down. The 1958 West Side Urban Renewal Plan in Manhattan, covering a twenty-block area between 87th and 97th Streets, was the first with rehab options and also incorporated a process for participation by residents. Relocation benefits were gradually increased until significant federal legislation in 1961 expanded benefits throughout the country. But by the time urban renewal hit the Upper West Side, organized grassroots opposition had already spread throughout the city. The press, particularly the *World Telegram and Sun*, ran exposés about land that had been cleared but never redeveloped, the huge numbers of people dislocated, and the terrible living conditions that faced tenants who were displaced and those who occupied some of the new housing. Hortense Gabel, a black planning commissioner who advocated for working-class communities against the urban renewal bulldozer, was a rare dissenting voice from within city government. A conservative estimate of the number of people displaced by the Moses bulldozer was 170,000 people between 1945 and 1953.[19] Later estimates by community advocates range in the millions.

Robert Moses did not need federal urban renewal powers for most of the 627 miles of highway he jammed into New York City (almost as many miles as subway tracks). He simply utilized the local power of eminent domain. It was (and is) normally assumed that highways are built for a "public purpose," the courts' test that ultimately decided the fate of scores of neighborhoods. Moses also used the abundant federal funding available at the time to build new public housing. Unlike public housing in the 1930s, the postwar units were often built for poor people displaced by urban renewal (and public housing itself displaced over 100,000 people, almost a fourth of the current number of public housing tenants). Since the displaced people were disproportionately people of color, whose options for owning and renting housing in the city were limited due to discrimination in the housing market, the projects became segregated ghettoes, even more segregated than the neighborhoods they replaced. Public housing was no longer a jobs program as it had been in the Depression. It was now an instrument to facilitate urban renewal while at the same time maintaining a modicum of social peace.[20]

Urban renewal hit tenants hard, but even without urban renewal tenants were subject to the everyday deficiencies of slumlords. And these also led to intense protests. The Harlem rent strikes of the 1950s and 1960s were militant protests against mostly absentee white landlords. Like the urban renewal battles, the Harlem rent strikes also dovetailed with the growing national civil rights movement. In the early 1960s, Jesse Gray, who went on to lead the National Tenants Organization, an organization of public housing tenants, led a two-year series of rent strikes in Harlem's private apartment buildings.

In his analysis of the Harlem rent strikes, Mark Naison points out the limitations of strictly tenant-based actions. Tenants mobilize first of all in their individual buildings. Their reactions to landlord abuses are spontaneous and often militant. However, to create a durable movement, tenants must organize politically, develop legal strategies, and build broader alliances throughout the city. To the extent that the Harlem rent strikers were able to do this, they were successful.[21] The Metropolitan Council on Housing, today the largest citywide tenant organization, was formed in 1959 by activists Jane Benedict in Yorkville and Esther Rand, who had fought against urban renewal on the Lower East Side. As a citywide tenant organization, Met Council is an arena for expanding the capacity of local tenant groups and tenants as a citywide constituency to engage in the legal and political struggles to benefit tenants as a whole. However, tensions between Met Council and the Harlem rent strikers, partially rooted in turf and racial differences, were also symptomatic of the built-in limitations of tenant organizing when it is not connected to a larger, diverse citywide housing movement.

For tenants to achieve broader goals—such as rent and eviction controls, control over the incursions of urban renewal, and general improvements in the quality of life at the neighborhood level—they must at least pose the questions of community control. Although Met Council helps rent strikers move in that direction, they have generally stopped short of strategies for community control. In short, they tend to deal with housing and rent but not land.[22]

The community struggles in the postwar period contributed to the demise of Robert Moses, but fundamental changes happening nationally made Moses increasingly irrelevant. Moses was a creation of his times, and to paraphrase Bob Dylan, the times "they were a'changin'." Funds for public works dwindled as the postwar liberal coalition began to unravel. Whites went to the suburbs, and blacks (still without a big-city mayor until Cleveland's Carl Stokes in 1969) were not to receive loans and other benefits of the welfare state, only grants of public assistance. By the time blacks achieved a majority and took control of local government, the welfare state had moved to the suburbs.

Just as the City Planning Commission gave birth to a new vision for the grand modernist city (which was embodied in the 1961 Zoning Resolution), an alternative vision emerged from the community movements. In 1961, Jane Jacobs, a Greenwich Village activist, published *The Death and Life of Great American Cities*, which was based mostly on her experience and observations of urban renewal, public housing, and urban planning in New York City.[23] Jacobs set out a scathing critique of elitist, top-down planning and urban renewal and developed an enduring series of principles for understanding, preserving, and developing central city neighborhoods. More than just the personal viewpoints of an outspoken layperson, this classic critique of city planning in the United States incorporated the ideas of local activists who were struggling to save their communities. Her often-ignored concept of "integrated diversity" reflected a deep appreciation for the complexity of cities and the tensions between the needs to both integrate and preserve diverse elements. It helped create a public consciousness of the value of neighborhoods and the threats posed by large-scale development. Jacobs played a role in defeating the proposed Lower Manhattan Expressway, one of the last Moses megaprojects that fell victim to the growing community movements and dwindling fiscal resources.[24]

Jane Jacobs came out of a sector of the community movement that had the resources and political strength to stop the urban renewal bulldozers in their neighborhoods. Although Greenwich Village was multiracial and the paramount Bohemian center of the city, the neighborhood was mostly white. Unlike the Harlem rent strikers, the grassroots groups in Central Brooklyn, or the Lower East Side radicals, the Village activists would soon send Ed Koch (hardly a radical) to Gracie Mansion. While Jacobs's *Death and Life* was acquiring the status of a classic work, the communities of color that were more vulnerable to displacement were not visible to the professional mainstream and did not have their manifestos reprinted and distributed. They may well have told a different story about street life and public housing. This doesn't diminish the epochal significance of the work by Jane Jacobs, which today is required reading in city planning programs around the country.

Other resources for communities emerged from within the city planning profession in the 1960s. Walter Thabit, a planner who worked closely with Lower East Side residents and businesses who stopped the Cooper Square urban renewal plan (see the next chapter for more details), was a founder of Planners for Equal Opportunity, a national organization (until 1974) involving hundreds of professionals who advocated for low-income neighborhoods. A group of architects and planners in Harlem founded ARCH (Architects Renewal Committee of Harlem) to assist neighborhoods that were fighting displacement. Paul Davidoff, an attorney and planner who would go on to help found the graduate urban planning program at Hunter College (part of the City University of New York), popularized the term *advocacy planning* as an approach that integrated social, economic, and ethical concerns with physical land-use planning (see chapter 1). Davidoff also founded the Suburban Action Institute, which challenged exclusionary suburban zoning laws. The Urban Underground in New York City was a loose network of urban planners in city government who supported community-based struggles. In 1975, advocate planner Chester Hartman founded Planners Network, an organization of planners and activists that remains active today and has a strong base in New York City.[25] These were some of the elements of the city planning profession that have been allies in struggles for community planning.

1968: Emblem of Revolt and Reform

There were many critical turning points in the 1960s, but one year stands out as emblematic—1968. This was a critical moment throughout the world. In Paris and other European cities, radical students took over streets and public places. They highlighted urban issues, many fought narrow trade unionism, and there were violent confrontations between students and workers. Many students criticized the unions and left parties for ignoring housing and community issues, among others. The New Left trend in the United States and Europe challenged narrow economistic arguments that the only valid media for working-class organization were unions and left-wing parties. In the United States, the civil rights movement, led by a broad coalition of black churches, students, and progressive labor, was the leading national force for progressive social change. Martin Luther King Jr. joined the battle for racial justice with the working-class goal of economic justice and at the same time joined the rising opposition to the U.S. military aggression in Vietnam.

These trends resonated at the community level in New York City. Black Panthers and the Young Lords launched community-service programs even as they advocated armed struggle. In New York City, the Young Lords launched a dramatic protest against garbage that would prefigure the environmental justice movement over two decades later.[26] The New Left, seeking new and progressive meanings in the housing and community movements, focused on local organizing. And the women's movement brought into focus the relationships between home and community and the leading roles played by women in defense of their neighborhoods. It later led to the establishment of community-based self-help clinics. Grassroots organizing in mostly white working-class communities was also supported by the work of Saul Alinsky and his Industrial Areas Foundation.[27]

In New York, the occupation of Columbia University's administrative offices and other facilities in 1968 by protesting students highlighted a new awareness of the complicity of large institutions, mainly universities and hospitals, in the land grabs that were displacing working-class communities of color.[28] Columbia had proposed to expand into nearby Morningside Heights by building a gym in Morningside Park, a hilly, poorly maintained city park that sharply divided Columbia from black Harlem. While West Side elites got a lot of press when they fought Robert Moses's plan to build a parking lot for the Tavern on the Green restaurant in Central Park, this was the first time that students from an elite school had joined with Harlem activists in a battle for community land. Columbia waited until the twenty-first century before it dared to propose another grand expansion plan.

President Lyndon Johnson's national War on Poverty was also an important backdrop to 1968. In New York City, the Mobilization for Youth, a grassroots organizing project started with foundation support on the Lower East Side, became a model for the War on Poverty's new Community Action program. One of the most ambitious War on Poverty initiatives was the Model Cities program, which was also a major precursor to community planning. It aimed at engaging the participation of residents and workers in low-income communities. Three Model Cities districts were established in New York—Central Brooklyn, Harlem, and the South Bronx. Model Cities for the first time gave official sanction and provided financial resources to support community-based planning and organizing and democratic participation in decision making.[29] While these programs raised great expectations for neighborhood empowerment, they came to an end after the 1968 election of Richard Nixon and the subsequent dismantling of Lyndon Johnson's Great Society programs.

In 1968, Martin Luther King Jr. was assassinated. This unleashed a wave of urban rebellions throughout the nation that brought together the issues of community control and black power. Republican John Lindsay was mayor of New York at this time and started a series of reforms that would open up City Hall to greater consultation with neighborhoods. Lindsay initiated dialogues with black political and church leaders in the neighborhoods. He created Little City Halls and linked community planning boards, started under the previous mayor, Robert Wagner, with his executive office. Lindsay declared 1970 "the year of the neighborhood." The community planning boards were loosely organized and somewhat ad hoc, and their significance was outweighed by the concurrent reorganization of city government by Lindsay into superagencies that further concentrated power in the hands of the mayor and technocrats. Lindsay's reforms also bypassed the powerful borough presidents, who were mostly Democratic Party loyalists. The feeble decentralization reforms were soon to be overshadowed by the fiscal austerity that followed the city's near-bankruptcy and culminated in a half-hearted charter reform in 1975 (more on this later).

Decentralization and White Backlash

The struggle for community control of schools is one of the least-recognized and perhaps most important foundations for community planning in New York City. It started with a school boycott in 1965, led to a teacher's strike in 1968, and came to a close in 1970 with the creation of community school boards.[30]

Black neighborhoods grappling with the issue of community control faced a school system about which they had little to say. Management and teachers with seniority were mostly white. Many drove to work from white suburbs and drove back home after the last school bell. Segregated neighborhoods were served by a segregated school system, the largest in the nation. White children had more opportunities to go to the best city schools that sent them to the nation's top colleges, and blacks struggled to stay in school.

Frustration burst into rage when parents and community residents launched a 600-school boycott in 1965. After much debate, the Board of Education set up three demonstration districts that were to involve neighborhood parents. This move challenged the teachers' power (they had won their first contract in 1960), and the predominantly white teacher's union, led by Albert Shanker, went on strike in 1968. The teachers mustered significant political support, demonstration districts were shut down, and in 1970 the mostly white state legislature created elected community school boards. In 2003, the school boards were abolished in a massive reorganization led by corporate lawyer Joel Klein, appointed by Mayor Michael Bloomberg as education chief in a new recentralized regime under mayoral control.

The lesson to be drawn from the thirty-three years of community school boards is a critical one for community planners and neighborhood activists. From the beginning, the local school boards were given little support and practically no resources that would allow them to serve as genuine links between community and school. Some were truly representative, some were patronage mills for the Democratic Party, but most never had the resources or recognition to fulfill their missions. Both administrators and teachers could easily point to them as proof that community control would never work. One could easily conclude that they were set up in such a way that they could only fail, validating top-down, white control of a school system in which students of color predominate. While Mayor Michael Bloomberg renewed strong central control and also created paid parent advocates, he left no durable structure for community involvement in decision making. He would continue the trend toward breaking up large schools into many small ones, creating charter schools, and playing with privatization. As New York City entered the twenty-first century, its schools, both large and small, were controlled by elite urban reform advocates like those of a century ago, preaching charity, efficiency, and scientific management through testing and quantitative performance measures, now with a neoliberal twist that justified privatization and a renewed offensive against the teacher's union. Community control of schools is still a distant possibility, especially in nonwhite districts.

The white backlash against blacks became legitimized in the administrations of Mayors Ed Koch and Rudolph Giuliani. Even as the city's population was shifting rapidly to a nonwhite majority, the entrenched minority consolidated positions that prevented the new majority from appropriating its fair share of political power. Mayor David Dinkins, New York's first African American mayor, elected with strong grassroots support in 1990, might have broken this trend but was narrowly beaten for reelection by the revanchist Giuliani in the 1994 elections. The white backlash of 1970 was much more than a union dispute or a matter of education policy. It was the opening of a decades-long effort of a disappearing white majority and a powerful financial sector to hang on to their privileged positions of political power.[31]

Taking Control of the Land

The demise of the Keynesian and Fordist models of economic development in the 1970s gave rise to the city's fiscal crisis in the 1970s and a wave of neighborhood abandonment (see chapter 2 for a more detailed discussion). As the private real estate market collapsed in many working-class neighborhoods, it created a vacuum that community organizers and activists filled with new alternatives. This laid the foundations for community control over land and greater community influence over official land-use controls.

Squatting, Homesteading, and the Rise of Community Land

In the bleak environment created by widespread real estate abandonment beginning in the 1960s, many residents asked themselves what they could do to save their neighborhoods. After the onset of the fiscal crisis, tenants and grassroots activists saw little help coming from local, state, or federal governments. But for many, it was an urgent matter of survival for themselves and their families. Surrounded by vacant lots, vacant buildings, garbage, and rats, entire neighborhoods were falling off the city's map. Police and fire entered only in emergencies, and they couldn't always be relied on even then. Police were perceived as an occupying force made up of whites who had moved to the suburbs (police and fire services were among the few exemptions to a law requiring that city employees reside in the city at the time of employment).

While the threat of displacement by new development struck many neighborhoods close to the city's business districts, other neighborhoods faced just the opposite. There were no developers, the much-vaunted magic of the real estate market wasn't working, and land was worth less than nothing.

Thus was born the idea of taking over neighborhoods and of people seizing their turf. Solidarity by race and class were often part of this idea, but it was a notion quite distinct from labor solidarity, New Deal solidarity, religious solidarity, and ethnic solidarity. It was the new ideal of *community land*—the idea that people who lived in local neighborhoods (and not speculators, absentee landlords, or the city) could control what happened on their land.

Squatters[32] and homesteaders[33] were among the first to take direct action. Thousands of privately owned and city-owned buildings in the South Bronx, Harlem, and central Brooklyn—areas devastated by abandonment—were taken over by tenants who resisted eviction and fought to stay. Other neighborhoods in transition where low-cost housing was at risk saw a new upsurge in tenant organizing. For example, in 1970, eighty-two families in Morningside Heights, mostly poor immigrants from the Dominican Republic, took over three buildings owned by Morningside House, a nonprofit run by the Cathedral of St. John the Divine. They fought for almost a decade against eviction attempts prompted by the church's plans to build a community facility. In the end, they lost one building and won the right to stay as a limited-equity coop in the other two.[34]

In the abandoned neighborhoods, landlords milked their buildings for rent and failed to pay taxes for years, and properties ended up in the hands of a poorly prepared city administration under a political leadership with little commitment to do much with them. Thousands of buildings were held *in rem*—a legal limbo in which the city temporarily controlled properties while they awaited the lengthy process of assuming full title. Many *in rem* buildings were fully occupied by poor tenants. Others were demolished because they were ruled to be unsafe (though they often were not). Some were redeemed by the original owners, who could negotiate a reduction in back taxes. And yet other *in rem* buildings that had been vacated or were partially vacated were taken over by squatters and homesteaders. Some organized themselves to do their own renovations, and the concepts of *sweat equity* and *self-help* were advanced as strategies for improving neighborhoods. Government, banks, and foundations gave modest support to such efforts as they often appeared to contribute to hoped-for trends toward gentrification, homeownership, and revival of the real estate market.

The Koch administration set the policy for *in rem* housing in accordance with the rising neoliberal philosophy that reigns today: make sure no human tragedies occur (that is, keep the boilers running in winter and vacate buildings about to collapse), and do everything possible to get the property back on the market. With little confidence in the public sector, city policy assumed that private owners would fix up the buildings and start paying taxes. This policy was openly supported by the real estate establishment, which did not want the city to become a major property owner and counterweight to the private market. However, it clashed with the harsh reality during the years of the real estate bust: there really was no market in distressed neighborhoods. The land had little or no value, and investors were not interested in buying a liability. The city also tried to sell the buildings to the tenants, but most could not afford the cost of bank financing and the responsibility for long-term maintenance, even after some initial public subsidies.

From the start, tenants organized to fight the city's policy. Some resisted attempts to sell their buildings to landlords, and others resisted attempts to sell the buildings to tenant-run coops, fearful that self-management would result in higher rents (*in rem* tenants paid modest rents). They organized building by building and neighborhood by neighborhood. At one point, they formed a Union of City Tenants. Eventually, hundreds of thousands wound up staying either as owners in new low-income coops or as tenants in what would end up in the 1980s as the nation's largest pool of municipally owned low-income housing.

At the instigation of progressive housing advocates, the city's new superagency for housing, the Department of Housing Preservation and Development (HPD) established the Division of Alternative Management Programs (DAMP), whose main instrument has been the Tenant Interim Lease (TIL) program, a mechanism for engaging tenants in the process of management and their eventual takeover of the building. The successful TIL buildings became limited-equity coops, others were sold to landlords and privatized, and yet others remain in the program.

The nonprofit Urban Homesteading Assistance Board (UHAB), established in 1973, has been a consistent advocate for limited-equity, tenant-run cooperatives. UHAB helped set up limited-equity coops for 27,000 families in 1,300 buildings. In these buildings, the tenant-owners cannot reap enormous gains in value that normally accrue due to land-value changes. These coops, along with most of the Mitchell-Lama coops, public housing, and supportive housing, are critical building blocks of community land.

The city's policy of selling off buildings also applied to vacant land. In addition to owning thousands of buildings, the city also ended up owning thousands of vacant lots. The city held public auctions and accepted bids from speculators and landlords. With few exceptions, no conditions were placed on the sales. In neighborhoods where the market was virtually inoperative, most vacant lots ended up as dumping grounds. Many small-time speculators bought up bunches of parcels without having ever seriously understood what it would take to get them developed. Some figured that they would just pay the bargain-basement price and sit on the land until gentrification or a city-initiated project would allow them to sell at top dollar. Most of these small investors didn't figure on the taxes they would have to pay even as the land stayed vacant, the fines they would get for dumping, or the outrage of community activists. Many of these properties ended up back in city ownership.

In the throes of the abandonment crisis, communities mobilized to stop the city auctions. Protests ranged from demonstrations at the auction sites to political campaigns to force borough presidents, City Council members, and community boards to intervene to stop the sales. For a short period of time under the Dinkins administration, the City Planning Department adopted a policy of considering neighborhood context before authorizing a sale, but the protests did not lead to any fundamental change in city policy, and the Giuliani administration later reverted to the old policy of selling off land without much oversight.

Some community groups proposed that the city consciously create a land bank in which vacant properties would be held for future development, but the city refused. A land banking strategy would have allowed government or neighborhood residents to come up with comprehensive redevelopment plans. With a single property owner, it would have been easier to establish a clear long-range strategy for preservation and development. City officials and their real estate partners opposed the idea of more city-owned low-income housing, but they absolutely dreaded the idea of city-owned land, and within communities there had remained a distrust of government planning ever since the federal urban renewal programs. Today, the city no longer holds tax-delinquent properties and now sells the tax liens fairly promptly to private entities. However, today there are many fewer abandoned buildings as the real estate market booms and as gentrification sweeps neighborhoods that were once abandoned.[35]

Squatting slowed through the 1980s but picked up again in the1990s. In East New York, squatters emerged spontaneously and benefited from organizing by one of the nation's largest community-based organizations, ACORN (Association of Community Organizations for Reform Now). Hundreds of units of low-rise vacant city-owned housing were occupied. In practice, this meant following Saul Alinsky's admonition to "rub raw the sores of discontent" and instigate confrontations with the powerful while at the same time preparing to negotiate a piece of the pie with them. These tactics produced city support for the rehabilitation of squatted buildings that would become part of a locally controlled mutual housing association (similar to a limited-equity cooperative). Also in East New York, East Brooklyn Churches, a coalition of neighborhood churches, built the Nehemiah Houses after persuading Mayor Ed Koch to turn over control of urban renewal land for development of Nehemiah's low-cost single-family homes.[36]

Perhaps the Lower East Side has gotten most recognition for squatting because of the 1991 battle for Tompkins Square Park and numerous high-profile evictions in the 1990s engineered by combat-ready police. However, unlike the squatters of the 1970s in communities of color, the more recent Lower East Side squatters were an eclectic mix. Many were engaged in a progressive struggle to ward off gentrification, others simply committed to living rent-free, and still others opposed to community-based plans for low-income housing on sites they had occupied.[37] There are still scores of squatter-occupied buildings throughout the city.

Community Development Corporations: Devolution Meets Revolution

What do you do once you have control of a building? This was the urgent and practical question faced by tenants, squatters, and homesteaders in buildings abandoned by landlords. Once you've stopped the urban renewal bulldozers, how do you get financing to make repairs? Once you've kicked out a slumlord, how do you gain legal title? How can you improve buildings and also ensure that they are still affordable to current tenants? These questions had to do with not just the building but the *land* on which it stood.

To address these questions, tenants formed their own associations, at first informally. They sought advice from professionals, sympathetic housing reformers, and foundations. Community development corporations (CDCs) were born in New York City and in other central cities around the nation that were facing widespread abandonment.[38] The pioneers in New York included groups like Banana Kelly and People's Development Corporation in the Bronx and Los Sures and Saint Nicholas in Brooklyn. They were set up as nonprofit development corporations under state law. They often began with a building or group of buildings and then mobilized wider support in the neighborhood. They became partners with institutions that had access to capital—churches, foundations, banks, and city government. Some were more openly critical of city policy than others. Some linked neighborhood decline with redlining, racism, and the city's policy of planned shrinkage. Others became typical landlords who were more concerned with protecting their property than providing decent services and undertaking a social mission. Some even deliberately excluded very low-income people.

The most progressive of the new neighborhood-based organizations organized against the city's *in rem* and auction policies and service cutbacks. They exposed slumlords, tried to persuade the city to take action against them, and attacked the federal withdrawal from cities and spending for the Vietnam War. But CDCs were all over the political map and served very different strata and ethnicities. Many were faith-based organizations whose sponsors could be progressive, activist clergy or conservative, paternalistic religious leaders who saw CDCs as charities. They could appeal for support to conservative advocates of homeownership and the American dream or revolutionaries in the Young Lords and Black Power movements. Overall, the one thing that most CDCs had in common in this early stage was a prominent local social mission—to reverse neighborhood abandonment by controlling the use of land and buildings and changing government policies.

After feeling the political pressure from below and understanding which way the federal winds were blowing, City Hall soon came to see CDCs as allies. The crash in real estate during the early 1980s made private developers even less interested in distressed neighborhoods, opening up legitimate space for CDC growth. While some CDCs were constant critics of city policy, many were already enmeshed in the official ideology of neoliberal devolution. The city saw CDCs as a favored option for getting rid of *in rem* buildings and downloading responsibility for neighborhood renewal. CDCs would become the local development packagers, pulling together financing from city, state, and federal governments, churches, foundations, and private partners. CDCs had roots in local organizing and could legitimize the city's housing policy, which at heart was to spur revitalization of the private real estate market in abandoned neighborhoods.

In effect, CDCs grew out of a convergence of two trends—grassroots efforts to take control of neighborhoods and City Hall's interest in washing its hands of responsibility for neighborhood renewal. Devolution met revolution. And real estate stood to benefit.

Today there are eighty to a hundred CDCs in the city, the largest grouping anywhere in the world, and altogether they have been responsible for the rehabilitation and management of some 80,000 units of housing.[39] Political pressure from tenants and neighborhoods, including CDCs, forced the city to invest in the rehabilitation of *in rem* buildings and convey them to CDCs for renovation and management. HPD treats them as the preferred redevelopers of city-owned buildings. However, when CDCs stand up to City Hall, they can lose their franchise. This was what happened with Housing Works, Inc., the city's largest producer of housing for people with HIV/AIDs, which was not bashful about its opposition to Mayor Rudolph Giuliani's social policies and as a result found its access to city housing subsidies curtailed.

Despite its vaunted partnership with CDCs, the city has never given them access to the big development plums. For example, since the 1980s the city has used established private developers to build one- to four-family homes on choice vacant land through the New York City Housing Partnership, turning to CDCs only for help in marketing the completed units. CDCs have rarely had a role in any giant downtown projects built with tax incentives and giveaways to private real estate developers.

CDCs face a continuing tension between their social mission and their role as local landlords.[40] Dependence on government and foundation funding can lead to political docility, and CDCs can simply become the enforcers of narrow, conservative city policies. When CDCs ignore their social mission, they act like selfish, for-profit landlords and developers, making sweetheart deals and evicting tenants arbitrarily. On the other hand, if CDCs ignore their responsibilities as property managers, they can easily go bankrupt, and their neighborhoods will lose precious low-income housing units. The larger and more successful CDCs, like the Fifth Avenue Committee (FAC) in Brooklyn, are more skillful at balancing the two roles. FAC recently launched a campaign for a displacement-free zone while maintaining a sizeable portfolio of low-income housing units.

Progressive CDCs that remain focused on their social mission are among the strongest supporters of community planning. It quickly becomes clear to socially conscious local developers that owning and operating a few buildings is a far cry from protecting all low-income housing in neighborhoods where tenants and homeowners face rampant displacement pressures. Constantly pulled into the nuts-and-bolts details of housing development and management, the more forward-thinking CDC staff also understand the need for long-range planning and strategies that address wider neighborhood concerns. They understand the difference between the control of buildings and community control of land.

Taking Control of Land-Use Controls

Reeling from the struggles against urban renewal and for community control, elites introduced a number of reforms in the 1970s and 1980s that promised some measure of community control over land use. The reforms were a response to growing neighborhood activism stemming from the struggles against urban renewal, for community control of schools, and against neighborhood abandonment. Nevertheless, the reforms have often been used by developers and the city administration to block effective neighborhood control or by exclusionary neighborhood groups to stop new development. Mayor Lindsay's decentralization experiments proved to be a sideshow that drew attention from the long march toward the imperial mayoralty. But the growing centralization of power only increased demands from neighborhoods for greater involvement in government and control over their land.

The city's most important land-use reform since the establishment of zoning in 1916 was the creation of community boards in 1975.[41] The New York city charter was revised, and for the first time community boards had a formal role in the official land-use review process. The city was divided into fifty-nine community districts, each of which would have a community board of up to fifty members appointed by the borough president (half of the nominations to be made by the City Council representatives). The charter change established the Uniform Land Use Review Procedure (ULURP), which included a role for the community boards in all major land-use decisions such as zoning changes, urban renewal plans, acquisition and disposition of city property, special permits, and City Map changes. However, community board votes were to be advisory only. The final decisions are reserved for the City Planning Commission (seven of its thirteen members are appointed by the mayor) and the City Council.

The most influential individuals and groups in the charter revision were Manhattan-based good-government groups and elite reformers. Grassroots organizers wanted a more powerful role and resources for community boards, but at the same time they distrusted the establishment's ability to create genuine local democracy. In the grips of the city's fiscal crisis, community boards were seen by many in government as a way to channel or co-opt dissent from communities through a controlled process. Perhaps, some thought, it would diminish the recourse by neighborhood groups to more militant tactics or the courts.

The opposite trend toward an imperial mayoralty did not abate even as the new forms of decentralized governance were taking shape. The charter revision included a recommendation that city service districts be coterminus with the new community district lines, a neat arrangement that appealed to efficiency experts in the mayor's Office of Management and Budget but was not applied to all services due to resistance in some agencies. Each community board had a District Service Cabinet that would bring together representatives from different agencies to coordinate services in that district. However, each community board had no more than one or two professional staff members and little authority to convene top agency officials or influence overall policy. The mayor's office tightened its control over the budget. Community board representatives had no significant role in budget-making, and the City Planning Department also lost its role as coordinator of the capital budget process. A further constraint was that community board members usually answered to the borough presidents who appointed them and found themselves unable to independently influence major land use decisions. The most important limitation, however, is that community board votes on all matters are strictly advisory. Only the decisions of the City Planning Commission and City Council are binding.

Flexible Zoning and Preservation

Despite these limitations, the growing involvement of neighborhood residents and activists with land-use issues, through community boards or other community-based organizations, spurred new changes in land-use policy. An important development beginning in the 1970s was the creation of a new array of flexible zoning techniques that would patch up the holes in the 1961 Zoning Resolution. The tower-in-the park incentive zoning was producing ground-level public spaces that were uninviting to the public. Also, zoning rules permitted the construction of tall buildings in low-rise neighborhoods, sparking instantaneous community opposition. Pressures from communities gave rise to *contextual zoning*, which would incorporate height, bulk, and setback rules that would make new development relatively compatible with the existing built form. However, the City Planning Department turned this appeal for community preservation into a new opportunity for developers. The department would routinely propose contextual downzoning[42] in residential areas along with the upzoning of strategic avenues, giving developers even bigger opportunities for growth than they had originally.

The first residential-industrial *mixed-use zoning* was instituted in the 1970s. In neighborhoods with mixtures of industry and housing, the 1961 zoning worked against industry if the land was zoned exclusively for housing and against housing if it was zoned exclusively for industry. Caught in the cross-fire between an industry that wanted to expand and residents who wanted it to contract and pressured by local residents, the city established a mixed-use zone in the Northside of Williamsburg (Brooklyn). In the new mixed-use zone, both industry and housing could expand within limits. The Northside mixed-use zone was the first attempt to codify the lively integrated mixed-use neighborhood celebrated by Jane Jacobs in *The Death and Life of Great American Cities*.[43]

After they established several other mixed-use districts, the City Planning Department developed a new mixed-use district in the 1990s that could be mapped anywhere in the city. In this case, however, it turned a legitimate community desire to find a way that industry and housing could be compatible and coexist into a boon for housing developers. DCP now puts mixed-use zones in mixed-use neighborhoods (like Greenpoint and Williamsburg, Brooklyn) that are rapidly gentrifying (as illustrated in chapter 6). Since mixed-use zones allow either industry or housing to develop as-of-right (without the public review that is required by going through ULURP), the outcome is bound to be a rapid conversion of the remaining industry to housing. Having the choice between the two, property owners would be foolish to keep industrial tenants when they can get ten times the rent from residential tenants. The mixed-use zone is, in effect, a back-door residential zone posing as a preservation tool.

Historic preservation was another new tool. The official landmarks established after the local preservation law in 1965 are mostly expensive buildings in upscale neighborhoods, but preservation is also being used as a tool by community activists throughout the city. Neighborhood activists in Harlem and Bedford-Stuyvesant, for example, have successfully fought for landmark districts as part of larger community-preservation and cultural strategies. They may reinforce internal differences based on income and class, but they can also be a refuge from disruption by speculators. The struggle in the 1990s to obtain landmark status for the Audubon Ballroom in Harlem, the place where Malcolm X was assassinated, was a key (partial) victory won by local activists who argued that landmarks could be more than just the lavish creations of the wealthy designed by elite architects. They could be cultural sites of significance to the history and consciousness of all people. This is especially important in working-class communities whose habitats and landmarks are more likely to be demolished to make way for new development. Traditional preservationists who failed to support the landmarking of the Audubon Ballroom pointed to the relatively uninspiring physical character of the building rather than looking at its cultural meaning.

The 1970s saw the proliferation of localized *special zoning districts* of all kinds. Special districts establish unique regulations and often require some sort of discretionary review for all development applications. This review includes the local community boards. Some of these instruments of local land-use control are tools for democratic control; others are exclusionary. One of the most notable cases in which special district regulations were used by community advocates to preserve low-income housing was the Clinton Special District on the West Side of Manhattan, established in 1973. On the other hand, the Battery Park City Authority obtained special district regulations for its megadevelopment in lower Manhattan that were shaped by its business-driven master plan, which ended up excluding low-income housing (though housing advocates won a provision that required a portion of profits be placed in a trust fund for affordable housing). Staten Island has the most extensive and detailed special districts that protect natural land features, the result of pressures from both environmentalists and opponents of residential development.

Finally, *environmental review* requirements established in the 1970s became part of the ULURP process. Environmental movements at the national level won passage of the National Environmental Policy Act in 1969, amendments to the Clean Air Act in 1970, the Water Pollution Control Act in 1972, and the Coastal Zone Management Act in 1973. City legislation required that all land-use applications going through ULURP include a detailed statement disclosing potential negative environmental impacts. City Environmental Quality Review (CEQR) regulations made developers of major projects with negative impacts do elaborate environmental impact statements (EISs) and propose measures to mitigate negative impacts. The EIS would provide neighborhood activists with the information that they needed to oppose or support projects. However, the EIS must simply disclose potential impacts to decision makers and the public and does not prevent the impacts from occurring. Today, the EIS has become an enormous, complicated document that is constructed by professionals who follow legal advice that is geared to prevent future litigation. Few decision makers have the time or patience to read an EIS, nor do the judges who are occasionally asked to rule on its adequacy.[44]

In the 1980s, neighborhood activists engaged with environmental issues in a more effective way, through the environmental justice movement, linking them to broader struggles for housing, community development, and social justice (see chapter 5).

Race, Class, and the Roots of Progressive Community Planning

Throughout the city's history, working people without wealth have been shunted from one city tenement to another, especially after they make improvements to their housing and neighborhood. As tenants and small business owners invest their time and money to gradually upgrade their neighborhoods, real estate investors become attracted to these areas and anxious to capitalize on the improvements. As investors large and small move in, they effectively appropriate the value generated by others. This is the essence of what is now known as *gentrification*. It is not simply a change in demographics. It is *the appropriation of economic value by one class from another*. It gives added meaning to a phrase coined by the French reformer Jacques Proudhon: "Property is theft." To prevent this theft, people in neighborhoods, those who had no property and those who would lose their property, began to fight back and declare, "We won't move."

The history of labor and communities in New York City is one of people's progressively greater involvement in efforts to stop displacement and gain effective control over land, even as capital dominates and gains increasing control over all spheres of social and cultural life. This is a contradiction of modern capitalism: the greater its influence, the more there arise spontaneous efforts to counter or adapt to its rule. As capitalism expands, so do inequalities, both at its center and periphery. The center is made up of the giant metropolitan areas like New York, Tokyo, and Paris, but each of these centers has its own internal peripheries.[45]

Sometimes they are at the geographic margins of the metropolitan regions, and sometimes squarely in the center. Protest and reaction in the peripheral communities are related to the growing power of the center, so the most organized community movements are found in the peripheries of global capitals like New York City, São Paulo, and Mexico City (as well as in rural peripheries that gave rise, for example, to Brazil's Landless Peasant Movement and Mexico's Zapatistas). Nevertheless, community responses to capitalist growth are wildly diverse, ranging from the political left to right, militant to moderate, and working class to elite.

Communities are by no means singularly progressive in the political sense. As their influence grows, so do the differences between them, particularly between the community organizations founded on exclusionary principles and the progressive community movements founded on principles of equity and social justice.[46] The earliest community-based organizations in the United States were associations of property owners whose basic unifying principle was to exclude others based on class and race. Today, exclusionary homeowner associations, many in gated communities, prevail in wealthy urban and suburban neighborhoods. New York City has thousands of block associations and community associations, many of them dominated by property owners who are devoted to preserving their exclusive enclaves. But they differ dramatically from one another socially and politically and often play contradictory and ambiguous political roles. The difference between exclusionary and inclusionary groups is fundamentally one of politics and doesn't always follow from the social composition of group members. For example, the People's Firehouse was an all-white organization in an almost all-white Brooklyn neighborhood that fought against the service cutbacks of the 1970s that had even greater negative impacts on communities of color. As the People's Firehouse developed, its members consciously allied themselves with communities of color in this struggle. And as shown in several stories in the following chapters, local business owners, homeowners, and real estate developers can be powerful allies of tenants. This was the case in Cooper Square, Melrose Commons, Red Hook, and Williamsburg, for example.

We now turn to the first community-based plan in New York City, the Alternate Plan for Cooper Square, and the Melrose Commons plan, both of which were seminal experiences in the struggles against top-down urban renewal programs and for community control of land. Both were pioneers of inclusionary, progressive community planning.

II
Community Planning Stories

4

From Protest to Community Plan

There is no social change fairy. There is only change made by the hands of individuals.
—Winona LaDuke

The struggles against urban renewal, abandonment, evictions, and landlord abuse in New York City generated political momentum for the land-use reforms mentioned in the previous chapter. At the same time, however, neighborhoods also started something of much greater significance. They started to do their own plans.

The earliest community plans were alternatives generated by neighborhoods that struggled against displacement, and often they were alternatives to official plans that were perceived as threatening the displacement of local residents and businesses. The Cooper Square Alternate Plan was the first community plan in New York City. It was prepared by an active neighborhood committee with the help of pioneer advocate planner Walter Thabit. The Cooper Square story is significant because the plan set forth a bold strategy for building and preserving low-income housing, and over the span of four and a half decades community activists worked successfully to achieve most of its goals. In a neighborhood with many other forms of community and social ownership of land, Cooper Square was also a model alternative to the private real estate market.

The Melrose Commons plan, prepared by We Stay! ¡Nos Quedamos! thirty-two years after Cooper Square's first plan, was also an alternative to an official urban renewal plan. But economic changes (a dynamic upswing in South Bronx real estate and New York's growth prospects) and political changes (a stronger community movement that no longer faced a powerful Robert Moses) helped shorten the period during which the alternative plan was approved. An authentic Bronx cheer, We Stay! became the name of a community-based developer that is now implementing its own vision for the future of the neighborhood. This was also one of the first examples of the fusion of community planning with the environmental justice movement.

These two plans are bookends in the first phase of community planning in New York City, and they both came out of struggles against top-down city-sponsored urban renewal plans. The Melrose Common leadership had roots in the environmental justice movement, and leaders in both plans identified with the civil rights movement. Thus, both of these plans exemplify strong ties between community-based organizing and broader social movements.

The Cooper Square Plan: New York City's First Community Plan

The earliest and longest-lasting community planning effort was the Cooper Square Alternate Plan that came out of Manhattan's Lower East Side. The first Cooper Square plan was dated 1961, fourteen years before community boards were started, two decades before community planning became a buzz, and three decades before the first official community plan was approved by the City Council. In 1961, the city's professional planners also finished an historic overhaul of the city's zoning code, but Cooper Square's plan would contribute to the vast evidence that zoning without a plan makes little sense to neighborhoods. Cooper Square was the precocious pioneer of community-based planning, and its history of nearly half a century proves that gentrification can be beat if communities organize to confront it before it starts.

"Give us back our land," demanded Frances Goldin, one of the founders of the Cooper Square Community Development Committee and Businessmen's Association,[1] before getting arrested with Ernesto Martínez and seven other activists at a 1970 meeting of the City Planning Commission. Goldin led the struggle for land in Cooper Square for forty-five years and is still going strong: "They thought they would outlive us, . . . but we weren't going to move."[2]

In the Cooper Square story, links can be found between the community activism of the 1960s and 1970s and the radical, socialist traditions of the early twentieth century. It is the story of how a multiethnic group with a large Latino membership acted forcefully against racial and economic exclusion. In Cooper Square, community organizing was inseparable from community planning. To see their plan implemented, a core of dedicated leaders built a wide network of allies in the neighborhood, around the city, and in government. And they persisted. The Cooper Square Alternate Plan was grounded in sound technical planning, won over many elected officials, was revised several times to take into account changing conditions, and withstood many surreptitious attacks from conservative technocrats. The Cooper Square Committee (the name the group usually went by) and its allies managed to gain effective political control over a significant patch of land where they maintained and created an unprecedented amount of affordable, low-income housing. They, not Robert Moses or land speculators, decided how the neighborhood would change.

The Cooper Square story isn't a fairy tale. There have been lots of failures and internal struggles along the way. It inspired many other struggles, but many others also gave up. Cooper Square is a saga of people who are fighting a global goliath and demonstrates that, to use the phrase of the World Social Forum, "a different world is possible."[3]

Robert Moses Meets His Match

In 1959, Robert Moses proposed bulldozing an eleven-block area of the Lower East Side, based on the information presented in a survey conducted by the Helmsley-Spear real estate company for the city (figure 4.1). The project would have displaced 2,400 tenants, 450 single-room occupants, 4,000 homeless beds, and over 500 businesses. The city

Figure 4.1
Street scene in Cooper Square, 1960s

planned to turn over the land to a union-backed developer who would have created 2,900 new units of middle-income housing, displacing more people, most of them with low incomes, than would have been housed in the new complex.[4] This scenario didn't make any sense to neighborhood activists. They opposed the city's development plan because it would have wiped out several blocks of solid residential buildings and shut down viable businesses. They had recently seen another new project, Seward Park Houses, become a privileged white enclave in a neighborhood known as a model of the city's diverse working class. The city's proposal failed to guarantee housing for the low-income tenants who were currently living in the neighborhood. Typically, the growth machine's Moses was more focused on conveying land to anyone who could put brick and mortar together than dealing with the housing problems facing the people who lived and worked in the neighborhood.

In response to the city's urban renewal plan, a group of local activists organized the Cooper Square Community Development Committee and Businessmen's Association. They did a study that showed that 93 percent of the people in the urban renewal area would not be able to afford the proposed housing. They met with Hortense Gabel, an assistant to Mayor Robert Wagner. According to Cooper Square's professional planner Walter Thabit, Gabel said, "Why don't you come up with an alternate plan and tell the city the way you think it should be done?"[5] After more than a hundred community meetings, the final Cooper Square Alternate Plan was prepared by Thabit and released in 1961 (figures 4.2 and 4.3). Frances Goldin says the basic philosophy of the plan was that "the people who live in Cooper Square must be the beneficiaries and not the victims."[6] The planning document opened with the following statement:

A renewal effort has to be conceived as a process of building on the inherent social and economic values of a local community. Neglecting these values through programs of massive clearance and redevelopment can disrupt an entire community.[7]

Thus, the conceptual foundation for the Cooper Square planning effort was in the human values present in the existing neighborhood, not property values.[8] While some staffers in the Department of City Planning were disdainful of the community effort and saw nothing wrong with disrupting the lives of thousands of people,[9] the Alternate Plan was compelling enough so that the chair of the City Planning Commission soon praised it publicly.

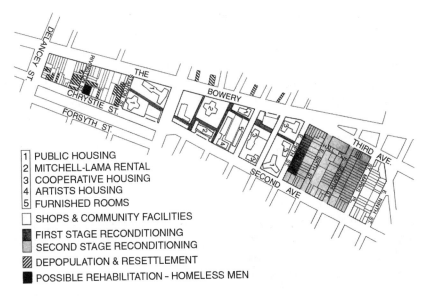

Figure 4.2
The Cooper Square Alternate Plan

Figure 4.3
Walter Thabit, community planner

The Alternate Plan started by exempting five blocks from any clearance and supported clearance and rebuilding on six blocks, with most site tenants to be relocated in stages within the urban renewal area. It proposed 620 new public housing units, 520 middle-income cooperative units, 300 moderate-income rental units, a single-room-occupancy building, and 48 studio apartments for artists. Almost half of all new housing units would be for low-income people.

In the next decade, Cooper Square's activists went back and forth with the city over plans for the renewal area, trying to reach agreement on the details of the plan. The city appointed a local project area committee (PAC) that, according to federal law, was supposed to be consulted about the planning and management of the urban renewal area. Some community activists were required to sit on the committee. However, according to Cooper Square activists, the city's appointees continued to act like bulldozer drivers. They launched a campaign against the PAC until the Cooper Square Committee itself was designated as the PAC in 1970.

The Cooper Square activists were aware from the start of the close connection between community renewal and zoning. But they were surprised when the city's planners tried to accomplish through zoning what they couldn't do with the urban renewal program. While the Cooper Square committee was working overtime to protect tenants in the urban renewal area and secure scarce public funds to build new low-income housing, the city's planning department announced that it wanted to upzone part of the neighborhood to permit market-rate housing four times as dense as the existing housing. The new high-density R-10 zone would have covered only parts of two avenues, but new market-rate buildings there would probably have sparked speculation and secondary displacement on surrounding blocks. Sixty-two speakers showed up at the City Planning Commission's public hearing to lobby against the rezoning. The proposal was dropped, but City Planning relaunched it soon after. This time, the opposition was even stronger, including a group of civic notables and organizations as diverse as the Architects Renewal Committee of Harlem, the Commerce and Industry Association, and the Urban Underground. It passed the Planning Commission but continued organizing killed it at the Board of Estimate, the city's main decision-making body.

In 1970, after years of planning, protest, and organizing, including the arrest of Cooper Square organizers, the city formally approved an updated version of the community's plan.[10] This ushered in a new stage of community planning that survived the city's fiscal crisis and "planned shrinkage" policies and went on to thrive into the 1980s and the new millennium.

The Plan and the Fiscal Crisis

The Cooper Square Alternate Plan would have died an early death if it weren't for the radical and often militant organizing behind it. In 1970, Cooper Square activists joined with the Esperanza Coalition, Chinatown Advisory Committee, and Action for Progress to form the Lower East Side Joint Planning Council (JPC). The coalition expanded to include many of the tenant groups and homesteaders, forming a political front to protect and expand low-cost housing in the neighborhood. The JPC became a forceful advocate for the preservation and development of low-income housing, lobbying before city agencies and the local community board and in Washington. The JPC was consciously dedicated to controlling land use in the neighborhood. In 1981, it started a campaign named This Land Is Ours, which called for antidisplacement zoning, land banking, and nonprofit housing development.[11] The JPC also supported citywide campaigns against the indiscriminate auction of city-owned land and buildings and for residential and commercial rent controls. Over the years, the Cooper Square Committee spawned other organizations, such as the Bowery Residents Committee, an advocate for decent single-room occupancy buildings, the Good Food Coop, the Third Avenue Artists, Good Old Lower East Side, and many tenant associations.

In the early 1970s, the Cooper Square Committee came close to sealing a deal with the state Urban Development Corporation (UDC) that would have employed federal low-income housing funds to build new housing. But cutbacks in federal funds during the Nixon administration, the state's fiscal woes, and the city's near bankruptcy interrupted this plan. Upstate conservatives who were nervous that UDC would also sponsor low-income housing in the suburbs were happy to see that agency thwarted. The Cooper Square Committee then backed a local developer, Reuben Glick, who won federal section 8 guarantees for low-income housing that he wanted to build on one of the largest vacant urban renewal sites. After many delays, 146 low-income rent-subsidized units were dedicated on May 19, 1984. Thelma Burdick Houses was named after the Cooper Square Committee's first president, who had been director of the Church of All Nations and University Settlement House. Even though it took more than two decades after the first Moses plan for the new housing to be built, 100 percent of all the new units were low-income units. The Cooper Square Committee worked closely with the developer at every stage of development, and the project included community gardens, stained-glass windows, a mural, and other artwork by local artists.

During the first twenty years of Cooper Square's history, saving existing housing was even more important than getting new housing built. The tenants in the buildings that had been saved from the wrecking ball suffered daily abuses by private landlords and the city. The Committee protested that the city operated the buildings under its jurisdiction like a slumlord. It organized rent strikes and picketed the city's site office. At one point, so much garbage was dumped in front of the site office that the staff couldn't enter for days. On top of poor or irregular maintenance, the city would fail to renovate and rerent vacant apartments and even strip them of plumbing and wiring. The city housing agency often failed to consult with the PAC as it was required to do. Cooper Square activists supported the city's innovative alternative-management programs that provided tenants with assistance to manage their own buildings. However, the ultimate objective of the city's housing agency was to sell these buildings to the tenants or private developers, and most of the tenants could not afford to buy. So the city always saw these programs as short-term solutions and limited investment in them.[12]

The Cooper Square Community Development Committee and Businessmen's Association was not narrowly focused on individual building projects but was concerned with every block, lot, and building in the area, asking how these parcels could contribute to or undermine the goals of the plan. Time and again they organized to persuade outside developers to respect the community plan. For example, when the Jewish Association of Services for the Aged (JASA) proposed to build a project for the elderly in 1983, the Committee discovered that other JASA projects in integrated neighborhoods were almost entirely white. Initially, JASA was unwilling to give priority to local people, who would have been largely people of color. After pressure from the Cooper Square Committee, JASA signed an agreement that required that 49 percent of units accommodate local tenants. Eventually, JASA would boast that its Lower East Side project was a model of racial diversity. The JASA victory validated Cooper Square's insistence on racial justice as an integral component of community development.

From the beginning, the Cooper Square Committee advocated for the protection of housing for homeless people and single-room buildings for low-income men, a population often forgotten and unwanted by local residents. For example, in 1979 the Committee responded to complaints about the Third Street Men's Shelter by holding community meetings and conducting a study. They supported rehabilitation of the decrepit building by the city and measures to address violence, alcoholism, and mental illness among the shelter residents. Another unpopular group that got the support of the Committee was low-income artists. Cooper Square fought for a city program to subsidize artist housing, a program that had a very short lifetime because of the lack of strong advocacy from other communities.

Mutual Housing and Community Land Trust

In the 1970s and 1980s, as community development corporations flourished throughout the city, circumstances pushed the Cooper Square Community Development Committee and Businessmen's Association to become more formally involved in the development process. Cooper Square was directly responsible for the renovation of over 320 apartment units and construction of the new Thelma Burdick project. One of the earliest and most difficult projects was the Cube Building (it looks like a cube). This city-owned building outside the urban renewal area was slated for a dollar sale to a speculator until the Committee organized to block the sale and persuade the city to sell it the building for a bit more than a dollar. Today it is a limited-equity cooperative with twenty-two units of housing for homeless families.

In the 1980s, the real estate market started to heat up, and the city was interested in selling off more of its vacant land to the highest bidder. The Department of Housing Preservation and Development (HPD) sent Cooper Square a proposal for leveraging low-income housing in an area under pressure by private developers. The proposal—called a *cross-subsidy plan*—was for every unit of market-rate housing to be matched by a unit of low-income housing. The money the city would make from selling to private developers would presumably go to subsidizing new low-income housing. Cooper Square rejected the cross-subsidy plan because it depended on market development, an example of increasingly popular linkage strategies for low-income housing. The cross-subsidy proposal became moot when the bottom fell out of the private market in the latter part of the 1980s.

In 1990, David Dinkins became the first African American mayor of New York City with strong support from community-based organizations. The climate in City Hall changed, and HPD moved to expedite an agreement on Cooper Square. A memorandum of understanding was

signed that gave the Cooper Square Committee responsibility for reno-
vating city-owned properties with financial support from the city's capital budget. It also included a formula for the development of the vacant
sites in the urban renewal area that mixed market-rate and low-income
housing and included new community facilities.

The agreement with the city recognized a new entity, the Cooper
Square Mutual Housing Association (MHA). This unique form of ownership, common in many northern European countries (Cooper Square
organizers got the idea from Holland), is essentially a form of nonprofit
ownership with tenant control. Unlike cooperative owners, MHA tenants
do not own shares, but they collectively make decisions about the
housing. Started in 1991, the Cooper Square MHA now manages eighteen buildings with 303 housing units. All of its projects are affordable
to low-income people who make less than 50 percent of the area median
income. With no bank loans for land and building costs, rents cover the
lion's share of maintenance costs. The Cooper Square MHA is one of
eight in New York City (not all of which are active), the largest grouping
in the United States. Three of these eight are in the Lower East Side.[13]

The Cooper Square MHA owns the buildings, but the land that they
sit on is owned by the Cooper Square Community Land Trust (CLT).
The terms of the trust mandate that the housing serve low-income
tenants in perpetuity. The CLT is one of the strongest legal instruments
for the preservation of affordable, low-income housing. Similar city-
owned buildings that were in the Tenant Interim Lease program were
sold to tenants organized as limited-equity coops, but the resale restrictions are limited in duration, the penalties for early resale at market
prices are limited, and the city does not monitor compliance. Cooper
Square thus pioneered in the establishment of one of the most effective
tools for the preservation of community land.[14]

However, the Cooper Square story reveals that communities do not
necessarily have to own the land to have effective control over how it is
used. Socially owned entities like MHAs, zoning, and partnerships with
private owners are also important tools for protecting affordable housing.
Together they can effectively reduce the speculative resale value of land,
a goal that progressives have sought to achieve ever since Henry George.
But the Cooper Square story also suggests that *the most important
element in perpetual affordability is perpetual organizing and protest,
particularly when the organizing and protest are tied to broader social
and political movements.* Frances Goldin and Esther Rand, two of the
Cooper Square Committee's key organizers, had been militants in the

socialist left—Goldin in the American Labor Party and Rand in the Communist Party. They both had been tenant organizers, and Rand helped to found the city's largest tenant organization, the Metropolitan Council on Housing. Perhaps their experiences with United Front and Popular Front organizing during World War II and the civil rights movement afterward led them to form the broad alliances needed to win on the ground. They could feel at home sharing the leadership with Thelma Burdick, a genteel woman for whom faith was more important than politics. They had no fear going up against Mayor Rudolph Giuliani, who considered the Lower East Side a special thorn in his side, and Antonio Pagán, a Giuliani ally who tried to destroy the Cooper Square Committee during his brief tenure in the City Council. And for all their shortcomings in this arena, the parties that Goldin and Rand had belonged to were the parties of W.E.B. DuBois,[15] Paul Robeson, and Vito Marcantonio, which put antiracism squarely in the middle of struggles for economic justice and community improvement.

At this writing, housing is going up on the last remaining sites in the Cooper Square Urban Renewal Area. Avalon Chrystie Place includes four buildings with 708 housing units, one-fourth of them reserved for low-income households; 85,000 square feet of retail space; and a community and athletic center to be operated by the University Settlement and the Chinatown branch of the YMCA. When all of the housing is built, about 60 percent of the housing units in the urban renewal area will be for low-income people and remain so in perpetuity. This is better than any other urban renewal project of this size (with the exception of those that became 100 percent public housing). The Cooper Square Alternate Plan and other community efforts played a role in stabilizing the neighborhood and limiting the impact of gentrification. Between 1960 and 2000, median incomes in the Lower East Side did not substantially change in comparison with Manhattan as a whole. While the period of abandonment led to a 29 percent loss in population, only 6 percent of housing units were lost as larger families and households gave way to smaller ones. Gentrification did expand inequalities, however. Whereas income levels in the neighborhood's twelve census tracts had been relatively uniform in 1960, by 2000 one tract had very high incomes and two had very low incomes.

Ironically, the sponsor of Avalon Chrystie Place is a real estate investment trust (REIT), the form of ownership that is closest to financial capital and furthest from the principles of community land. The meaning of this for the future of the neighborhood is not entirely clear. Could

Cooper Square's acceptance of a 75 percent luxury project reflect a weakening of the local constituency for community land, or is it an acceptable compromise that doesn't annul the achievement of a majority low-income urban renewal area? Will this particular REIT, known for investing in risky areas, be constrained by the lack of other available development sites in the neighborhood? The answer to these questions may rest on the outcome of current local battles to prevent middle-income coops and public housing from going private.

Within the Lower East Side, there are still tens of thousands of units within the reach of low-income people, even as the prospect of privatization of public units looms and gentrification floods many private blocks. The neighborhood's political history, social base, and racial diversity no doubt explain how so much public space has been carved out of the private city. According to Frances Goldin, "They were petrified that we would win our fight because then they said everyone is going to want this. And of course everybody wants it."

We Stay! ¡Nos Quedamos!

According to the We Stay! ¡Nos Quedamos! committee's literature,

We Stay! ¡Nos Quedamos! is a coalition of homeowners, tenants, property owners, institutions, and business persons who are resolved to remain a part of the Melrose community and become equal partners with the City of New York in the community's redevelopment. ¡Nos Quedamos! views the urban renewal process as not only encompassing physical regeneration but also addressing socioeconomic and environmental conditions in the area, with the goal of developing an economically productive, sustainable community and a healthy, livable environment. This vision is one that respects, supports, and involves the existing community in the formulation of plans and policies that address the issues of housing, open space, community renewal, and its sustainability; that are vital for the continued growth of Melrose Commons, the Bronx, and its role in the regional economy that fosters cohesion, growth, and responsibility. We believe that current members of the community must be afforded the opportunity not only to remain in the neighborhood as it undergoes renewal but also to play an active and integral role in determining the very process of development.[16]

We Stay! ¡Nos Quedamos! began when community activist Pedro Cintrón went to a local community meeting in 1992 and heard about the city's urban renewal plan that would have displaced 78 homeowners, 400 tenants, 80 businesses, and 500 workers. The result would have been the construction of low-rise homes for middle-income people and mostly unaffordable to current residents. He rang the alarm, protesting that the plan had been developed without the participation of community residents and businesses. Along with Yolanda García, another resident whose family had a business in the neighborhood, he formed We Stay! (figure 4.4). As with the Cooper Square Community Development Committee and Businessmen's Association, the organization was based on the idea that the people of Melrose Commons who struggled to stay there through the years of housing abandonment should have the right to stay as the neighborhood was redeveloped. We Stay! joined its struggle against displacement with the struggles for environmental justice—for more sustainable forms of development and against a medical-waste incinerator, waste-transfer stations, truck traffic, and other contributors to the exceptionally high levels of asthma and respiratory diseases in the South Bronx. It was one of the first examples of the fusion of the progressive community and environmental justice movements.

Since 1985, the city's department of Housing Preservation and Development (HPD), with the cooperation of the Department of City Planning (DCP), had worked on a plan for the thirty-block area in the south Bronx known as Melrose Commons. In 1990, the Bronx Center, a nonprofit organization supported by Bronx Borough President Fernando Ferrer, began to hold meetings and develop a plan for a larger area in the South Bronx, including Melrose Commons. The Melrose neighborhood had about 6,000 residents, mostly low-income people and mostly Latinos.

Figure 4.4
Yolanda Garcia, community planner. *Credit:* El Diario

After protest, discussion, and debate, We Stay! persuaded the city to agree to give it six months to come up with an alternative plan. The We Stay! committee held 168 public meetings to prepare its plan. The committee had the support of the Bronx Center, the borough president's office, and Ron Shiffman, a City Planning Commissioner and director of the Pratt Center for Community and Environmental Development (PICCED), a university-based planning group. They had the help of two planning firms that donated technical assistance.

The city then accepted the community's alternative plan, which passed the city's official Uniform Land Use Review (ULURP) process. The plan reduced significantly the number of people who can be displaced during development. Instead of the single-family homes proposed by HPD as part of its suburban-style strategy for urban renewal, the plan called for a variety of more dense housing. Instead of a large park proposed in the original plan, the community's plan called for a series of smaller open spaces that would be more accessible to and manageable by local residents and workers. The community plan identified the vacant Bronx Court House, an historic building, as a central place in the neighborhood and called for its rehabilitation and reuse.

Over 700 units of housing called for in the Melrose Commons Community Plan have been built (figure 4.5). We Stay! is now an established nonprofit organization that continues to work on community development issues, including housing, the environment, and economic development. It is developing the first affordable housing project in the city that conforms to green building standards.[17] It later stopped an attempt by the DCP to remove the design guidelines they had developed from the plan. But We Stay! lost a battle to keep the Bronx Courthouse from being sold by the city to a private speculator, who promptly proceeded to do nothing with the building.

Yolanda García, a founder and the first executive director of We Stay! ¡Nos Quedamos!, was a largely unrecognized planning hero of New York City. Her family owned a small business in Melrose that survived the worst years of abandonment. Without any formal planning education, she became an expert in community planning. Yolanda García died in 2005. She has been an inspiration to many activists in communities of color who are confronted with official plans about which they have had no say, and the Yolanda García award for community planners was established in her memory. The retrospective studies of Robert Moses are unending. Jane Jacobs is quoted profusely. But urban historians have

Figure 4.5
The Melrose Commons community plan. *Credit:* We Stay! ¡Nos Quedamos!

largely overlooked stories of people like Yolanda García, a Puerto Rican woman from the Bronx, and the many other working-class people throughout the city whose organizing and ideas have left an imprint on the city. Yolanda García follows in the footsteps of lifelong activists like Frances Goldin, Esther Rand, Marie Runyon, and Jane Wood, women who played leading roles in the city's community and housing struggles from the 1930s.

The We Stay! plan challenged a particular aspect of the neoliberal model of urban redevelopment that has characterized official community planning since the 1970s. As one way of justifying cutbacks in federal subsidies for low-income multifamily housing, government set up as an alternative model the low-density community of homeowners, the suburban American dream in an urban setting. The Bronx's high-density community of working-class renters was destroyed in the period of post–World War II abandonment along with the Keynesian model of economic growth. In its place, government proposed the low-density community of homeowners. It started with the infamous single-family homes in Charlotte Gardens, promoted by President Jimmy Carter in his well-publicized visit to the South Bronx and inaugurated in 1984, and continued under the program of the New York City Housing Partnership, a public-private venture that developed vacant lots using city subsidies on city-owned land and private lots that were assembled using the city's urban renewal powers. Because of this policy and the backlash against it by communities, the largely rebuilt South Bronx today is a patchwork of low-density one- to three-family homes mixed in with medium- and high-density apartment buildings.[18]

The story of the abandonment of the South Bronx was repeated in other devastated areas of the city such as Brownsville, Bushwick, and East New York in Brooklyn. As neoliberal policy took hold in the 1970s, these neighborhoods were left on their own to be restored by the magic of the free market. When the market didn't materialize and local residents and businesses organized, protested, and occupied buildings and land, government began to enter the picture in a modest way. As it did in the Great Depression when market magic failed, government eventually facilitated land development for interested private developers. But apart from the belated efforts of government, the abandoned neighborhoods of the South Bronx, Central Brooklyn, and Harlem were rebuilt largely through the efforts of the people who lived there, organized at the building, block, and neighborhood levels. City government and banks were pressed into making investments.[19] We Stay! followed in the footsteps of groups like Banana Kelly, the People's Development Corporation, the Mid-Bronx Desperados, and the Northwest Bronx Community and Clergy Coalition, community-based organizations that took control of their neighborhoods as both capital and government withdrew. Later, capital and government reentered when community activists challenged redlining practices and service cutbacks. The federal Community Reinvestment Act (CRA) also forced banks to disclose their lending practices and prodded them to search for potential investment opportunities as property values began to increase.

Conclusion: Unity and Conflict

The Cooper Square and Melrose Commons plans were two important milestones in New York City community planning. They both arose from community struggles to protest official urban renewal plans. They offered development alternatives that were more accessible to people who lived in the neighborhoods, and community organizers ultimately helped implement the plans. Significant and sustainable political unity in these diverse communities made their achievements possible.

But the planning process in both cases was by no means orderly and harmonious. In both cases, there were substantial internal conflicts over land-use priorities, the importance of compromise with the city, and approaches to plan implementation. One of the sharpest conflicts in both cases was over community gardens. Housing activists in the Lower East Side struggled for many years to force city government to develop vacant lots for low-income housing. When the city finally gave in, some of the vacant lots had been converted by neighboring residents to community gardens. The Lower East Side had one of the largest and most diverse collections of community gardens. Many of them had been formally adopted by the City's Green Thumb program, which did not provide them any guarantee of permanency since the city reserved the right to develop the land when it chose to do so. While some housing activists were adamant in asserting that low-income housing had been a long-term community priority, others sought to negotiate compromises. In Melrose Commons, the conflicts were similar, and there were also gardeners who maintained that they were not aware of the community plan and were not included in the process. In both cases, the local community board, elected officials, and city agency representatives played a role in mediating the disputes, but the conflicts were deep and reflected an enduring internal division within communities over the way that community land should be used.[20] We now turn to the stories of the diverse array of contemporary community plans, including those that arose through environmental justice struggles and confronted not so much the large-scale displacement of official urban renewal programs but the more gradual erosion of gentrification.

5

From Environmental Justice to Community Planning

Why is there a prevalence of incompatible land use and zoning policies in minority communities? What normative planning policies were ignored? What sectors, if any, within planning attempted to prevent this type of negative land use? Why hasn't the profession actively intervened to mitigate and resolve these conflicts?

—David R. Diaz, *Barrio Urbanism*

While today a few neighborhoods confront urban renewal plans like the ones that the Cooper Square Community Development Committee and Businessmen's Association and We Stay! ¡Nos Quedamos! responded to, many of them have instead constructed community plans in response to the complex dual threats of environmental hazards and gentrification. The demise of the federal urban renewal program in the 1970s removed a major source of financing for urban renewal. State and local governments continued to use their powers of eminent domain for urban redevelopment, sometimes assuming financial responsibility for the former federal urban renewal areas. However, with a decline in local spending in the 1970s fiscal crisis and a decrease in widespread abandonment during the 1980s, urban renewal ceased to be the major displacement threat.

Many of the current generation of community plans arose from the struggles for environmental justice in the 1980s and 1990s that arose because of the high concentrations of environmental and health hazards in low-income communities of color, and a concurrent concern with displacement resulting from gentrification. Some of these plans were officially endorsed by New York's City Planning Commission and City Council as 197a plans (discussed further in chapter 6), while others were never submitted for official approval. Some were broad comprehensive plans, and others were focused on zoning issues. This chapter discusses some of these stories.

Confronting Noxious Facilities and Gentrification

By the early 1980s, the wholesale abandonment and displacement of neighborhoods began to wane. Neighborhood movements had been successful in stopping the bulldozers of the federal urban renewal program and slowing down the city's cutbacks in services. Real estate also went into a cyclical period of boom, thanks to the excess capital released during the early years of the Reagan revolution with its military buildup and cutbacks of federal spending on social services. The local real estate industry profited from the abandonment disasters that they themselves had been complicit in creating. Those who had speculated by buying up vacant land and buildings would now renounce demolition and the use of eminent domain by government. Gentrification became the name of the game.

While real estate investors both large and small were buying up occupied buildings with low-income tenants and converting them to market-rate coops, they also became interested in the overall improvement of neighborhood services and the quality of life in the city. Although city government continued to profess austerity in spending, Mayor Ed Koch's $5 billion housing program, contrary to the prevailing neoliberal ideology that rejected government spending to fuel the local economy, primed the real estate market by helping to stabilize once-abandoned neighborhoods and stimulate land-value increases. Advocates for low-income tenants and homeowners applauded community improvement but with a proviso. They had a different interpretation of what goes into quality of life and sought better neighborhoods without displacing the people living there. "We won't move" continued to be the rallying cry as gentrification took hold although the target for organizing was not as easy to discern as it had been during the urban renewal struggles.

Despite the improvements in many neighborhoods, in some areas of the city community improvement of any kind, with or without gentrification, was thwarted by the presence of environmental hazards, including waste-transfer stations and proposals to build new noxious waste facilities. Many of these neighborhoods were located in older industrial waterfront districts, and all of them were low-income communities with large populations of people of color. Local preservation and development efforts by community-based organizations, community development corporations, and small property owners were thwarted by these LULUs (local unwanted land uses).[1] In other neighborhoods, the federal Community Reinvestment Act had stimulated banks to reverse decades of redlining practices, start issuing mortgages, and open up bank branches, but neighborhoods with LULUs were left behind. The city upzoned manufacturing land in wealthy neighborhoods to encourage new residential and commercial development but ignored the neighborhoods with LULUs.[2] Waterfronts in Manhattan and upscale neighborhoods in the outer boroughs were greened or promptly turned over to private developers, while waterfronts in working-class areas were left to languish. This was the context for the emergence of the city's environmental justice movement.

The decisions about locating existing and proposed waste facilities were made either by private businesses or officials in city agencies. Judging from the outcomes, it would appear that they based their decisions on informal, sketchy, and subjective cost-benefit analyses. Perhaps, however, "nondecision making,"[3] in which the prevalent action was to do nothing, prevailed among officials. It would appear that low-income communities of color were invisible. Whether the result of private or public actions or inactions, elite neighborhoods with high land values were priced out of the market following the principle of finding the highest and best use of land (see chapter 1) and were off the map when decisions were made about locating public waste-management facilities. The decisions were not made in the context of any comprehensive planning, nor were local residents and workers involved. In locating public facilities, there was no conscious attempt to apply a fair-share principle, which would have meant that no neighborhood should have more than its share of burdensome facilities (the 1989 city charter revision incorporated the fair-share principle, but the city failed to provide strict regulations to enforce it). The city's planners allowed better-off neighborhoods to remain free of LULUs and failed to intervene to restrict them in poor neighborhoods. Sometimes, this imbalance would even be justified by equating, by definition, protest against an unfair burden with the exclusionary, not-in-my-backyard (NIMBY) philosophy.[4] In practice, however, as demonstrated by the Organization of Waterfront Neighborhoods plan and other proposals from the environmental justice movement described in this chapter, environmental justice advocates embraced inclusionary approaches to planning. The environmental justice movement became perhaps the most vocal proponent of progressive and inclusionary community-based planning in the city. In addition, the movement gave birth to a new generation of community planners with considerable knowledge and skills in environmental science and regulation.[5]

Since its inception, the central concern of the environmental justice movement in the United States has been the disproportionate impact of noxious facilities on low-income communities of color. Beginning in the 1980s, campaigns for environmental justice emerged throughout the nation, as a space in which the issues of the civil rights and environmental movements converged. A landmark 1987 study sponsored by the United Church of Christ documented how hazardous facilities were more likely to be located in communities of color than white communities.[6] In 1991, the first People of Color Environmental Leadership Summit was held in Washington, DC. It brought together activists and professionals from throughout the United States who had struggled in local campaigns and through regional networks (a second summit was held a decade later). Environmental justice activists distinguished themselves from the mainstream environmental movement, which had roots in the elite conservation institutions and were perceived as focusing on the preservation of relatively pristine rural enclaves and ignoring urban environmental problems such as asthma.[7] One of the first undertakings of the movement was to seek legitimacy for its claims that environmental policy in the nation did not take into account the disparate effects of environmental hazards on communities of color. Leaders of the movement relied on political and legal rationales borrowed from the civil rights movement and rallied allies from the civil rights communities. In 1994, President William Clinton issued Executive Order 12898 on environmental justice, for the first time directing federal agencies to address disproportionate environmental burdens in carrying out their mandates (this order was ignored by the subsequent administration of President George W. Bush). Despite the scant progress made in the realm of federal policy, mainstream environmental groups now acknowledge environmental justice as a legitimate concern, and several have initiated environmental justice programs, though the effect on overall practice appears to be uneven.

Environmental justice advocates in New York City were influenced in their formation by the global discussions about *sustainability*—the process of meeting the needs of the present without compromising future generations (see chapter 1). The concept of sustainable development forced people to look beyond pollution to more complex, holistic approaches to the environment that incorporated issues of economic development and social equity. The historic 1992 United Nations Conference on Environment and Development in Rio de Janeiro, attended by many New York City activists, broadened thinking everywhere about environmental problems. The developing countries that took part in the Rio conference did not pose environmental quality and economic development as either/or choices, nor would activists from communities of color in the United States.[8] This set the framework for an approach to community planning that attempts to balance environmental and growth issues.

In New York City, the decade of the 1990s witnessed the acceleration of a local economic boom and a real estate bubble large enough to survive several stock market crises. This protracted upswing in the property market increased concerns in many neighborhoods about gentrification and displacement at the same time that activists were fighting against noxious facilities. In 1990, Mayor David Dinkins took office with the support of a broad coalition of community, environmental, and other social movements. The elections of Dinkins and William Clinton as president raised hopes among neighborhood groups for greater involvement in decision making.

From its inception, therefore, New York City's environmental justice community had to deal with the fundamental dilemma: LULUs held gentrification at bay, and if activists were successful in getting rid of the LULUs or reducing the risks they posed, residents would then face the threat of being displaced by rampant gentrification. Activists who struggled for a healthier community were rewarded with rising rents and land values that forced them to move out of the community. On the other hand, if they were passive, they would continue to suffer the serious health risks that went along with the LULUs.

This led community organizers to planning: *community planning was the means to address both LULUs and gentrification, environmental quality and economic development*. The central strategy would be to improve the environment while at the same time pursuing development strategies that protected them against displacement. Thus, the movements for environmental justice and community development converged to advocate for progressive, inclusionary community-based planning. This approach stands in stark contrast to the elite, exclusionary community-based planning whose ultimate result is to reinforce the negative effects of gentrification.

Let us look briefly at how the environmental justice movement emerged in New York City and then, through several stories of community plans, show how it led to inclusive approaches to community planning.[9]

It All Started on the Waterfront

Most of the city's port facilities were moved to New Jersey by the 1970s. Feverish real estate development and Robert Moses–era highways had left little upland space for the port to expand, and technology shifted to containerization, which required more land for container storage. Expansion of the global economy also increased the volume of imports, and competition between East Coast ports required economies of scale for ports to survive. After New York's port moved to New Jersey, prime Manhattan waterfront land was transformed for recreational use, but in the outer boroughs there remained large amounts of underutilized industrial land, particularly in Hunts Point (Bronx); Greenpoint, Williamsburg, Red Hook, and Sunset Park (Brooklyn); Long Island City (Queens); and Harlem (Manhattan). These waterfront areas, which abut large residential communities, remained zoned mostly for heavy manufacturing (M3). This meant that waste facilities and toxic uses could locate on abandoned industrial properties, usually as of right (without public review or approval).

In 1988, three Harlem community activists—Vernice Miller, Peggy Shepard, and Chuck Sutton—started West Harlem Environmental Action (WE ACT), an organization that became one of the most active and effective environmental justice organizations in the city. West Harlem is the site of the North River sewage-treatment plant, one of fourteen such facilities that the city was forced to build to comply with the requirements of the federal Clean Water Act. The West Harlem plant went into operation in 1986. Partially in response to community protest, the city got the state of New York to build a huge park on a platform above the sewage plant. The Riverbank State Park is the only state park in Manhattan and one of only two in the city. It has three swimming pools, an amphitheater, a skating rink, and ball fields. It helps balance the deficit of parks and recreation facilities in Harlem, a neighborhood that Robert Moses consciously ignored in his green building crusade because of his fear that whites would have to mix with "colored people."[10]

Despite its crown of green, the sewage plant smelled. Community activists were concerned that the plant would add to the public health crisis in Harlem, which has one of the highest asthma rates in the nation. Harlem already hosts most of the Metropolitan Transportation Authority's Manhattan bus depots, where diesel emissions add air-borne particulates to an already polluted environment (New York City and state have the highest levels of diesel contamination in the nation).[11] "The Sewage Seven"—a group of Harlem community leaders—were arrested on Martin Luther King Jr.'s birthday in 1988 as they led a peaceful protest in front the plant. WE ACT took the city to court and won a $1.1 million settlement, which was used to set up a fund to address community concerns.[12]

In the late 1990s, WE ACT developed its own plan for the Harlem waterfront, *Harlem on the River.*[13] Today the organization is a major voice in many community planning arenas. It is involved in planning for the 125th Street corridor and the community plan developed in response to Columbia University's West Harlem expansion plan. Like many environmental justice organizations, WE ACT combines activism and planning with a focus on improving environmental health.

The history of the North River plant suggests that environmental racism has deep roots that go back to the earlier urban renewal, "Negro removal" issues. The plant was originally to be sited further south in Manhattan's gentrifying Upper West Side near prime waterfront real estate that would later become home to Trump City, a huge upscale residential complex. At the urging of the City Planning Commission, which was committed to Robert Moses's West Side urban renewal plan, the plant site was moved uptown above 125th Street, the central artery running through the historic heart of Harlem. It has long been the dream of Harlem's business and community leaders that this street would become a magnet for community economic development. Despite opposition from Harlem residents, the city approved the Harlem treatment plant site in 1968 and started construction in 1972. The end result was a major infrastructure project that increased health risks in black Harlem while facilitating urban renewal, real estate development, and the displacement of blacks and Puerto Ricans in the nearby Upper West Side. Also, the new West Side real estate development may have eventually helped push the North River plant to operate beyond its planned capacity, creating greater risks of the release of odors and untreated sewage in the adjacent river.

The Air in the Bronx

In the 1990s, the South Bronx Clean Air Coalition successfully fought to close the Bronx Lebanon Medical Waste Incinerator, built in 1991 by Browning Ferris Industries to burn forty-eight tons of the region's medical waste every day. The incinerator was built in a low-income neighborhood near a public housing project and several schools. Contrary to claims by its operator and public authorities, the incinerator frequently discharged toxic air. The official environmental review of the proposed plant had concluded there would be no significant negative environmental impact. Engineers who relied on theoretically safe designs did not factor in the prospect that even a single failure in operations could have a catastrophic effect on people living around the facility.

An intensive community protest campaign forced the incinerator to shut down in 1998. Governor George Pataki responded to the organizing campaign, which included large demonstrations, by negotiating the facility's closure, using as leverage the $15 million in tax-free industrial-development bonds and tax exemptions, public subsidies that had been given to the developer. Just as Harlem's waste-treatment plant migrated from a wealthier neighborhood, the Bronx incinerator had first been proposed in Rockland County, a suburb to the north. In yet another instance of conscious targeting, in 2005 the city started construction on a water filtration plant in a park in the low-income North Bronx neighborhood of Norwood after rejecting a site in upscale Westchester County.[14]

The Bronx gave birth to many other grassroots environmental justice campaigns that spawned community plans. The South Bronx is traversed by the Cross-Bronx Expressway, the Robert Moses megastructure that now hosts the largest number of trucks entering New York City daily. The diesel trucks that stream across the expressway also saturate the South Bronx's mixed-use neighborhoods. In response to these conditions, the grassroots organization Mothers on the Move forced the city to improve its regulation of heavy truck traffic and developed a plan for rerouting trucks. The Hunts Point Rangers, a group of teenagers, patrol the neighborhood and report trucks that violate the city's laws against idling. Youth Ministries for Peace and Justice has helped protect and develop community gardens, public open space, and successful youth education programs. Youth Ministries developed plans to restore the polluted Bronx River and to tear down the Sheridan Expressway, another Robert Moses creation. The Sheridan plan would replace the expressway with new community facilities and public open space. Unlike the Embarcadero Expressway teardown in San Francisco, the main proponents of this idea were neighborhood organizers. The Point Community Development Corporation and Sustainable South Bronx[15] are two active CDCs in the South Bronx, both of which were created by activists who merged environmental activism with cultural development and community planning. These groups are developing plans for the Bronx waterfront, new public spaces, and housing as they are battling the concentration of waste facilities in the South Bronx. They are among the strongest advocates for community planning in the borough, and the mayor's office and city agencies have acknowledged their role as they formulate development policies in the South Bronx.

The Incinerator in Brooklyn

Brooklyn's Williamsburg and its northern neighbor Greenpoint together host the largest concentration of waste facilities in the city. These include dozens of privately operated waste-transfer stations, over a hundred industries handling hazardous materials, seventeen petroleum and natural gas storage facilities, a nuclear waste-transfer station, a waste-water treatment plant, and the largest underground oil spill in the nation.[16]

One of the city's earliest environmental justice campaigns defeated a plan to build an incinerator in Williamsburg, at the Brooklyn Navy Yard. The Community Alliance for the Environment (CAFE) brought together the Puerto Rican, Hasidic, and other communities in a rare display of interethnic and class solidarity. The central environmental justice group in this struggle was El Puente Academy, founded and led by Luis Garden Acosta, an educator and former Young Lord. The proposal to build a mammoth garbage incinerator in the Navy Yard (a decommissioned defense facility owned by the city and leased for industrial use) was the decades-long dream of the city's sanitation specialists, who touted state-of-the-art incineration technology that would limit environmental risks to the surrounding neighborhood. Approval of the plant was engineered by Norman Steisel, Mayor Ed Koch's Sanitation Commissioner and a former waste industry executive.[17]

The first proposal to build an incinerator was in 1979. Some national environmental groups passed over questions about toxic ash and dioxin that the plant would produce and went along with the plan to turn waste into energy because they were able to extract concessions from the city, including a commitment to stricter emission controls and a citywide recycling program. The project was attractive to the bond market as a utility investment (since the plant would generate a valuable 465 million kilowatt hours of electricity annually) and attractive to the real estate industry (since it could build more housing, confident of an increased power supply). The facility's planners had to admit, however, that the tons of toxic ash generated by the plant would be buried within the city.

A broad community coalition was the key factor in the ultimate success of the campaign to stop the incinerator. Other neighborhoods were powerful enough to get their incinerators taken out of the city's Solid Waste Management Plan (SWMP), but activists in Greenpoint and

Williamsburg were initially unable to kill this proposal to open a new one. In Williamsburg, there had been frictions between the large Hasidic and Latino populations, and they rarely worked together on issues. In both communities, large families with low incomes competed for public housing units, and the Hasidim had lost a landmark court case brought by the Puerto Rican Legal Defense and Education Fund that showed how the New York City Housing Authority excluded blacks and Latinos from Williamsburg projects in favor of whites. Although the Hasidic community leaders were privileged with a political inside track in the Koch administration and its successors, they found themselves without the leverage they needed on the citywide matter of a new incinerator. But after all groups joined together in a major symbolic march across the Williamsburg Bridge to City Hall in 1993, elected officials found it no longer advantageous to pursue the incinerator.[18] Mayor Dinkins slowed the project down, and Mayor Giuliani let it lapse. In a war of position, as many community groups that face overwhelming odds have discovered, delay proved to be a powerful tactic.[19]

Incinerators all over the country had given way to more profitable landfills, and this may have made the decision more palatable for the city's sanitation experts. But there were still active incinerators across the Hudson River in New Jersey, upwind of New York City. The Brooklyn victory was therefore only a partial one.

Also in Williamsburg, a group of young people who adopted the name Toxic Avengers undertook research and monitored sources of environmental risk in this mixed industrial and residential neighborhood. Toxic Avengers was a project of El Puente Academy and followed a pattern of youth mobilization around social issues that also developed in Sunset Park (Brooklyn) and the South Bronx. They were examples of what Jason Corburn calls "street science"—community-based analysis of environmental and health risks and the application of scientific knowledge to address critical community health issues.[20]

The coalition formed during the incinerator struggle was a foundation for the coalition that prepared the Williamsburg and Greenpoint 197a plans (discussed in chapter 6). El Puente and environmental justice activists in these neighborhoods, which have the largest concentration of environmental hazards in the city, were organizing to reduce the number of waste-transfer stations, enforce restrictions on industrial polluters, and limit heavy truck traffic, and they also joined together with established CDCs and advocates for community preservation to become leading participants in community planning.

The Sludge Battles: Red Hook and Sunset Park

In 1988, the City of New York was legally enjoined from dumping the sludge from its waste-water treatment plants in the ocean, as it had done for many years.[21] *Sludge* is the gooey, watery residue that is left after sewage is treated. It may contain active bacteria, viruses, and toxic chemicals. Each day, the city produces about 1,200 tons of sludge in its fourteen treatment plants. Today eight of these plants dewater the sludge, after which it is taken away by companies that have long-term contracts with the city. The sludge ends up being used for compost or spray irrigation on farms. Many toxic substances enter the waste system through the city's ancient sewer network, which combines storm and sanitary waste, and serious doubts remain about the health consequences of using New York City sludge in the food-production process (organic farmers will not use it).[22]

In an effort to give the city a stake in the fertilizer business (and vice versa), David Dinkins's First Deputy Mayor Norman Steisel, former head of a Bronx-based sludge plant and once an operative of the Lazard Frères bond firm, proposed to build eight sludge plants in the city that would convert the waste to fertilizer pellets and sell them to local and national markets.[23] He proposed two plants each in Manhattan, Brooklyn, and Queens and one each in the Bronx and Staten Island (the Manhattan sites were on Wards Island, between Manhattan and Queens). The city's consultants chose sites in and near low-income communities and communities of color where land values were lower and large vacant parcels of land were zoned for industry. All of the sites were in waterfront communities.

Red Hook in Brooklyn was to get two plants on its industrial waterfront. One would be at the site of the Revere Sugar Refinery, which had stood abandoned for over a decade, a victim of the free-trade shift from refined sugar made from imported raw materials to corn sweeteners made from surplus U.S. corn. The other would be on Erie Basin, the site of a recently failed fish port started by the Port Authority of New York and New Jersey (thanks to poor planning by the Port Authority and competition from Japan on the global market for fish).

Following the orthodox "highest and best use of land" planning approach, Red Hook was a top candidate for LULUs. It was one of Brooklyn's poorest communities and had been bypassed by the global marketplace and the gentrification that blanketed nearby Carroll Gardens and Park Slope. Over 70 percent of the population lived in public housing, there was a good deal of vacant industrial land, and it was isolated from the rest of Brooklyn by a Moses-era expressway. But opposition to the sludge plants brought together residents and businesses in a rare display of unity. They organized demonstrations, lobbied elected officials, and managed in a relatively short period of time to persuade the city to withdraw its plans. Red Hook's victory helped create the personal and organizational ties in the neighborhood that led to a community plan (described further in chapter 6).

After the city dropped its plans for the two Red Hook plants, it decided to combine both plants into one giant facility on the Sunset Park waterfront, just a couple of miles south of Red Hook. The Sunset Park sludge proposal elicited widespread opposition from the neighborhood's Latino, Asian American, and Italian American communities, which had rarely worked together. The United Puerto Rican Organization of Sunset Park (UPROSE), led by civil rights attorney Elizabeth Yeampierre, played a pivotal role in bringing the opposition together and argued that the sludge proposal was a classic example of environmental injustice. The proposed plant would have been located on the waterfront, and the residential population closest to the site was mostly Puerto Rican. UPROSE attempted to build an alliance with the Asian American community in New York City's third largest Chinatown, located more than a mile from the site. In 1993, the city withdrew its plan, and later the community came together to develop its own Sunset Park waterfront plan. The heightened consciousness of environmental hazards among youth led UPROSE to sponsor a youth group, the Environmental Enforcers. The Sunset Park waterfront plan was sponsored by Brooklyn Community Board 7 and followed some of the ideas set out in a previous community-generated plan. Its alternative for the waterfront was a mix of industrial preservation, new public open space, and preservation of residential blocks with a mostly Latino population. UPROSE became one of the neighborhood's most vocal advocates for community planning.

After losing the fight in Sunset Park, the city's Department of Environmental Protection dropped plans for the new sludge facilities. It would use and expand existing capacity for dewatering sludge at eight treatment plants and rely more on private contractors. Still, up to 40 percent of the city's sludge is processed at the New York Organic Fertilizer Company in the South Bronx, whose odors provide a constant reminder to environmental justice groups that a more equitable solution lies ahead.[24]

There are many other environmental justice groups in the city's working-class neighborhoods, such as the Magnolia Tree Earth Center in Bedford-Stuyvesant (Brooklyn), the Southern Queens Park Association, and the East New York United Front, which worked to defeat a proposed incinerator in neighboring Long Island. They and other groups mentioned here formed the New York City Environmental Justice Alliance (NYCEJA), a citywide coalition.

One might ask why there was a need for new environmental groups when New York already hosts several well-established environmental organizations such as the Natural Resources Defense Council (NRDC), Sierra Club, and Environmental Defense Fund (EDF). The following excerpt from *City Limits* magazine suggests how distant the established environmental movement has been from the concerns of communities of color. The article is about Majora Carter, a South Bronx activist and director of Sustainable South Bronx, who expressed concern that established groups failed to consult her when discussing support for her work:

So she was surprised to learn this summer from a friend that a new group called the Waterfront Park Coalition, assembled by the politically influential state chapter of the League of Conservation Voters, wanted to adopt and promote her project. Headed by some of the same players behind Manhattan's new Hudson River Park, the coalition spent this summer searching for promising community-generated ideas that might merit big-dollar investments from public and private funders. Its canvassers called borough presidents, community boards and city agencies. But no one—not the coalition nor any of its member groups, which include the NRDC, EDF, Trust for Public Land and the Open Space Institute— ever contacted Carter.[25]

In a more serious and complicated case in which local environmental justice groups came up against a mainstream environmental group, the South Bronx Clean Air Coalition and other community groups opposed a proposal for a large recycling facility backed by the NRDC. The plant had the support of Banana Kelly, one of the oldest CDCs in the Bronx. It would have meant hundreds of jobs and might have helped reduce the flow of waste and trucks through the South Bronx. But the nonprofit developers were not able to put aside the accumulated distrust of outside forces that had done little in the past to address their particular and grave environmental problems, especially because the solution took the form of yet another large waste factory. The NRDC proposal died.[26]

Waste-Transfer Stations and the Waterfront

One of the most important citywide struggles for environmental justice was waged against the concentration of privately owned solid waste-transfer stations in working-class communities and communities of color (figure 5.1). These struggles led community activists to develop their own citywide waste-management plan. This became the first citywide plan to be developed by communities and an historic precedent for community-based planning. In 2002, recently elected Mayor Michael Bloomberg reversed the policies of his predecessor, Rudolph Giuliani, and accepted the basic principles of the community plan.

The Organization of Waterfront Neighborhoods (OWN), with the Consumers Union, produced the first citywide plan based on principles of equity to be adopted by city government. OWN is a coalition of twenty-six neighborhood groups that are fighting against waste-transfer stations. They were founded in 1996 with support from the New York

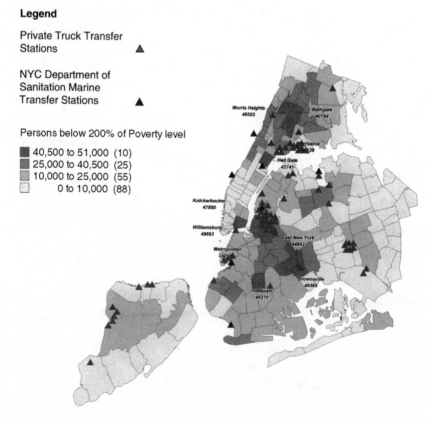

Legend

Private Truck Transfer
Stations ▲

NYC Department of
Sanitation Marine
Transfer Stations ▲

Persons below 200% of Poverty level

■ 40,500 to 51,000 (10)
■ 25,000 to 40,500 (25)
□ 10,000 to 25,000 (55)
□   0 to 10,000 (88)

Figure 5.1
Map showing waste-transfer stations and below-poverty-level neighborhoods in New York City. *Credit:* Pratt Institute Center for Community and Environmental Development (PICCED)

Lawyers for the Public Interest, NYCEJA, and the Consumer Policy Institute. Among its membership are communities that also instituted community plans as proactive statements against waste facilities and other LULUs. These include Red Hook, Greenpoint, Williamsburg, and Sunset Park in Brooklyn; Hunts Point in the Bronx; and Harlem in Manhattan.[27]

There was a period in the city's history when trash wasn't just taken out and thrown away. In 1881, the Department of Street Cleaning took over from the police, and by 1895 the city had an active recycling program that lasted until 1918. At the same time, refuse in working-class neighborhoods was commonly used as input for local craft production. Rubbish was sorted for marketable materials, rag merchants recycled old clothes, and food waste was used to make grease for soap and fertilizer.[28] But in the 1920s and 1930s, the city adopted the modern notion that waste is something to be gotten rid of and not material to be reused or recycled. City government, not its households, took responsibility for collecting and disposing of waste. At that time, when large parts of the outer boroughs were still undeveloped, the city had twenty-two incinerators spewing toxic fumes into the air and eighty-nine landfills. In 1994, the last incinerator was shut down, and real estate became too valuable to keep using it for landfills that might be undevelopable for centuries—an action that is consistent with the conservative planning principle of highest and best use (see chapter 1).[29] In sum, the city's waste policies had produced serious environmental hazards and also restricted development outside Manhattan. This soon led to a policy of exporting all waste, displacing the problem to other communities and states.

In 1987, the city raised the fees it charged to private haulers to dump in the Fresh Kills landfill, the last of the city's landfills, the largest in the world, and an environmental hazard for the area in Staten Island where it is located. These carters then established some eighty-five waste-transfer stations in the city where waste could be sorted and put on large tractor trailers for export out of state. For their transfer stations, they went where land was cheapest and zoning permitted them. As a result, about 70 percent of all putrescible waste (all commercial waste, including food, except for construction waste and fill) went through transfer stations in north Brooklyn and the south Bronx, in and near low-income communities. The carters brought with them heavy truck traffic, diesel fumes, noise, odors, vermin, and increased risks for asthma and other respiratory diseases. Despite legislation (Local Law 40) requiring the

Department of Sanitation to issue siting regulations for these facilities, the department had failed to do so for years. In 1993, regulations were proposed but never passed; in 1997, the city was ordered by a court to issue regulations; in 1998, the city issued regulations that would have no effect on the concentration of sites; these were unsuccessfully contested in court by OWN, but the Department of Sanitation was forced by political pressure from community organizers to tighten up on enforcement.[30]

In 1998, Mayor Rudoph Giuliani announced the closing of the Fresh Kills landfill, in part to pay a political debt to the Borough of Staten Island, a largely European American borough that had given Giuliani the margin of votes he needed to win the election. In 2001, the last city sanitation truck made its delivery to Fresh Kills. Giuliani had helped get rid of the mob-controlled network of small private garbage haulers but handed over control of the waste stream to a few price-fixing transnational corporations. Today three transnational waste companies control half of all the waste in the United States. In other words, the garbage went from one mob to another.

Most of the city's waste is now handled by private carters or exported under contract with the city. Waste-transfer stations are still concentrated in poor neighborhoods with large populations of African Americans, Latinos, and Asian Americans who have high levels of asthma and respiratory disease, conditions that are exacerbated by the increased truck traffic, odors, noise, and vermin.

The Department of City Planning has never addressed the concentration of waste facilities or the applicability of the city's fair-share rules. Instead, it defers to the Sanitation Department, which, according to OWN activists, acts as if their only job is to "take out the trash." The Chicago City Planning Department at least acknowledged, in a 1985 report, the environmental injustice underlying the location of sanitary landfills in that city:

Four fifths (80 percent) of the garbage generated in the City of Chicago is disposed of in sanitary landfills located on the Southeast Side [where a large percentage of African Americans live]. While still the cheapest method of waste disposal, primary reliance on landfills *has become unacceptable to adjacent neighborhood residents*, results in environmental degradation, and is of limited physical capacity.[31]

While New York City's planners did not address the disparity in the siting of waste facilities, environmental justice organizers utilized planning to do just that.

The OWN Plan

The OWN plan was the first citywide community-based plan. The OWN/ Consumers Union solid waste-management plan[32] is based on three principles, each of which the professional staff of the Department of Sanitation had consistently resisted:

• Retrofit the existing marine waste-transfer stations, which are underutilized but relatively evenly spread throughout the city, to handle both domestic and commercial waste streams, and substitute barges for tractor-trailers;
• Fully support recycling; and
• Enact measures to prevent and reduce waste.

The plan belies the common prejudice against community-based organizations that says they are necessarily exclusionary and advocate NIMBY politics. Here is a citywide plan that seeks to implement the principle of fair share—that is, no neighborhood should have to take a disproportionate amount of the city's garbage. OWN accepted the presence of waste-transfer stations in waterfront neighborhoods, including communities of color, but only if the city's transfer stations were to be distributed more equitably around the city and took the garbage from the private haulers, used barges instead of trucks to get the waste out of the city, and promoted recycling and waste prevention, measures that would reduce the total volume of waste going to transfer stations. OWN criticized the city's export-based waste-management strategy, and the policy of issuing *ad hoc* contracts, both of which masqueraded as planning in the city's Solid Waste Management Plan.

OWN's strategy was based on the understanding that to resolve each individual neighborhood's problems there had to be a just plan for the entire citywide waste stream. If it was to gain allies from other neighborhoods, it would have to come up with solutions that ensured that nobody's backyard would be overburdened by waste. However, the few neighborhoods with environmental justice claims that would wind up with expanded marine transfer stations took the most difficult step of accepting the plan out of solidarity with the other neighborhoods and with an understanding that resolution of the overall waste problem was essential and would bring relief to everyone.

OWN activists demonstrated, lobbied elected officials, and met with the mayor and his aides. In 2002, Mayor Michael Bloomberg announced that the city was planning to retrofit its existing marine waste-transfer stations. The city would adopt the basic principles of OWN's solid-waste plan, and this was an historic moment for all activist-led planning in the city.

OWN continues to struggle for implementation of the plan. In 2005, Manhattan's Upper East Side residents and their powerful City Council representative, Council Speaker Gifford Miller, tried to prevent reopening of the marine transfer station in their backyard while allowing the others to move forward. This demonstration of NIMBY sentiment came from the city's wealthiest neighborhood and was fought most vehemently by the very community advocates who were accustomed to being called NIMBYites. In 2006, the City Council approved the new SWMP, including the marine transfer station on the Upper East Side.[33] Retrofitting of the marine transfer stations is proceeding slowly, and city efforts to improve recycling and reduce waste have been limited, but the main outlines of New York's waste policy definitively shifted in response to the OWN plan.

The OWN plan made good sense to the mayor's office because it would cut costs and remove a potential obstacle to gentrification in waterfront neighborhoods they were targeting for new housing development. But the plan was resisted by the bureaucratic core of the city's Department of Sanitation (DOS). The DOS throw-away culture has governed waste management for almost a century. DOS fought recycling, waste-reduction programs, and siting regulations for transfer stations and claimed that its job was only to "take out the trash."[34]

The OWN story brings to light one of the many myths surrounding Mayor Rudolph Giuliani that are widely propagated outside the city—that he cleaned up the city. To be sure, his quality-of-life campaign led to a visible decline in the amount of trash on the streets around the financial districts of Manhattan. But this was in large part the work of business improvement districts (BIDs) that were started during the Dinkins administration. On the other hand, in neighborhoods with waste-transfer stations, there was more garbage. Giuliani also left his successor a costly garbage crisis with no government strategy other than exporting all the garbage. The Sanitation Department's operating expenses shot up from $590.5 million in 1997 to almost $1 billion in 2001, about where it remains today.[35] By 2003, 240,000 DOS trucks were taking trash out of the city every day, mostly to an incinerator in Newark, New Jersey (which is upwind of New York City), and some 250,000 tractor trailers were hauling waste to landfills in other states.[36] While it appears that landfill costs are now going down nationally, this may not last, and the cost to New York of getting the waste to the landfills, and the environmental and health impacts, are still substantial. This calls into question another Giuliani myth—that he made government more efficient.

After OWN, another coalition of neighborhoods was founded to protest the concentration of energy plants in the city. Communities United for Responsible Energy (CURE) responded to the unleashing of private power plant developers on communities of color by energy deregulation. In 2001, the state admitted that power plants were sited disproportionately in low-income areas.[37] According to Julie Sze:

> CURE also called for a community-based planning process that included access for underrepresented constituencies, the protection of the waterfront, and the need to promote open space for recreation (this issue is a key one for waterfront communities, which have fewer areas of recreation and open space than other neighborhoods).[38]

Transportation Justice

The campaigns against diesel buses in Harlem, the Sheridan Expressway in the Bronx, and diesel trucks in the South Bronx and Sunset Park were among the first transportation justice campaigns in the city. The Gowanus Expressway Community Stakeholder Group brings together diverse neighborhoods in opposition to the state's plan to rebuild the 2.6-mile Moses-era elevated Gowanus Expressway. The neighborhood coalition favors replacing the old viaduct with a tunnel or surface roadway.[39] Community groups in Bedford-Stuyvesant (Brooklyn) also organized, successfully, to prevent the MTA from shutting down the Franklin Street shuttle and subway station there.

These campaigns follow a long history of successful neighborhood struggles against expressways, including the Lower Manhattan Expressway and Westway, both massive projects in Manhattan that would have worsened air quality, favored a small group of upper-income car users, and benefited downtown real estate. Both projects were defeated after decades of struggle by community-based organizations.

The Transit Workers Union and Straphangers Campaign are two notable citywide advocates of transportation justice, though they are not community-based. They tend to oppose fare increases that hit working people the hardest and advocate for improvements to the city's mass transit system, which working people with modest incomes rely on disproportionately. New York is the only city in the country where almost half of all residents do not own a car. Every weekday, over 7 million people use mass transit. Yet 54 percent of all air pollution is due to transportation, mostly motor vehicles, according to the national Surface Transportation Planning Project. Even though New York City gets the biggest mass transit subsidy in the country, subway riders pay 75 percent of all operating costs, a higher proportion than in most systems around the world.

Transportation Alternatives (TA), founded in 1973, is the city's largest advocacy group for bicyclists and pedestrians. The city's 120,000 daily bicyclists include a growing cadre of commuters, messengers, delivery people, children, and the elderly. TA has also supported neighborhood efforts to improve the environment for pedestrians and cyclists. Though it is not mainly a neighborhood-based group, TA does have local chapters and is constantly forced to organize locally to support local bicycle and pedestrian projects and confront NIMBY sentiments among neighborhood-based resident and business groups and community boards. While the city's Department of Transportation is mainly focused on moving more motor vehicles at faster speeds, TA promotes a more balanced system that ensures pedestrian and bicycle safety and the quality of public spaces. TA has struggled for implementation of new on-street bicycle lanes, bike parking, and improved safety measures (see chapter 6 for a discussion of TA's role in the city's Bicycle Master Plan). TA's efforts to reduce traffic and improve safety in communities with high asthma rates support the goals of environmental justice. For example, in 2004, TA supported community protests when a truck turning the corner in a Brooklyn neighborhood killed two Latino children, whose lives could have been saved if the Department of Transportation had implemented a simple adjustment to the traffic light (called a *leading pedestrian interval*) that gives pedestrians an advantage over turning vehicles.[40] TA works closely with its regional partner, the Tri-State Transportation Campaign.[41]

Public Health and Environmental Justice

The environmental justice movement has called attention in a dramatic way to the correspondence between chronic diseases affecting low-income communities of color and the city's land-use and environmental policies. As documented by the city's Department of Health, high childhood hospitalization rates for asthma tend to be concentrated in communities of color (figure 5.2). These neighborhoods host toxic industries, waste-transfer stations, and expressways that carry large volumes of truck traffic.[42] Environmental justice advocates were also central to the battle against lead poisoning, which is concentrated in low-income

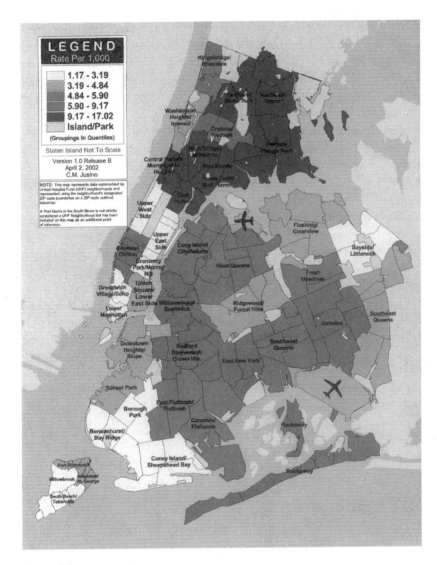

Figure 5.2
Map showing asthma hospitalization rates in New York City. *Credit:* Carlos M. Jusino, West Harlem Environmental Action, Inc. (WEACT)

neighborhoods, and were successful in getting the City Council to pass tough legislation improving the regulation of apartments with lead paint. Childhood obesity rates are also highest in low-income areas (and auto-dependent Staten Island), and more recent initiatives by environmental justice advocates are aimed at expanding information about healthy food and opportunities for recreation.

Since so many chronic public health problems are place-based, solutions often lend themselves to neighborhood-level strategies. The City's Department of Health has begun to move more vigorously toward place-based strategies by establishing community health districts, working with bodegas to improve access to quality food, tightening regulation of fast-food outlets (which predominate in low-income areas), and promoting safer pedestrian and bicycle options. But the DCP has yet to weigh in on efforts to improve community health. The idea that community planning can help create healthier living environments by integrating housing, transportation, open space, and recreation through comprehensive planning is articulated publicly by environmental justice activists. It is to be found in many comprehensive community plans. But DCP remains narrowly fixated on zoning to promote development. Community-based planning for environmental justice is based on a holistic view seeking healthy communities and requires crossing the boundaries that separate agencies, academic disciplines, and professions. But the city's planning agency appears to have abandoned the concern for public health that was originally an integral part of its foundation.[43]

6

Making the Plans Official

A conservative government is an organized hypocrisy.
—Benjamin Disraeli

Since the 1961 Cooper Square Alternate Plan, community planning in New York City has focused on preserving and developing housing for people with modest incomes and reversing years of abandonment and neglect. In the 1980s, community planning reemerged as communities set their sights on broader objectives and tried to come to terms with two complex and contradictory elements—the concentration of environmentally hazardous local unwanted land uses (LULUs) and gentrification.[1] The environmental justice movement played an important role in the emerging community-planning efforts in the South Bronx, Red Hook, Greenpoint/Williamsburg, Sunset Park, and Harlem. But planning also broke out all over the city. Advocates of transportation, housing, parks, and open space developed comprehensive long-range plans and contributed to substantial changes in city policy. They often beat the city at the planning game, much as the Organization of Waterfront Neighborhoods (OWN) did with solid waste. A major revision of the city charter in 1989 made it easier for community plans to be officially approved. Community participation in planning became legitimate as elite neighborhoods started planning, and some major real estate development plans, including the plan to rebuild lower Manhattan after 9/11, incorporated elements of public participation (see chapter 7). At the dawn of the twenty-first century, community planning had arrived. The next struggle, which is addressed in the final chapter, is to guarantee the implementation of community plans and create a more equal partnership between city government and community-based planning.

The 197a Stories

In 1989, voters approved a revision to the city charter that legitimized the efforts of neighborhoods to plan for their futures. For the first time, the city charter, which functions as the city's constitution, explicitly enabled communities, through the fifty-nine community boards, to submit official plans for approval by the City Planning Commission and City Council (under section 197a). The call for community-based planning made by City Planning Commissioner Beverly Moss Spatt in 1971 seemed to have been answered.[2] However, seventeen years after the charter change initiated the era of 197a plans, only ten have been adopted.

The main reason for the charter change in 1989 was the U.S. Supreme Court ruling that the Board of Estimate, the city's main governing body since 1898, violated the constitutional principal of one person, one vote. The Board of Estimate included the presidents of each of the city's five boroughs, but since each borough had vastly different numbers of people, representatives from the smaller boroughs—Staten Island, for example—wielded power that was disproportionate to the constituencies they represented. The 1989 charter change was meant to be a victory for civil rights, and the commission charged with changing the charter was further pressed by community leaders to give more power to communities through the City Council and community boards. However, community boards were not a major focus of charter revision, and there was little interest in expanding community-planning powers among the community board representatives who had been comfortable in their positions for many years and represented influential upper-income districts. In these community boards, protest was muted, there were few environmental justice issues, and community planning was not on the agenda. Some progressives were also leery of giving more power to community boards that they perceived as patronage sinkholes. Progressives focused more attention on expanding the powers of the historically weak City Council and ensuring greater racial equity in districting. Although City Council members recommend community board members that are then appointed by the borough presidents, their powers are diluted because the boundaries of City Council districts are not coterminus with community board districts, and any proposals to make them coterminus would have met with strong resistance from both borough presidents and advocates of a strong mayoralty.

So the 197a reform was relatively mild and demanded nothing of the city's planning establishment. The charter revision promised each community board a professional planner, but city administrations have interpreted this requirement as already fulfilled by the Department of City Planning (DCP) borough offices. The city stuck to this interpretation even when DCP cut its borough staff (in the Dinkins administration) and when Mayor Giuliani forbade DCP staff members from talking with community board representatives without express permission from City Hall. In the end, the 1989 charter change ended up shifting more power to the imperial mayor, perversely frustrating the civil rights objective of greater democratic representation of minority communities. Staten Island's conservative political weight did not wane but figured significantly in the elections of Rudolph Giuliani and Michael Bloomberg—evidence that changes in government structure by themselves do not necessarily yield changes in political power. Advocates of greater centralism wanted to go even further and entirely eliminate the borough presidents, but failed. Borough presidents and the fifty-one City Council members mediate between communities and the imperial mayor. Borough presidents play the leading role in appointing community board members, have an advisory vote in the land-use review process, and have a small discretionary budget for local projects. While their powers have been severely curtailed, they often lend support to community boards when they are neglected by the mayor's office. Manhattan Borough President Scott Stringer, for example, has undertaken a major reform of that borough's community boards and supported strong board leadership. On the other hand, since borough presidents control community board composition, they can also stand in the way of the development of strong, independent bodies of local governance and thwart genuine participatory democracy. For example, in 2007 Brooklyn Borough President Marty Markowitz failed to reappoint nine members of Brooklyn Community Board 6 because of that board's position opposing the Atlantic Yards project (see chapter 7). Elected City Council members have less influence in community boards because they only recommend appointees to community boards and Council members usually have to divide their attention among several community boards. In the final chapter, the potential of community boards is discussed in greater detail.

When David Dinkins took office in 1991, there was great optimism among the grassroots organizations and civic groups that had supported him that power could be decentralized. The optimism was short-lived.

Conservatives in civil society and the media pounced on Dinkins for reacting deliberatively to the Crown Heights riots that had pitted blacks against
Jews, undermining support for Dinkins among some key Democratic
Party constituencies and making his reelection unlikely.[3] In 1993, Giuliani
won the mayoral election by a narrow margin and immediately sent the
message that he was in charge and that City Hall would reign with or
without community boards. In 2002, Michael Bloomberg continued
Giuliani's policy of benign neglect of community boards, though instances
of confrontation were greatly reduced. However, as is shown in the case
of Greenpoint/Williamsburg later in this chapter, though the mayor
speaks with a softer voice, listens to others, and is sometimes willing to
negotiate, he is still the commander-in-chief of an imperial body.

To his credit, David Dinkins appointed a City Planning Commission
strikingly more diverse and representative, in terms of ethnicity and
gender, than any preceding one. The body that had been accustomed to
rubber-stamping the mayor's decisions now openly debated planning
issues and major development approvals. Commissioners Ron Shiffman,
community-planning advocate and long-time director of the Pratt Institute Center for Community and Environmental Development (PICCED),
and Brenda Levin, Borough President Ruth Messinger's appointee, broke
the tradition of allowing staff recommendations and developer assertions
to pass without questioning, and others followed suit, much to the
chagrin of the agency's top staff.

In 1991, in an environment of optimism and change created by charter
revision and the new administration, the DCP issued rules for the processing of 197a plans.[4] The rules assumed a traditional rational-comprehensive planning process, which included setting goals and objectives,
analyzing problems, and outlining recommendations. The rules were
broad enough to allow for plans that covered small or large geographic
areas and focused on a diverse array of community problems. They could
be comprehensive or narrowly focused on a specific issue. However,
conservative approaches to planning by DCP staff held sway on three
crucial elements that would come back to haunt community planners.
First, while the rules stated that "an adopted plan shall serve as a policy
to guide subsequent actions by city agencies," there was a gaping loop-
hole that would let them ignore community plans: "The existence of an
adopted 197-a plan shall not preclude the sponsor or any other city
agency from developing other plans or taking actions not contemplated
by the 197-a plan that may affect the same geographic area or subject
matter."

Second, while the rules gave the DCP responsibility for performing the required environmental review for community board plans, the agency—in a pragmatic effort to save the city from having to do an enormous and expensive environmental impact study—declared that 197a plans would not result in any significant changes to the physical or social environment. What first looked like a hedge around the cumbersome and expensive environmental review process became an excuse to treat community plans as meaningless pieces of paper. Third, there was a strong tilt in the new rules toward traditional development-driven planning. The rules allowed plans that "promote the orderly growth, improvement and future development" of communities but said nothing about preservation, equity, or environmental quality.[5]

Despite these limitations, the charter revision encouraged at least a dozen communities to pull together plans and submit them as 197a plans.

The Bronx Got There First

In 1992, the City Planning Commission and City Council approved a plan developed by Bronx Community Board 3 (CB3), *Partnership for the Future.*[6] It was the first community plan to be approved under section 197a and is now one of ten officially adopted 197a plans.[7] The first 197a plan had actually preceded the charter change but was not a community plan. The citywide Waterfront Revitalization Plan was developed by DCP in accordance with a state mandate and approved in 1982. The only other city-sponsored 197a plan, adopted in 1987, was for the Nassau Street Mall in lower Manhattan.

The Bronx CB3 plan called for affordable housing production in a variety of configurations, including three- to four-story owner-occupied units and midrise rentals, which would increase the population in neighborhoods that had been devastated by abandonment and "planned shrinkage." It also proposed improvements to the local infrastructure and services. This path-breaking plan would not have been possible without the hard work of Ricardo Soto-López, who prepared the plan while working in the Bronx office of DCP. He played a critical though atypical role in securing information from city agencies and coordinating with the Consumer Farmers Federation, which provided valuable technical assistance in the person of Eugenia Flatow, an industrial engineer who had worked with City Hall, the Model Cities program, and the City Planning Department. Flatow describes her role as "helping the community to plan rationally" and belongs to the same generation as Beverly Moss Spatt and Hortense Gabel, strong early supporters inside government of community-based planning.[8]

As it turned out, many of the vacant lots identified in the CB3 plan were eventually developed by the New York City Housing Partnership, a public-private partnership administered by HPD. The Partnership's preference was for suburban-style one- and two-family homes, following the model established in Charlotte Gardens. However, this inefficient and inequitable approach was soon to be challenged by We Stay! ¡Nos Quedamos! in its 1993 plan for Melrose Commons, which included a small part of CB3 (see chapter 4).

The city's willful neglect of the policies advocated in the CB3 plan set a pattern for its approach to subsequent 197a plans: the plans were approved and quickly ignored, and the city took no responsibility for implementing them. According to the current CB3 District Manager John Dudley, who helped usher the plan through to City Council approval, "It doesn't really have any teeth." He doesn't think anyone in government is guided by the plan, and "maybe once or twice I've looked at it."[9]

In 1990, Bronx Borough President Fernando Ferrer sponsored *New Directions for the Bronx*, a comprehensive planning study that sought to incorporate diverse development proposals. The Bronx Center plan, sponsored by the Urban Assembly, a private nonprofit group with foundation funding and backed by Ferrer, was a strategic overview that projected an optimistic future for a borough that had suffered years of abandonment. It was not a community-generated plan but opened the door to discussions about planning that were accessible to community organizers and community boards. Ferrer was one of the few borough presidents to engage in any kind of planning, supported the We Stay! plan, and later was the only mayoral candidate to fully endorse the principles of the Campaign for Community-based Planning in the 2001 election campaign (see chapter 8). Manhattan Borough President Ruth Messinger, who had strong roots in neighborhood organizing, was the only borough president to sponsor 197a plans: the plan for the Manhattan waterfront and the plan for Stuyvesant Cove were both approved in 1997.

While only ten 197a plans were approved in the more than fifteen years since the charter change, the Municipal Art Society Briefing Book, which catalogs community plans in the five boroughs, shows that there are over 100 community plans. Thus, most communities have chosen not to go through the years of negotiation with the DCP and other city agencies to get their plans approved as 197a plans and then find them of no use in changing city policies.[10] Many community planners have had no contact with DCP at all, others have little confidence that the city will implement their plans if approved, and some simply do not trust the agency's planners. It is both significant and remarkable that despite all of the skepticism and problems, communities continue to forge ahead to do planning. It would appear that even without official approval there are benefits to community planning, and they have to do with bringing together diverse community forces, developing common political strategies, and identifying ways to gain control over community land.

Planning versus Zoning: The Chelsea Stories

Since the city's first, last, and only master plan died on arrival in 1969, and since capital budget responsibilities were taken away from the City Planning Commission (CPC) after the fiscal crisis of the 1970s, the city's planning agency has tightly clutched its zoning powers, as if this were the one and only tool of planning. In effect, the agency treats the city's three-volume Zoning Resolution as *the* plan for the city. For DCP, it is perfectly natural to ignore community planning because without plans the agency retains maximum flexibility to change zoning rules. This narrow focus on zoning as a tool of land-use control offers maximum flexibility for the real estate industry, which can use its influence at City Hall to get zoning changes when and where they need them. DCP also yields to pressures from City Hall and changes zoning to limit or prevent real estate development in politically connected neighborhoods. Aside from a handful of experienced land-use lawyers in the city, DCP's veteran zoning specialists are perhaps the only ones who even understand the arcane multivolume Zoning Resolution. So it should not be surprising that the agency would turn its back on planning and fight to preserve its control over zoning; for DCP as an institution, zoning is power.

DCP's obsession with zoning allows it to wash its hands of responsibility for everything else going on in the city and bow to the line agencies on every matter of substance. For example, when it comes to building or preserving affordable housing, DCP defers to the Department of Housing Preservation and Development (HPD), an institution fixated on housing production. As a result, no city agency is responsible for questions of community services, displacement, and gentrification that may be involved in HPD projects. However, some community groups have been successful in securing from a reluctant city planning establishment zoning changes that protect and encourage low- and moderate-income housing.

A case in point is the Clinton inclusionary zoning requirement. Facing an HPD urban renewal plan in the 1980s that would have destroyed a good deal of affordable housing, activists in the Clinton/Hell's Kitchen neighborhood of Manhattan did their own plan, which they intended to get approved as a 197a plan. They also prepared a proposal for a special zoning district that mandated that 60 percent of new housing units be reserved for low- and moderate-income people and that housing be low- to mid-rise in scale, consistent with existing development. The community plan was put aside but the zoning proposal passed. Today Clinton remains a haven, though increasingly encircled and embattled, for low-cost housing in the very shadows of a booming Times Square and Michael Bloomberg's West Side expansion.[11] However, by using inclusionary zoning as the main tool, fulfillment of goals for new affordable housing will always depend on new market-rate development, which has been slow to come because of the high proportion of existing and proposed low- and moderate-income housing, something private developers shy away from.

Another early example of planning for inclusionary housing is in Chelsea. In 1986, Manhattan Community Board 4 started to work on a plan for Chelsea, just south of Hell's Kitchen, that they hoped would control new development and both protect and encourage affordable housing in this gentrifying neighborhood. Until 1990, they (like CB 3 in the Bronx) lacked the resources to prepare their own environmental assessment of the plan, and the city's planning agency had no rules or procedures for dealing with community plans. They realized that ultimately they would need to address zoning because this was the principle legal instrument for controlling land use. But since they had entered DCP's domain, they had to play by DCP's unwritten rules. After ten years, the Chelsea 197a plan was finally approved in 1996. Its major recommendations were for a series of zoning changes that fit into the overall housing goals outlined by the community board. But since zoning can only be changed by a Uniform Land Use Review Procedure (ULURP) action (under section 197c of the city charter), the community board then had to undergo another lengthy process, which lasted several more years, to actually change the zoning.

The Chelsea plan highlights a dilemma for community planners in New York City. If the 197a plan does not produce the needed zoning changes, then isn't it just an extra step that takes years of work, after which there is no guarantee of implementation? Those at DCP who consider zoning as the perfect tool for land-use control must be the first to relish this dilemma. If the plan is irrelevant and ultimately communities have to deal with DCP on zoning, then DCP has effectively eliminated any incentive to plan through the 197a process.

In the following cases of Red Hook, Greenpoint, and Williamsburg, DCP went along with community plans, though not without causing significant delays, and then turned around and presented rezoning proposals that contradicted the community plans. DCP's posture sent a discouraging message to all who would dare to undertake a 197a plan. Yet in the case of upscale Riverdale in the Bronx, DCP ushered the community board through a 197a plan in 2004 with lightning speed in less than a year, and it did not miss a beat when they immediately followed up with a rezoning that helped meet the community's exclusionary objectives (see below for more on Riverdale).

Red Hook: Environmental Justice Meets the 197a Plan

The Red Hook *Plan for Community Regeneration* was the first 197a plan closely linked to environmental justice. In the late 1980s, the Red Hook Civic Association and Red Hook Tenant Associations (East and West) were joined by local businesses in struggles to shut down several giant waste facilities. They pursued two large privately owned waste-transfer stations until they forced them to shut down. They successfully faced down the city's proposal for two sludge plants. Two local organizations, the Groups against Garbage Stations (GAGS) and Red Hook Civic Association, engaged in the neighborhood's environmental justice struggles and later became members of the citywide OWN (see chapter 5).

Long-time Red Hook residents and business owners had in their collective memory an understanding of the power of planning. A half-century ago, the Red Hook peninsula was cut off from the rest of south Brooklyn by a Robert Moses expressway. Moses also displaced local residents to build the Red Hook Houses, a large public housing project, without planning for the retail and community services that every community needs. For six years in the late 1960s, as the Port Authority was shifting its port operations to New Jersey, the city developed a plan for Red Hook that would have wiped out a large swath of housing and industry. The plan was kept under cover, but it was enough to cause "planners blight": uncertain of their future, small property owners sold to speculators and moved out. Red Hook lost half its population and many of its small industries, further isolating public housing tenants. In part due to resistance at the regional port authority to the retention of any port facilities in Brooklyn, the full-scale condemnation foreseen in the plan never occurred, and instead a small container port was built, leaving the rest of the neighborhood with acres of vacant lots.[12] The new port facility employed only a handful of dockworkers while unemployment became a chronic problem for Red Hook residents.

The impulse to do a 197a plan came after the defeat of the sludge plants and the closure of two privately owned waste-transfer stations. An important event triggering the plan was the shooting death of Patrick Daly, a highly respected white elementary school principal (in a largely black and Latino neighborhood), when he went to visit the family of a student who had left his school. He got caught in cross-fire around Red Hook Houses. This event brought together residents and businesses and made news on the national wire services. Red Hook was on the map. The question was whether the map would change at all in the future.

This neighborhood of 12,000 residents was no less fragmented than other neighborhoods. Public housing tenants, accounting for 70 percent of all residents, were represented by two tenant associations and appeared to have more influence on the city's Housing Authority than on community planning or the community board, and even that was limited. Residents and businesses in "the Back"—a section of the neighborhood with a small group of homeowners and shop owners and a larger group of renters—were more connected to local elected officials and the community board. Yet another element was the rise of Greg O'Connell, a retired police officer who bought up vacant waterfront properties and began to renovate them for industrial and commercial tenants. O'Connell became the main business leader in Red Hook and driving force in the South Brooklyn Local Development Corporation (SBLDC).

Each of these forces had its own reasons for supporting a community-planning process, and in the early 1990s the potential for consensus among them was substantial. First to approach Brooklyn Community Board 6 about the prospect of doing a community plan were residents in the Back who saw the potential for new housing and retail development on land that was zoned for industry. At this time, DCP was preparing its first-ever citywide waterfront plan, which included proposals for zoning changes and public access to the waterfront.[13] O'Connell was interested in securing zoning changes that would give him greater flexibility to develop his waterfront and upland properties, including the option of converting industrial space for residential use. The tenants in Red Hook Houses started their own internal discussions about the future of the neighborhood and were interested mainly in new economic opportunities, education, and community services.

Community Board 6 formed a 197a subcommittee and began to hold meetings in different parts of the community district, a district of mostly middle- and upper-income neighborhoods of which low-income Red Hook is only a small fraction (about 10 percent of the district's population). This aroused the suspicion of public housing tenants and led to a clash over the openness of the planning process. The issue was resolved by an agreement to hold future meetings in Red Hook and expand the number of representatives from Red Hook Houses on the planning committee. Underlying the disagreement over planning process were historic class and race fractures within the community. However, these were temporarily overshadowed by a consensus on a vision for the future of the neighborhood that incorporated diverse agendas.

The Red Hook 197a plan challenged the conventional development scenario reinforced by the existing zoning regime. Zoning separated land uses and real estate developers tended to prefer this separation in old industrial areas to maximize the value of new residential development. This was especially true on the waterfront, where separate enclaves sell well. New residential projects separate from public housing would also get better prices. The Red Hook 197a plan instead called for preservation of a mix of industry, retail, and housing vaguely defined as "mixed-use development," particularly along the waterfront. In the plan, the Back and Red Hook Houses were to be physically linked by connecting streets and a string of community facilities along them, and each residential community would be physically linked with the waterfront. Education Way and Ecology Way were to be two axes of development in the plan that would help bind all elements of the neighborhood together and encourage public access to the waterfront (both of these were first suggested by residents at community meetings). They would intersect at Education Plaza, a new town center bridging Red Hook Houses and the Back. The plan included short-term, medium-term, and long-term proposals, and projects that were already underway. Even while the planning process was still underway, the plan became a political force. For example, Red Hook Tenants and CB6 both cited the plan they were developing as they successfully lobbied the city and won public access to the waterfront at the end of Columbia Street, a major artery through the public housing complex that was named "Education Way" in the plan.[14]

One of the major problems faced by the community planners in Red Hook was the limited amount of developable land in the public domain. Unlike other neighborhoods that had experienced massive abandonment during the 1970s and beyond, there were very few parcels of city-owned vacant land. Properties that were taken over for nonpayment of taxes were immediately auctioned off and held by speculators. Many of them were used to store heavy equipment and trucks or became dumping grounds. Given the past experience with the threat of condemnation, there was little support in the Red Hook community for using eminent domain, despite the fact that this was one of the few instruments community planners would have to control future land use. Instead, Greg O'Connell assembled vacant parcels and forged partnerships with other property owners, preempting any public control of land assembly. Although O'Connell's general vision of a mixed-use Red Hook that would develop incrementally and in an integrated way was not that far from the vision outlined in the Red Hook Plan, he ultimately undercut specific recommendations in the plan that conflicted with his business interests. After the plan was approved with overwhelming support by Community Board 6 and endorsed in writing by O'Connell and the SBLDC, the businesses independently lobbied the CPC to severely limit rezoning for mixed use and residential development, eliminate Education Plaza to protect the existing property owners there, and make other changes in plan elements that had not been popular with local industries.

In 1995, CPC Chair Joseph Rose praised the original plan, calling it "the best we've seen." He said that "the process behind the plan and the product itself should be a model for how neighborhoods plan for themselves in the future."[15] Less than two years later he and the Planning Commission overruled the community board's continuing support for the original plan and accepted all of the changes proposed by the business leaders, undermining the integrity of the community planning process. Several years later, the CPC would turn around and grant a zoning change to facilitate an O'Connell project that was very similar to one proposed in the original plan but rejected in the final version because of his opposition. This move reinforced City Planning's use of zoning primarily to support individual development proposals while at the same time it undermined the legitimacy of a community plan that proposed zoning changes consistent with a community plan for future land use.

This was a harbinger of things to come in Greenpoint/Williamsburg and other communities.

In 2004, the CPC approved a zoning change for a section of the Red Hook waterfront to allow the construction of a big box store. IKEA, the Swedish-owned furniture store, wanted to create the kind of isolated traffic-generating commercial waterfront enclave that had been universally rejected by the community planners. IKEA got support from the Red Hook Tenant Associations, and neither community board leaders, the borough president, nor City Hall challenged IKEA's racialized marketing plan, which portrayed the opposition of mostly white environmental advocates as inimical to economic and racial justice. This corporate campaign exploited the historic failures of the local political establishment to incorporate public housing tenants in meaningful decision making and cynically undermined the principle fought for by the environmental justice movement and the Red Hook community planners—that the issues of environment and social justice were intimately related and not separable. An unsuccessful lawsuit highlighted the CPC's failure to even consider the Red Hook 197a plan before changing the zoning.[16] The IKEA battle reflected an intensification of the gentrification process in Red Hook, as other big-box developers began to buy up sections of the waterfront and do what the community plan had attempted to prevent—drive industry out, segment the neighborhood into separate enclaves, and further divide it by race and class.[17]

Eddie Bautista, who had grown up in Red Hook, was an organizer for New York Lawyers for the Public Interest who worked with tenants at Red Hook Houses on environmental justice campaigns and then the community plan. Bautista is a leading example of a new generation of community planners that come out of the environmental justice and community movements. Bautista would become one of the city's leading experts in community planning and a central figure in the OWN plan. He would go on to earn a master's degree in urban planning, become the local legislative director and special assistant to Mayor Michael Bloomberg, and be part of the staff that developed the city's sustainability plan, PlaNYC2030.[18] Shortly after completion of the Red Hook plan, Bautista summed up his personal vision of community planning:

1. People develop, articulate and implement their vision for future development, in all aspects;
2. Everyone comes along for the ride, not just the politically wired;
3. The poorest and the powerless become priorities, not liabilities;

4. People commit to true empowerment, so that communities aren't just struggling against oppression but fighting for justice;
5. The people regain control over their land.[19]

In these reflections on the Red Hook 197a plan, Bautista independently ends up with the same proposition this book has advanced from the start—that democratic control over land is an essential element in community planning.

Zoning Trumps Planning: The Greenpoint and Williamsburg Plans

Not far north of Red Hook, Greenpoint and Williamsburg are among the oldest mixed industrial and residential neighborhoods in the city, located along the East River waterfront and linked to lower Manhattan by the Williamsburg Bridge. About a third of all residents in this densely populated mixed-use area of 150,000 people are within walking distance of their jobs. There is a mix of incomes in the mostly working-class neighborhood and large Polish, Latino, and Hasidic populations. In the 1980s real estate boom, tenants who were priced out of lower Manhattan apartments migrated to Greenpoint/Williamsburg, accelerating gentrification and the displacement of long-time residents. The new residents included artists forced out of Soho and the Lower East Side. Displacement pressures were also felt by industries as loft conversions, both legal and illegal, ate away at affordable industrial space. And on top of all this, vacant industrial waterfront properties were being eyed by residential developers who were eager to capitalize on waterfront views of Manhattan. As described in chapter 5, Greenpoint and Williamsburg are home to one of the city's largest concentration of noxious industrial and waste facilities and the largest underground oil spill in the nation.

In 1989, the first community meetings were held with the intention of putting together a community plan for the waterfront. After many ups and downs and internal turf wars, reflecting the wide spectrum of income, age, and ethnic diversity in the neighborhood, a decision was made to do separate plans for Greenpoint and Williamsburg. In 1998, with the assistance of PICCED, draft plans were prepared for each neighborhood. While there were important shades of difference between the two plans, they both reflected two constant objectives that underlay community activism:

• *The environment* Eliminate the environmental hazards associated with the concentration of LULUs. In this, they coincided with the aims of the environmental justice movement even if not all community groups saw racial and class inequities as issues.

• *Affordable housing*   Allow new, contextual mixed-use development on the waterfront without displacing people by providing affordable housing opportunities.

Around these two objectives swirled the central dilemma of progressive community planning—how to address LULUs without fostering displacement.

The 197a plans for Greenpoint and Williamsburg were approved by the City Council in 2001. Two years later, the DCP proposed to rezone a large 175-block area in the neighborhood, including the waterfront, and claimed that the rezoning was based on the 197a plans. Immediately realizing that DCP's rezoning plan violated the most basic principles of the community plans, residents and businesses organized, formed new committees, coalitions, and task forces, and presented critiques and alternative proposals for rezoning. After two more years of discussion and debate, DCP was forced to make several important concessions, due mostly to community organizing and the eventual mediation by elected officials. A lengthy memorandum from the mayor's office detailed these concessions, and among the most important were inclusionary zoning incentives for affordable housing that DCP had adamantly resisted in the past by claiming, contrary to the experience in scores of other cities including San Francisco and Boston, that inclusionary zoning does not work. Despite strong evidence that inclusionary rules should be mandatory, the city adopted a voluntary program, which could leave the neighborhood with far fewer than the promised 30 percent affordable units.[20] Community activists and planners also won a promise for a waterfront park where the 1,100 megawatt TransGas plant had once been proposed and opposed by Communities United for Responsible Energy (CURE) members. In the end, however, after almost two years of heated debate, DCP got the high rises on the waterfront that real estate developers had wanted for years—a scenario that had been explicitly rejected throughout the twelve years of community meetings that led up to the 197a plans. The community board voted against the DCP zoning proposal, but since its vote was only advisory, the zoning plan passed.

The Greenpoint/Williamsburg plans and the subsequent zoning battles revealed the tensions within the neighborhood's diverse population over questions of social justice and the environment. Williamsburg's Northside, the social base for more progressive politics, has an active Latino community, established CDCs with strong track records, and two OWN members (Neighbors against Garbage and the El Puente Academy). The Northside mixed-use zoning district, established in 1975, was a model of planning for compatible industrial and residential use. If any place, this is where the concept of sustainable mixed-use development integrating jobs and housing, as opposed to gentrification's monoculture, took hold.[21]

On the other hand, Greenpoint's large white working class, often represented by the Catholic Church, was more focused on replacing polluting industries with solid residential development, included many individual homeowners, and left the door open to gentrification. The draft Williamsburg plan had explicitly stated its objective was to "prevent gentrification on the waterfront." The Greenpoint plan was not as specific, and there was room within its vision statements for the latent homeowner desires to cash in on land-value increases triggered by large-scale development on the waterfront. White Greenpoint residents had also more than once turned their backs on racial justice and solidarity with their Latino neighbors.[22]

Despite the important concessions it led to, the DCP rezoning of Greenpoint and Williamsburg was a setback for community planning. It sent a message to communities that even after more than a decade of community meetings and a couple of years of negotiating changes to the plan with DCP, the principles of the community plan could be abridged. DCP would be free to use its zoning powers as it saw fit and disregard community plans. It could state publicly that it consulted the community plan, as required by law, but it was free to come away with any interpretation of the plan it believed to be reasonable. In other words, rezoning could trump community planning.

In 2007, the sharp divide between community planning and DCP's zoning powers arose again in West Harlem, where Columbia University's large scale expansion plan confronted a 197-a plan developed by Manhattan Community Board 9. The Columbia-supported rezoning and the community-backed 197-a plan were approved simultaneously by the City Planning Commission. The 197-a plan reflected local concerns about the displacement of West Harlem residents and businesses and emphasized community preservation. But the zoning changes gave the university almost everything it needed to proceed with its expansion. The only obstacle remaining were the tenants and business owners who refused to sell to Columbia. The university had been able to buy up most properties, but to help sway landowners the school officials asserted that a state authority, the Empire State Development Corporation, was willing to use its power of eminent domain to make the Columbia expansion a reality.[23] By approving the rezoning, the City Planning Commission basically nullified the 197-a plan it formally approved.

This lack of commitment by DCP and other city agencies to the 197a planning process and the implementation of community plans was a major reason for creation of the Campaign and Task Force on Community-based Planning a decade after the 1990 charter reform. The Campaign is aimed at getting the city to support community planning and create mechanisms for implementing community plans (see chapter 8 for more detail).

The Partnership Plans

One of the most powerful influences in community planning over the last two decades has been *strategic planning*, an approach that originated first in the Pentagon, migrated to the business world, and penetrated the ideology of community development and planning. The basic idea is to bring together *stakeholders*—everyone who has a possible interest in the community—to develop common goals and objectives, analyze *opportunities* and *constraints* in the community, and outline comprehensive strategies around which consensus can be reached.[24]

Strategic planning is in some ways a newer version of the rational-comprehensive planning that was used as a foundation for the orthodox approaches to urban renewal, master planning, land use control and zoning (see chapter 1). As a set of techniques for planning, it is neutral and can be used in a variety of ways to promote inclusive or exclusive planning. However, the conceptual roots of strategic planning are likely to take community planners back to the original notion of using planning to build consensus around a corporate strategy—not, as Eddie Bautista believes, "true empowerment" and "fighting for justice." Strategic-planning approaches tend to emphasize public-private partnerships. In practice, the private partners are the most powerful and can control the agenda. Strategic plans tend to be seen as management tools rather than tools of popular democracy.

Many planning initiatives in the city have been modeled on the strategic-planning approach or borrow from its toolkit. In the early 1990s, a group of foundations supported six CDCs in the South Bronx in developing a Quality of Life Physical Plan for their neighborhoods. They called it a Comprehensive Community Revitalization Plan (CCRP).

In 1998, four of the CDCs formed another nonprofit to implement programs with foundation support.[25] The CCRP approach may have helped
the foundations better utilize their funds or helped CDC management to
operate more efficiently and creatively, but it is not clear that they helped
empower people. The foundation world often changes its priorities and
creates demonstration projects without long-term commitments to
follow-up. The CCRP model has not been repeated in New York.

In some ways, city government has undertaken long-term planning
partnerships with representatives of local communities. HPD has essentially adopted CDCs as exclusive partners for housing development in
their neighborhoods. But partnerships such as these do not necessarily
involve any broader community participation. In a few rare cases, like
that of the abandoned Rheingold Brewery site in Brooklyn, HPD helped
organize a community-planning process that resulted in a concrete proposal for the development of affordable housing and services on the site.
This was initiated by a local nonprofit with the support of a powerful
local elected official and remains one of the few exceptions to HPD's
usual practice of negotiating development deals with CDCs.

Pressed by local elected officials, DCP undertook an unusual partnership in the development of the 1993 Downtown Flushing Plan in Queens.
However, the central focus of the plan is to encourage new downtown
real estate development.

In recent years, the city's Economic Development Corporation (EDC)
has shown a much greater interest in comprehensive strategic planning
than DCP. EDC is a nonprofit corporation, wholly owned by the City
of New York. It was set up after the fiscal crisis under the neoliberal
dictum that economic growth without regulatory restrictions would save
the city from collapse. Its internal structure is more fluid than that of a
city agency and rather resembles a private corporation. As it is technically not a city agency it is not subject to ULURP or oversight by the
City Council. Since the Koch administration, when it was the Public
Development Corporation (PDC), it has been used as the mayor's instrument for negotiating tax breaks, city land deals, and infrastructure benefits to developers, fulfilling the neoliberal philosophy that government
should follow and provide incentives for market trends. While neither
EDC nor its predecessor has opened its doors widely to community planning, it is an aggressive practitioner of strategic project planning and
more adept at the use of participatory planning. For example, EDC
spearheaded, with DCP assistance, a community-planning process to

plan development along Sherman Creek in Manhattan's Washington Heights neighborhood.[26] This was possibly the first city-sponsored planning process carried out in both English and Spanish. EDC is also central to planning in the Hunts Point section of the South Bronx, working with a broad collaborative including community-based organizations and environmental justice groups.

These are clearly steps forward in community planning, but they are bound to be limited by EDC's mandate, which is to promote "economic development." This is most often interpreted as meaning any project that entails investment by the financial, insurance, and real estate (FIRE) sector. For example, EDC generated a master plan for the Willets Point area of Queens based on Requests for Expression of Interest issued to the investment community, not a participatory planning process (see the next chapter for more details). Planning for EDC is thus a tool for securing public consensus for development projects that generate significant interest among investors.

The Plans That Didn't Make It

Since the 1989 charter revision, more than a dozen community boards have stated their intentions of preparing 197a plans. Some started the process with the aid of pro bono assistance from one of the city's four graduate urban planning programs. Most never got off the ground. The reasons for this are varied. Community boards do not have the staff to support the lengthy planning process, and DCP's role is not proactive. Each community board has a full-time district manager and assistant, whose days are filled with answering complaints and going to meetings. Most are not trained in planning. Successive city administrations have avoided providing effective professional planning assistance to community boards, despite the mandate in the city charter to do so.

Among the plans that didn't make it is the plan for the Old Brooklyn District, a large area near downtown Brooklyn that includes DUMBO (Down under the Manhattan and Brooklyn Overpass).[27] The 1996 draft plan was not embraced by DCP or the Brooklyn borough president's office, which were engaged in private negotiations with downtown developers about zoning changes. DUMBO's industrial buildings were being converted to residential and commercial uses, and building owners preferred zoning changes and variances to the less predictable process of community planning. The community board plan also might have incorporated public housing tenants in a broader discussion about the future of the mostly white area. Within a decade after the 1996 draft plan, DCP upzoned DUMBO and most of downtown Brooklyn to facilitate real estate development and residential conversions without a comprehensive plan.

Another plan that didn't make it was in Manhattan's West Village. Manhattan Community Board 2 withdrew its proposal for a Special Greenwich Village Hudson River District when it faced potential conflict with other waterfront and redevelopment projects. Manhattan Community Board 10 (Central Harlem) started working on a plan with the help of a Hunter College graduate urban planning studio class in 1993. A preliminary draft plan was submitted to DCP in 1999, but nothing further has been done. Manhattan Community Board 11 (East Harlem) initiated planning efforts in 1990 with El Barrio Convention, a community assembly, and got help from the Hunter College graduate planning program in 1993. They submitted a draft plan to DCP in 1996 and a revised version in 2000. Both of these draft 197a plans in Harlem received staff support from Manhattan Borough President Ruth Messinger, but her successor did not follow through, and the planning staffs of all borough presidents were severely reduced during the Giuliani and Bloomberg years. Neither plan has been approved. Thus, the list of plans that didn't make it through the 197a process is long and growing.

Plans in the Pipeline

At this writing, several 197a plans are in various stages of preparation.

The Point CDC and other community-based organizations have been working on a plan for Hunts Point in the Bronx that includes public access to the waterfront and sustainable mixed-use development. A plan for the Sunset Park waterfront in Brooklyn, which includes public access to the waterfront and the greening of the port facilities, has been evolving for over decade under the sponsorship of Community Board 7. Also in Brooklyn, Community Board 3 is drafting a plan that seeks to control rampant conversion of an industrially zoned area to residential uses through ad hoc variances.

Even though these plans have not been officially approved, they continue to serve as organizing tools and reflect political strategies around which community organizers may coalesce. Draft community plans are often invoked in organizing campaigns even if the plans are far from the approval stage.

Planning by Sector: Housing, Transportation, and Open Space

As shown in chapter 3, community planning has strong roots in the tenant and housing movements. While tenant organizations remain focused on both individual buildings and citywide rent controls and CDCs focus on the preservation and development of affordable housing units in specific neighborhood-based projects, there are a host of organizations and coalitions that address citywide housing policy, including Housing Here and Now!, the Association of Neighborhood Housing Developers, Citizens Housing and Planning Council, and Community Services Society. Through their continuing involvement as both critics and supporters of city housing policy, they contribute to the formulation of policy and are de facto participants in planning for the city's future. Recently, the New York City Campaign for Inclusionary Zoning[28] was formed and brings together these and other housing and community-planning advocates.

The broadest housing coalitions include private real estate developers, whose focus is principally on expanding production and eliminating regulatory barriers but who share with community-based organizations the goal of increasing government subsidies for low- and moderate-income housing. This is one of the clearest examples of a durable community and real estate alliance and indicative of a profound contradiction within real estate over affordable housing (see chapter 2). For community and housing activists, questions such as who runs the alliance and who gets the subsidies are paramount. The tension between the real estate industry's deregulatory stance and the progressive housing movement's push for expansion of the public realm and rent regulation is built into this alliance. One recent challenge to this alliance has been the growing use of inclusionary housing programs (see more on this question in chapter 8).

In the area of recreation and open space, there are also established citywide organizations and coalitions, such as the Neighborhood Open Space Coalition and New Yorkers for Parks. Because parks and open space are anchored in neighborhoods, their preservation and development depend on continuing engagement with community planning. Some parks advocates focus on expanding the public commitment to parks and the improvement of public places, while others, like Partnership for Parks, support the establishment of local conservancies to raise private money and recruit volunteers to work in the parks. This difference in emphasis reflects more general tensions between policies that preserve community land and the neoliberal privatization of the commons. Since the Department of Parks gets little or no financial support from state and federal governments, it is one of the city agencies most vulnerable to discretionary budget cuts by the mayor. Well-endowed public-private partnerships, such as the Central Park Conservancy, are smoothing the way toward greater privatization of parks and contribute to inequalities in parks maintenance. Neighborhoods that cannot attract wealthy donors depend on a decimated Department of Parks staff for maintenance, and a recent study by New Yorkers for Parks showed that maintenance in these parks tends to suffer.

A community plan for a section of Brooklyn's waterfront has been the battleground for an important privatization war. In the 1980s, a coalition of Brooklyn groups defeated a proposal by the Port Authority to sell its abandoned piers and upland property for luxury housing that might have blocked the waterfront views of Brooklyn's wealthiest neighborhood, Brooklyn Heights. What followed was a decade-long process of planning by the Brooklyn Bridge Park Coalition that involved dozens of neighborhood organizations and that reached consensus around a proposal to create a regional park with a minimal amount of commercial space to finance park maintenance. The community coalition thought it was getting a regional park, but the underlying neoliberal assumption of privatized public space eventually was allowed to overwhelm the progressive idea of a regional park. In 2005, a local subsidiary set up by the Empire State Development Corporation (ESDC), a state authority, to implement the plan announced they would include a high-rise luxury apartment building that (along with the hotel and convention center that were already part of the plan) transformed the plan into a commercial enclave with some public access instead of a regional park with a few businesses.[29]

The neoliberal planning principal that public open space must be generated by private and not public investment governs the city's waterfront zoning, which was adopted in 1993 by the City Planning Commission. Waterfront zoning requires that all new residential and commercial development on the waterfront incorporate a public promenade and leave open public streets and corridors leading to the waterfront. The practical effect of this is both to relieve government of responsibility for building publicly accessible waterfront parks and to facilitate the development of open space that, because of its position behind waterfront towers, effectively functions more as a backyard for private buildings than as public space. In the contentious battles to rezone the industrial waterfront in Brooklyn, advocates for high-rise residential development often claim that greater density is needed so that developers can afford to build and maintain the public areas.

Just as progressive parks advocacy came out of the environmental movements of the 1970s, advocates for sustainable alternatives in transportation planning have banded together to help change city transportation policy. Streets and sidewalks are the city's premiere public places, but they are not planned for in a systematic and sustainable way. One of the chronic problems identified in neighborhood plans is safety for pedestrians, in particular children and the elderly. Activists with Transportation Alternatives (TA) in the Bronx got the city's Department of Transportation (DOT) to launch a Safe Routes to School campaign, which was to use traffic-control measures around city schools. In the 1990s, TA introduced the concept of traffic calming to the DOT, an institution dedicated to moving traffic as quickly as possible instead of planning how to move people. TA has been critical of DOT's policies for promoting safe pedestrian and bicycle circulation. Major thoroughfares like Queens Boulevard and Ocean Parkway (Brooklyn) function as speedways and surrogate highways when they could be shared by pedestrians, bicyclists, and motor vehicles. Thanks to TA's advocacy, DOT has now installed over 1,000 speed humps on local streets, experimented with neck-downs and other traffic-calming devices, and redesigned dangerous intersections to improve safety.

Sustainable transportation planning got a huge boost with the completion of the city's first Bicycle Master Plan in 1997. The Transportation Division of DCP produced this landmark document with the involvement of DOT, TA, and a host of civic groups. It is not likely that this plan would have happened without federal highway funding that for the first time allocated a portion of local transportation funds for modes other than cars. As with 197a plans, however, implementation of the Bicycle Master Plan has been a slow and difficult process. DOT is the agency responsible for implementation, and its traffic engineers continue to give priority to cars, even as New York City remains in noncompliance with federal clean air regulations.[30] Citywide and neighborhood advocacy groups have had to fight for every inch of new bicycle lane, every car-free hour in the city's parks, and every new inch of sidewalk for pedestrians. The city is still a dangerous place for cyclists and pedestrians. TA's Executive Director Paul Steely White recently wrote:

While the DOT deserves credit for taking baby steps with its limited Safe Routes to Schools program and piecemeal pedestrian safety improvements on a few of NYC's most dangerous streets, it has not yet made the sizable policy shift required to meet the enormous public demand for safe, traffic-calmed streets.[31]

Among the advocates of sustainable transportation is a small but resilient group that seeks to turn around the city's complete lack of interest in light rail. Ever since the nation's largest trolley system got shut down in the 1950s, the Metropolitan Transportation Authority (MTA) has turned its back on light rail, simply claiming that buses are cheaper. But the biggest deficit in the city's otherwise extensive mass transit system is its rickety surface transit system. It is the main reason that the city that has the largest subway system in the nation also has the longest average commutes. Most people have to walk long distances to subway stations, bus connections are unreliable, there is no bike parking at transit hubs, and few bike lanes get people to those hubs. The city has the slowest buses in the nation. Cross-town buses in Manhattan, for example, are slower than the average walker. Buses are loud, polluting, and too often stuck in traffic. While buses are run by a state authority, the MTA, the city's DOT has done little to create exclusive bus lanes, build safe bus stops, or reduce traffic volumes so that buses can move more quickly. In this context, the plan for a 42nd Street Light Rail system, which has been discussed by several city administrations, stands out as what could be a large first step in reversing city policy. This proposal would cost a fraction of Mayor Bloomberg's proposed extension of the 7 subway line and could be coupled with traffic-calming measures to reduce traffic in heavily congested Midtown.[32]

In sum, there is a lot of community planning going on all over New York. From the Cooper Square and We Stay! plans to the generation of community plans nurtured by environmental justice advocates and the 197a plans, community planning has caught on. Although only a handful of plans have gone through the official 197a process, government agencies are beginning to preempt local planning, even in modest ways, which indicates that community planning is starting to affect the way that government operates. The Bicycle Master Plan and Sherman Creek plans are perhaps important beginnings. However, in Red Hook, Chelsea, Greenpoint/Williamsburg, and in far too many other cases, city policy has evaded community planning and favored the use of zoning to promote real estate development.

In one way or another, community plans seek to help local residents and businesses gain control over a community's land. The plans that are sketched out here are generally inclusionary and, contrary to the charge of NIMBYism, usually call for more housing and public services, not less. They seek equity in the allocation of LULUs and measures that will reduce the environmental risks of all infrastructure, no matter whose backyard they are located in. This trend of progressive community planning faces a much more powerful trend of exclusionary, market-driven planning dominated by sections of the powerful real estate industry, in collaboration with government. The next chapter looks in depth at planning for rebuilding the World Trade Center site, the Midtown West plan, Olympics 2012, Atlantic Yards, and other examples in which inclusive planning was evaded, diverted, or undermined.

7

Community Planning for the Few

By the powerful we mean, of course, those who are able to realize their will, even if others resist it.
—C. Wright Mills, *The Power Elite*

Citizen participation[1] is as American as apple pie. The concept was popularized during the federal War on Poverty in the 1960s, which sought to widen opportunities for participation in civic life by poor people and African Americans.[2] Civic engagement and participation have been hailed by many as fundamental hallmarks of democracy in the United States. Alexis De Tocqueville's admiration for eighteenth-century civic life in the United States is often presented as evidence.[3] However, the notable opportunities for civic participation that De Tocqueville observed were accompanied by the exclusion of slaves, women, indigenous people, and those who owned no property from the main venues for participation. Democracy for the few would be a more appropriate way to describe the history of civic engagement in the United States.[4]

Citizen participation in New York City continues to reflect a complex array of underlying power relations (including differences in class, race, and gender) and they are manifested in spatial disparities. Working-class communities and communities of color have had to struggle to participate in civic life as equals, and community planning is one of the mechanisms they have chosen. But powerful New Yorkers, including the leading real estate and financial institutions, continue to rely on civic engagement when it supports their interests and are particularly skilled at engaging neighborhoods and the resources of the local state to legitimize their efforts.

Community Participation in Planning

Community participation is not simply an instrument for wielding power but a fundamental component of power. It is imbedded in the web of social and political relations within and among communities and between communities and the state. The city's wealthiest neighborhoods have highly developed networks involving resident participation. Manhattan's Silk Stocking District and other elite enclaves in the five boroughs have committees to combat every nuisance and a direct pipeline to the city's problem solvers. These neighborhoods disproportionately use the city's new 311 hotline, and since policy makers in City Hall pay attention to trends in 311 complaints, their collective voices are often heard. The "plan" in these neighborhoods often takes the form of an unwritten, informal consensus about how to maintain the status quo. Some of them do have formal plans, and a few have 197a plans that have been approved by the City Planning Commission and City Council. But in contrast to the insurgent community-based planning that arose in the struggles against displacement and environmental hazards in poor communities of color, these plans tend to be more limited in scope, exclusionary, and truly parochial. Formal community-based planning is not as urgent in these more stable neighborhoods because unwanted speculators and developers often fear to tread there in the first place. They know they are likely to meet resistance from residents and businesses that, unlike poor neighborhoods, have politically powerful connections, deep pockets, and recourse to legal remedies. Often the community board chair needs only to make the right phone call to scuttle the deal. So the pressure to plan in a formal way is not as urgent.

Community Planning and Exclusionary Zoning

Previous chapters show how small homeowners and businesses in Cooper Square, Williamsburg, and Red Hook allied themselves against urban renewal and for inclusionary community-based planning. Yet in a number of other neighborhoods, homeowners and businesses have supported exclusionary planning.

The 197a plan for Riverdale in the Bronx was approved in 2003. Riverdale is the wealthiest neighborhood in the Bronx. The plan, called *A River to Reservoir Preservation Strategy*, recommended thirteen separate areas for rezoning. Within a matter of two years, more than half of the areas were rezoned by the Department of City Planning (DCP). Most of the zonings reduced the potential for new development in areas where single-family homes predominate. A Special Natural Area District was created, a zoning measure protecting pristine green space that has been used in only four community boards in the city, all of them in high-income white neighborhoods.

The DCP was faithful to the Riverdale 197a plan's exclusionary goals. In contrast, when it came to rezoning in Greenpoint/Williamsburg and West Harlem, the agency violated the 197a plans' inclusionary principles and concerns about gentrification.[5] It took Greenpoint and Williamsburg over twelve years to produce their plans and several years to get them approved, but DCP moved the Riverdale plan through the approval process quickly. The Riverdale rezonings were also part of a larger array of downzonings in other homeowner neighborhoods like Bensonhurst, Brooklyn, and Springfield Gardens, Queens, where political support for the mayor's reelection would be critical.[6] The downzonings removed most of the potential for new development in these low-density neighborhoods. In working-class Greenpoint and Williamsburg, on the other hand, upzoning multiplied problems related to gentrification. Displacement pressures on low-income tenants and small industries grew at the same time that opportunities for them to move to outlying neighborhoods were being curtailed by downzonings there. In sum, these comparisons suggest that government gives priority to the implementation of plans in elite neighborhoods while other plans are put on the shelf.

In previous lower-density rezoning schemes, DCP had sought to balance downzonings with some upzonings in the same area. Sometimes the upzonings were more symbolic than real because there was little market interest in new development in the upzoned areas. But if applied wisely, the principle could encourage greater density in areas served by mass transit and balance both development and preservation. However, the extensive downzonings prior to the last mayoral election offered relatively little balance within neighborhoods.

An early example of a community plan in an upscale neighborhood had a somewhat different outcome because DCP insisted on balancing downzoning with upzoning. The proposed 197a plan for Douglaston and Little Neck in Queens called for the establishment of a special natural area zoning district and downzoning to limit new development. This community is a 75 percent white, upper-income residential community with many areas dominated by single-family homes. The stated purpose was to protect a 33-acre salt marsh and upland area bordering Nassau County. In this area, the city had already acquired substantial land for preservation as a park. According to long-time Queens

Community Board 11 Chair Bernard Haber, then-CPC Chair Joseph Rose wanted to balance the proposed downzoning with an upzoning along Northern Boulevard, a busy commercial thoroughfare. "We wanted to rezone Northern Boulevard for low density residential and local retail," said Haber, but Rose wanted to rezone to R6 or R6A—higher-density residential. "The R6 on Northern Boulevard was the killer issue."[7] When faced with the prospect of upzoning to balance a down-zoning, the community board dropped its plan.

Developer-Driven Planning

Developer-driven planning is another example of community planning for the few. When companies in the hegemonic sector of the real estate industry (the corporate giants and leading clans) are central players, the planning process tends to be highly controlled and participation limited. Decision making tends to be less open, transparent, and democratic. Democracy for the few frustrates participatory community-based planning. Using Sherry Arnstein's model of a "ladder of citizen participation," which goes from diffused power at the bottom to control over decision making at the top, the developer-driven plans for lower Manhattan after 9/11, for Midtown West, and for Atlantic Yards in Brooklyn come out at the bottom, where many people participate and have very little power.[8] In other words, for those at the bottom of the ladder, no matter how much participation there is in public discussions, the power to make decisions is reserved for the few.

The story of planning to rebuild lower Manhattan after 9/11 is a tale of how community planning was dealt with by one of the city's most powerful real estate clans and its partners in government. The plan for Midtown West was put together to favor the rising power of real estate interests with intimate connections to powerful sectors of globalized finance capital, including the new real estate investment trusts (REITs) (see chapter 2). This plan resulted in a battle by residents and businesses to save the Hell's Kitchen neighborhood from being wiped out by new development. The Atlantic Yards plan in Brooklyn is one among several recent attempts by powerful developers to revive the use of eminent domain as a tool for large-scale redevelopment schemes. This project also spurred a lively protest movement and alternative community plan.

These megaprojects raise strategic questions for community planners. How important is it to engage in the public debates over these mega-projects if they are supported by the most powerful real estate interests, have strong government support, and pose formidable organizing challenges? In the past, megaprojects like them (the Lower Manhattan Expressway and Westway, for example) were defeated only after years of organizing and the expenditure of enormous energy by community activists. To what extent would community-based organizations better serve their neighborhoods by retreating from such struggles and focusing on the relatively peripheral areas where they may have greater ability to actually influence outcomes? Or are the potential ripple effects of these large-scale projects on land values and rents and therefore displacement and gentrification so great that it is worth building broad coalitions to confront them? Do the high-profile battles at the centers of regime power offer unique opportunities for building broad coalitions to defend and expand community land? There are no simple answers to these questions. The lower Manhattan case suggests that in some situations the prospects for real change in decision making are extremely remote and call into question any extensive participation. The Atlantic Yards case, however, suggests that when potential ripple effects on neighborhood life are great, the option of retreating may not be a very attractive one.

The Plan to Rebuild Lower Manhattan

Immediately after September 11, 2001, there was a flowering of participation in the public discussion about how to rebuild lower Manhattan. The press was filled with ideas by architects, artists, philosophers, residents, and people from all over the world. At first, it looked like decisions would be made through an open, transparent, and deliberative planning process. But to avoid such a process, powerful elected officials acted decisively to narrow the discussion and expedite decision making. Early on and throughout the five years following the World Trade Center disaster, the planning process was taken over and managed by an elite group of officials and professionals who practiced public relations more than public participation. In the end, they ensured that most of the benefits of rebuilding would accrue to property owners in the area, particularly Larry Silverstein, the major leaseholder on the 16-acre World Trade Center site and a scion of one of the city's powerful real estate clans.

Advocates of community-based planning learned two important lessons from the lower Manhattan experience. First, the public participation process can be diverted and narrowed to focus on minor issues, technical details, and conflicts that concern mostly the real estate and finance sectors instead of the larger issues raised by others. Conflicts within the real estate sector can open up opportunities for an inclusionary process, but as long as the powerful are in control, these opportunities to influence the outcome will be limited.

Within less than a year after 9/11, the main conflict in the public eye was between Governor George Pataki, avid supporter of Silverstein's maximum rebuilding program, and Mayor Michael Bloomberg, who wanted to limit office development in lower Manhattan to minimize competition with his Midtown West project. This conflict was also reflected in the debates between David Childs, Silverstein's architect, and Daniel Libeskind, the author of the master plan, over matters of detailed design and execution of the plan. For the thousands of people who lost their jobs, housing, and family members and who were ill from the toxic dust and fumes, these were distant battles of little apparent import. These conflicts about urban design and infrastructure were the focus of media attention, and the benefits of rebuilding went disproportionately to property owners. Only a small portion of the relief funds went to heal the human wounds. The focus stayed on buildings and infrastructure, not people.

The second lesson is that the planning process can easily be diverted from discussions about hopes for the future to an obsession with fears of the present. Planning to rebuild lower Manhattan opened up a public debate on the question of how to create safe urban environments—an issue of concern in community planning everywhere. But this debate saw the rise in legitimacy of approaches that appeal to human fears. Physical design and planning were dedicated above all to the protection of private spaces and control over the use of public places, with the introduction of more barriers and surveillance and the curtailment of basic freedoms. Doomsday voices predicted the end of cities and touted the virtues of suburban sprawl, rejuvenating the well-established antiurban biases that have been the foundation of U.S. city planning.[9] The manipulation of fear and antiurban ideology and the disproportionate emphasis on physical design may be contrasted with the integrative and optimistic approaches to planning found in the community-based plans described in the previous chapters.

How the Participation Process Got Hijacked

On September 11, 2001, two hijacked planes were crashed into the World Trade Center (WTC) and reduced two 110-story buildings to rubble.[10] The media immediately burned the image in the public psyche of the twin towers as a symbol of global capital, the heart of U.S. financial power, and the anchor of the Wall Street district in Manhattan. This helped generate an emotional and defiant response that demanded expedited reconstruction of the WTC in its original form. Mayor Rudolph Giuliani appealed to New Yorkers to return to business as usual, and the federal Environmental Protection Agency, with no serious analysis to back up its assertions, declared there were no public health risks even as fumes from the debris wafted over lower Manhattan months after the incident.

The Alliance for Downtown New York, the Association for a Better New York, the New York City Partnership, and the Real Estate Board of New York (REBNY)—the elite of the city's business community—endorsed the rush to rebuild commercial space in a clear policy statement:

We know it is important that downtown remain and grow as a powerful engine of the city's, region's and nation's economies. The best living memorial to those who perished in the World Trade Center attack is to make sure that lower Manhattan emerges from this tragedy as a spectacular center of the global economy. The rebuilding effort must assure that this function is secured and enhanced.[11]

These groups went on to form a joint venture, NYC Rebuild, that advocated restoration of the 11 million square feet of office space that had been lost on 9/11 by creating a new commercial icon resembling the North and South Towers as a flagpole for the financial industry and in patriotic defiance of terrorism. They later had to concede a fraction of the square footage, but in the end their plan would be adopted. In 2004, REBNY President Steven Spinola reminded New Yorkers that "Larry Silverstein clearly has the right to build 10 million square feet [at the World Trade Center site,] and he plans to do that over 10 to 15 years."[12]

Patriotic rhetoric aside, it was logical that Larry Silverstein would want to maximize development on his property and win big on his insurance claims by maximizing his presumed future gains (or losses). And who could blame the big-time architects who joined him in his heroic mission if they could earn handsome commissions and help shape the skyline of the city? Said Robert A. M. Stern, dean of the Yale School of Architecture, "It is important to build. . . . We have always expressed our confidence through tall buildings. We are still a brash, new, swaggering country."[13] To complete the roster of growth machine regulars, New York's construction unions pledged allegiance to the rebuilding flag as long as there was plenty of building to do.

The Rise and Fall of Public Participation

The obsession of the U.S. media with the 9/11 disaster reflected in part a deep shock in a population that had never directly experienced the horrors of war. In the last century U.S. troops engaged in combat far from the nation's shores, and since Vietnam the military has used superior air power and advanced technology to distance themselves from the human suffering of others and reduce risks to U.S. forces. Cities in Europe had suffered terrorist attacks on civilians for decades and before that had survived two world wars and centuries of tribal and national military conflicts, but there was an ocean between Europe and America. Not since the U.S. Civil War had the ravages of war been directly felt by so many North Americans, but even in that war many of the battles were at the fronts between armies of conscripts. Although there had been an earlier attack on the WTC in 1993, it was not perceived as a global event in the way that 9/11 was.

After 9/11, the local and national media featured an extensive rogues gallery of the perpetrators, all of them from the Middle East and South Asia, that contributed to a growing climate of anti-immigrant prejudice. The *New York Times* ran daily articles with personal profiles of the WTC victims as President George W. Bush declared a war without end against terrorism, invaded Afghanistan, planned the invasion of Iraq, and announced the doctrines of preventive war, the global U.S. monopoly of military power, preventive detention, and other usurpations of civil and human rights. These doctrines reflected a new Manifest Destiny on a global scale, but they also served as the political and ideological context for the planning discussions about rebuilding lower Manhattan, where patriotism, the war on terror, and calls for a powerful state informed public debate.[14]

Even as the public was asked to trust in elected commanders-in-chief—the president, governor, and mayor—there was a surprising flood of grassroots discussion about what needed to be done. Myriad voices spoke out about rebuilding: the victims' families, volunteers in the rescue efforts, architects, planners, and others who translated shock, anger, and distress into reflections about the meanings of war and peace, life and death, public and private space, and the future of cities. Many artists, architects, families of the victims, and even Mayor Rudolph Giuliani felt that the site should remain undeveloped as a memorial or a sacred place. Others saw an opportunity to correct Manhattan's serious lack of open space and create a miniature version of Central Park at the southern tip of the island. Local residents and small businesses looked beyond the

WTC site and saw an opportunity for new development that would be integrated with their growing residential neighborhood, unlike the monumental twin towers that stood apart from them. Manhattan-based civic groups called for broad participation and extensive discussion, in some cases beyond New York City and the United States. Some were distressed at the bottom-line commercialism of the business community's program, but most focused on alternatives.[15]

Among the first to move into action was a coalition of local residents, small businesses, and design professionals, Rebuild Downtown Our Town (R.dot), which put together principles for rebuilding. The coalition's version of lower Manhattan included the residential areas of Battery Park City, Tribeca, and parts of Chinatown. It advocated for an approach that would integrate commercial and residential uses, expand community facilities, and promote innovative and environmentally sound design practices.

Two major civic and professional coalitions emerged. The Civic Alliance to Rebuild Downtown New York was convened by the Regional Plan Association and brought together more than eighty groups, including civic and professional organizations, foundations, a few unions, and universities. In addition to the unprecedented Listening to the City events that it organized, the Civic Alliance was able to muster professional oversight and opinions on the various proposals and environmental reviews. The Civic Alliance advocated for continuing open participation in the planning process, but as the process became more technical and narrow, only its professional core was left. It was unable to expand much beyond its Manhattan base, and even at the Listening to the City events two-thirds of all participants were white.

NY New Visions was a coalition of sixteen architecture, planning, and design groups that were convened by the New York chapter of the American Institute of Architects. This group encouraged innovative planning and design approaches, including green building, and echoed the need for a comprehensive planning approach. However, professionals with architectural firms that would be involved in the project were active participants, thereby raising issues of conflict of interest.

Imagine NY, a project of the Municipal Art Society, held 230 workshops throughout the city and region to catalog the diverse visions for rebuilding. The visioning sessions included populations throughout the region that had not been attracted to participate in other forums. The organization published the proposals that came out of these sessions and called them the People's Visions.[16]

The Labor Community Advocacy Network (LCAN) brought together groups that were largely excluded from public discussions, including tenants from low-income neighborhoods and representatives of labor. This network included groups from the Lower East Side like Good Old Lower East Side (GOLES) and progressive labor unions like the Chinese Staff and Workers Association. They were perhaps the most vocal critics of the official rebuilding priorities and the exclusionary planning process. LCAN criticized the lack of financial support for the workers and small businesses that were devastated by the 9/11 attack. In an environment of suspicions about immigrants in general, LCAN asked how government aid would reach immigrants who were too afraid to approach public agencies. Also, Mobilization for Youth launched Rebuild for Whom? Spotlight on the Poor as a network of grassroots organizers, advocacy groups, professionals, and community-based organizations and service providers, mostly from the Lower East Side and Chinatown.

Asian Americans for Equality (AAFE) criticized the exclusion of Chinatown representatives from the planning process even though Chinatown was among the most severely affected communities. On top of its longstanding problems of poverty and overcrowding, Chinatown lost proportionately more jobs after 9/11 than any other neighborhood in the city. A study found that five months after 9/11, forty Chinatown textile factories had shut down, and 70 percent reduced their hours.[17] Almost 25 percent of all Chinatown workers lost their jobs. Restaurants and tourist shops were empty for months. And since many workers in Manhattan's Chinatown live in the Chinatowns of Queens and Brooklyn, the impact was felt much farther afield. AAFE started its own planning process and developed a strategic plan for the redevelopment of Chinatown.

Several associations of the victims' families emerged, including Voices of September 11. Peaceful Tomorrows was the most progressive and stood out because it sought "effective, nonviolent solutions to terrorism" and "to break the cycle of violence and retaliation engendered by war." The most powerful group was the Coalition of 9/11 Families (discussed later).[18]

Planning through the Independent Authority

Despite this wide array of spontaneous organizing, the official decision-making process was tightly controlled through an independent authority appointed by Governor George Pataki. Shortly after 9/11, Pataki created the Lower Manhattan Development Corporation (LMDC), a subsidiary of New York State's Empire State Development Corporation (ESDC). Like Robert Moses, Pataki had become skilled at using independent authorities that were established under state law and could bypass local elected officials in the planning of development projects. Pataki appointed seven of the eleven LMDC board members. The first board was almost entirely white males from the business world, a demographic that would identify with the downtown business community's approach to the site.[19] The LMDC would be the lead planning agency and control most of the $21 billion of federal rebuilding funds. Pressed by the influential real estate bloc, Pataki from the beginning and regularly throughout the planning process reassured the public that he would move expeditiously to rebuild the site, while at the same time his LMDC director adopted a public attitude of patience and respect for all views. In less than a year after 9/11, however, while the rubble from ground zero was still being carted away to the Fresh Kills landfill in Staten Island and without any significant public involvement, the LMDC commissioned plans for restoring the 11 million square feet of office space. The plans included six alternative configurations by one hand-picked local architectural firm, Beyer Blinder Belle. The public reaction to the LMDC plans was overwhelmingly negative. According to architecture critic Ada Louise Huxtable,

The only concept apparent in the six concept plans released by the Port Authority and the Lower Manhattan Development Corporation is the restoration of all the commercial real estate by dumping it back in the same place in a slightly different form. . . . This is déjà vu all over again for those who remember the urban renewal destruction of lower Manhattan in the 1960s.[20]

In July 2002, civic and professional groups sponsored a Listening to the City event, an online dialogue and assembly at the Jacob Javits Convention Center that engaged over 5,000 people to discuss and debate the future of ground zero and New York City.[21] At this event, in the press, and in local political circles, the verdict was a huge thumbs down for the LMDC-commissioned plan. "People voiced strong objections to elements of all six proposals, particularly the dense office and commercial development they called for," stated the Listening to the City report.[22]

Listening to the City was a critical turning point in the planning process. The cumulative effect of the organizing by communities and professionals was to change the terms of the debate, but the diverse voices were interpreted in ways that were convenient for those in power. Deputy Mayor Daniel Doctoroff, the advocate of thinking big, stated, "If I had to sum up what I heard today in one phrase, it would clearly

be: Don't settle. Do something great."[23] In the meantime, the drumbeats
to start building increased in tempo. The *Wall Street Journal* denounced
"the city's anti-development activists . . . the nightmare of delay and litigation" and declared that "the best way to honor the dead is by reviving
normal life and commerce."[24] Amid the myriad calls for a memorial,
affordable housing, sustainable design, and equitable solutions, one
conclusion must have made Larry Silverstein smile: 71 percent of the
participants went on record as saying that "it is very important to add
a signature element to the skyline."[25]

After Listening to the City, the LMDC quickly coopted the public
debate and narrowed it to focus on questions of physical design. The major
media followed along. *New York Times* architecture critic Herbert Muschamp convoked leading architects from around the world, who advanced
new alternatives with flashy design innovations, all of them assuming that
11 million square feet of office space would be reconstructed in lower
Manhattan. In their exuberance, many wanted room for even more building space.[26] The LMDC then issued a new and more flexible program that
allowed for a moderate reduction of office space, placement of up to 40
percent of the office space within a thirty-block area around the WTC site,
the preservation of the footprints of the twin towers as a memorial, and
a variety of other uses including cultural space. Based on this program,
the LMDC held an international competition that resulted in the selection
of the striking and creative design by architect Daniel Libeskind in early
2003. Libeskind's design reflected some of the ideas that emerged from
the professional and civic discussions.

The attractions of the Libeskind design, however, obscured the essence
of the LMDC program, which had not significantly changed since Listening to the City. In October 2003, one of New York City's most prominent black architects, J. Max Bond Jr., lamented the social exclusion that
characterized the decision-making process. "If there had been a greater
variety of people, someone *would* have questioned the program," he told
the *New York Times*.[27] Bond pointed out how it has always been difficult
for people of color "to get access to the upper realms of Wall Street
towers" and that the tight security measures made it unlikely that many
immigrants would take part.

When the competition was launched, much of the public discussion
was about design, and the fundamental questions of economic and social
equity faded from view. Once the competition was over, public discussion was about how to get it built. REBNY's original mission would thus
be fulfilled. The bottom line—restoring office space—was to be met.[28]

After Libeskind was selected, the planning process moved behind closed doors where elected officials, Silverstein and his architects, the LMDC's staff of fifty full-time professionals, and a small circle of local elites worked out their conflicts and consensus with input from about eight advisory councils that they set up and managed. Many LMDC meetings and community hearings were by invitation only, prompting protests from community groups. Silverstein hired David Childs, leader of the staid business architectural firm Skidmore, Owings & Merrill, to give expression and credibility to his bottom-line strategy. In a torturous year-long process of arm-twisting and after a lawsuit filed by Libeskind, the architect's innovative designs were twisted to fit Silverstein's business strategy. Libeskind was forced to work collaboratively with Skidmore, Owings & Merrill, whose designs never went below the bottom line. As early as July 2003, the *New York Times* was already declaring Silverstein the winner: "Last week, Mr. Silverstein's high hopes of early 2001 seemed, if anything, too modest. He emerged victorious in the struggle for control of ground zero, elbowing aside Daniel Libeskind."[29] In September 2003, the program was changed to increase the height of the office towers, reduce their cores, add ground-level retail space, and generally convert it to a typical rectilinear office park.[30] By the end of 2004, Silverstein was guaranteed almost $5 billion in insurance earnings, less than the $7 billion he asked for but clearly the biggest pot of money on the rebuilding table. By 2005, Libeskind's striking irregularly shaped design for the 1,776-foot Freedom Tower, the centerpiece of his plan, came out looking like one of the old rectangular WTC towers. A new team of prestigious architectural firms was formed under Silverstein's command. In the end, the developer got his way. The "highest and best use" orthodoxy of urban planning won the day (see figure 7.1).

Memorial to Real Estate

The whole question of a dedicated memorial space became submerged in the rush to rebuild. The objectives of the Coalition of 9/11 Families were that the memorial should take priority over everything else, that it should be planned first, and that redevelopment should be planned around it. Just the opposite occurred. The memorial is the afterthought, and at this writing it is still not clear how it will be developed or paid for. The families did win the reassurance that the footprints of the twin towers would not be built on and that there would be a museum and cultural center on the site. But they opposed all of the rebuilding

Figure 7.1
Rendering of the latest plan for the new World Trade Center site with designs by architects Santiago Calatrava, David Childs, Norman Foster, Fumikiko Maki, and Richard Rogers. *Credit:* Silverstein Properties.

alternatives because every one started with the office space as the overriding element and the memorial as a footnote.

While the Coalition's demand that the site be a repository for the remains of the 9/11 victims was not met, the LMDC proposed that portions of the footprints be used for other purposes. The proposed cultural center was challenged as one of its two prospective tenants, the Drawing Center, withdrew because Governor Pataki, reacting to reports that one of its exhibits put George W. Bush in an unfavorable light, demanded that the center pledge that no exhibits would be "anti-American." The other tenant, the International Freedom Center, headed by a former George W. Bush business partner, complied.[31] Perhaps the greatest irony in the memorial discourse was Rudoph Giuliani's strong support for the work of the Coalition. Although as mayor he had shown little interest in preserving spaces that were being taken over by the real estate machine and actively sold off scores of community gardens that were built on city-owned land in the nearby Lower East Side, at ground zero he discovered, in his own words, "the significance of the place."[32]

While the mostly white leadership of the Coalition of 9/11 Families was able to exercise some influence in planning for a memorial, nothing of the kind was possible for the families of the victims of American Airlines flight 576, which crashed in Belle Harbor, Queens, a mostly white neighborhood, on November 12, 2001, only two months after 9/11. Most of the victims and their families were from the Dominican Republic, the destination of flight 576. A provisional memorial went up at the crash site, with flowers, pictures, and mementos of the victims. But the owner wanted to develop the property, and it had to go. The *New York Times* astutely reported, "Grief Aside, Some Memorials Are More Equal Than Others."[33] A modest permanent memorial was later built at another location.

The Struggle within Real Estate: Limited Growth at Ground Zero?

Larry Silverstein's ownership of the ninety-nine-year lease to the World Trade Center site was, as the saying goes, nine-tenths of the law. Some suggested that government could use its powers of eminent domain to get Silverstein to go away, and others proposed that the city could swap the land that it owns under the Port Authority's two airports—LaGuardia and Kennedy—for the WTC site, but these proposals never went very far. From the beginning, Silverstein's interests were protected by the real estate establishment and, among elected officials, Governor George Pataki. Other real estate interests, however, gave Silverstein a run for his money.

Without directly criticizing Silverstein, incoming Mayor Michael Bloomberg and Robert Whitehead, the first head of the LMDC, talked publicly of lower Manhattan as a mixed-used diverse community. They proposed the incorporation of residential, commercial, and memorial functions on the World Trade Center site and in the surrounding area. Unwilling to publicly endorse any crass commercial proposals while the public was reeling from the WTC attack and imagining better ways to use the land, they called for consensus and neither applauded nor thwarted Silverstein. But tension was bubbling beneath the surface and could be seen by comparing Pataki's exuberance for rebuilding office space and the cautious words of Mayor Michael Bloomberg. Bloomberg warned of the temptations of overbuilding. "The Twin Towers' voracious appetite for tenants weakened the entire downtown market," Bloomberg declared.[34] He knew that there was already a glut of office space in lower Manhattan, 40 million square feet in all Manhattan (about a 12 percent vacancy rate, considered normal in the real estate world), and a few new giant office buildings were about to be completed uptown, including his own corporate headquarters. He also was in the midst of promoting a massive plan for the redevelopment of Hell's Kitchen as the "last frontier" for office development (see next section) and did not want lower Manhattan to get in the way.

During his election campaign in 2001, Bloomberg had stated that a new development corporation was not needed to rebuild lower Manhattan. But after entering City Hall, he quickly changed his tune and saw the value of having an independent entity that was immune from ULURP and neighborhood participation and could override local zoning and planning. Bloomberg never considered undertaking a 197a plan, which would have mandated an open, transparent process of public participation. As he had done so often in his business career, Bloomberg made a deal. The governor would have control, but the mayor would be a player. The governor would rebuild lower Manhattan and the mayor would be in charge of Midtown. There would be an ongoing dialogue[35] about lower Manhattan, but it would take place behind closed doors. Silverstein and Pataki could rely on their business-friendly mayor to throw in the services and user-friendly open space that lower Manhattan residents were asking for, while the centerpiece of redevelopment would still be office space. Bloomberg would cooperate in rebuilding the local infrastructure and could carry the bag for those interested in good design. Deputy Mayor Doctoroff told the *New York Times*, "The guiding force has to be excellence of design and creating the right demand for commercial, retail, cultural and other attractions."[36] A key player in the Bloomberg/Pataki dance was Roland Betts, the LMDC board member who oversaw the design competition. Betts owned Chelsea Piers, a major commercial recreation center on the Manhattan waterfront, supported Bloomberg's Midtown West plan, and was a member of the City's 2012 Olympics Committee but also enjoyed the confidence of Pataki and the Republicans (he was a business partner of George W. Bush and thus had Washington connections).

Bloomberg's planning strategy for lower Manhattan, announced in December 2002, officially endorsed the growing residential and mixed-use community in lower Manhattan and proposed its expansion and integration with the WTC site. Some elements in the plan had been suggested by local neighborhood and downtown business groups. The Bloomberg strategy included the creation of a major public space, Greenwich Square, a green market, a new waterfront park, the development of 10,000 new housing units over the period of a decade, and the creation of a transit link between lower Manhattan and Kennedy and Newark Airports.

Bloomberg understood that today lower Manhattan, though often thought of as just the financial district, has more residents than it did a hundred years ago. Nearly 300,000 people live below 14th Street in a collection of diverse, lively neighborhoods that function long after the three-piece suits leave their office suites and the lights go out in the Stock Exchange. Even in the smaller area below Canal Street within a one-mile radius of ground zero, more than 35,000 residents live in a twenty-four-hour-a-day, seven-days-a-week community. This was in fact one of the fastest-growing neighborhoods in New York City.

Perhaps receptiveness to neighborhood requests was considered normal in City Hall because this neighborhood had joined the ranks of the wealthiest in the city. Median income is twice the citywide average. It is largely white and is represented in Albany by the powerful speaker of the assembly, Sheldon Silver, Governor Pataki's oft-time nemesis but also an important power broker for both New York City as a whole and his home district in Manhattan. Bloomberg must have understood the political importance of this community when he named the one (and only) local community representative to the first LMDC board—Madelyn Wils, chair of Manhattan Community Board 1, who came from this area. Later Carl Weisbrod of the Alliance for Downtown New York, a powerful business group, was appointed to the LMDC board.

The First Disaster: Creation of the World Trade Center

Bloomberg's statement of caution about overbuilding has some foundation in the history of the World Trade Center. The opening of the WTC in 1973 was the first disaster to strike lower Manhattan. Its immediate effect was to raid office space in the surrounding area, leaving millions of square feet of space in vacant buildings. There were still not enough tenants to fill the two towers, and government offices were moved in to fill the gap. Initially, state offices occupied 60 percent of one of the towers, a huge bailout for the bondholders of this giant project. Even then, the two buildings had vacancy rates in the double digits until the 1980s real estate boom. In *The Abuse of Power*, Jack Newfield and Paul DuBrul declared, "Public revenues desperately needed for transit improvements in two states have been sequestered to pay off bond-holders in the biggest white-elephant construction project in history."[37]

From the start, the WTC's neighbors got the worst part of the deal. In addition to the vacant office space it created, the WTC wiped out industrial space in lower Manhattan. Radio Row, a concentration of small electronics businesses, was leveled to build the WTC. Thousands of small manufacturing businesses and warehouses in Tribeca were forced out by rising rents in the 1980s following the construction of Battery Park City, an exclusive residential and commercial enclave built on landfill from the WTC. Tens of thousands of jobs were lost, yet there were still millions of square feet of vacant office space in lower Manhattan. In the 1990s, the City of New York, responding to pressures from distressed property owners, made zoning changes that allowed for the conversion of lower Manhattan vacant office and industrial space to residential use.

Thus, a new residential community was spawned by the WTC adventure. Battery Park City, a meticulously planned luxury enclave, gave Tribeca's gentrification a big push (as did the conversion of nearby Soho from industry to housing), and the icing on the cake was the converted office buildings that rescued building owners in the Wall Street area. Paradoxically and contrary to the intentions of the developers, the World Trade Center *hurt* the financial district most and gave birth to a new residential neighborhood.

Until its final days, the WTC remained an enclave that was isolated from the thriving city that grew up around it. Many of its workers went in and out through the WTC subway stops below the building, never interacting with the world at street level. This was a supreme example of extravagant, high modernist architecture. The monumental towers overpowered all. They were surrounded by desolate wind-swept concrete plazas, an eerie no-man's land that divorced buildings from their environment. They truly met LeCorbusier's objective of destroying life on the street. This was the tower-in-the-park model without a park.

As construction of the WTC neared completion, the Pruitt-Igoe public housing project in St. Louis, designed by Minoru Yamasaki, the same architect who designed the WTC, was demolished, a precedent-setting rejection of modernist architecture's promise that the rational organization of physical space by itself would improve the human condition. The towers in lower Manhattan that were supposed to be beacons for the future were destined to be tombstones for modernist excess. More important, these two fateful building projects demonstrated the prevalence and cohabitation in public policy of both a lack of public commitment to house poor people and the readiness to subsidize downtown office development, two sides of the neoliberal coin (reducing social welfare programs and expanding subsidies for private development).

Putting aside the rhetoric about the promotion of world trade, the Rockefeller adventure in lower Manhattan was an ambitious real estate deal meant to expand the value of the family's lower Manhattan property, in particular the new Chase Manhattan Center. It was the lynchpin of the plan authored by Rockefeller's Downtown-Lower Manhattan Association that included the failed proposal to build the Lower Manhattan Expressway, a project killed after a twenty-five-year battle by community groups.[38] The downtown plan was based on a vision of lower Manhattan as a high-rise business district, with no housing or community facilities. But the victory of neighborhood groups, coupled with the decentralization of the financial, insurance, and real estate (FIRE) sector in the last quarter of the twentieth century, cut the Rockefeller dream down to size.

The Local Real Estate Deal and the Global Financial Center

The assumption underlying the plan to rebuild lower Manhattan was that it was the global center of trade and finance, but this was part myth and part reality. New York City's largest financial center is now in Midtown Manhattan, not downtown, and Manhattan's two financial centers are only a small part of the financial centers that stretch across the region and beyond. Terrorists and tourists may see it as a symbol, but the World Trade Center is no more or less the center of global capital than the nondescript Liberty Plaza across the river in Jersey City, the Metrotech Center in Brooklyn, or the Citibank building in Long Island City. Gradually, after the WTC was opened in 1973, the FIRE sector began leaving lower Manhattan in search of cheaper land. The Regional Plan Association now recognizes eleven business centers in the New York region.[39] It took the *New York Times* a full year from the 9/11 disaster to announce what had long been obvious to urban planners and the captains of global finance for quite some time: "Current trends militate against future growth in financial services downtown, or even in New York City, according to a range of people who have knowledge of the district."[40] That is why the September 11 attack produced little more than some extra static in an already troubled downtown real estate market.

Underlying the clash over how much to build was the tension between a powerful local real estate clan and corporate, global capital. Though they shared common interests, the two groups had different priorities. Financiers first of all watch the global marketplace, while local property owners keep their eyes on their territory. New York's current mayor, Michael Bloomberg, the twenty-ninth wealthiest man in America and number seventy-two internationally, made his billions in financial news and analysis. He is a big-picture executive who was elected without the need for contributions from local real estate developers, so he might be less committed to the immediate needs of a handful of downtown Manhattan property owners than to the long-term interests of the financial sector. In his capacity as mayor, Bloomberg also has had to look out for the interests of the city's bondholders, who are based all over the world and care about local real estate only to the extent that revenues from property taxes, which are based on the market value of real estate, are adequate to balance the city's budget. But in New York City, property taxes account for only 20 percent of all city revenues, and some 60 percent of all properties pay no taxes.

The tension between real estate and finance capital is only a part of the picture. Contrary to the media image sent out by City Hall, Michael Bloomberg is not just a disinterested financier. He is as deeply involved in Manhattan real estate as David Rockefeller was—as an interested party and through the business people he is friendly with and who help out his administration. The Bloomberg circle of friends and confidants includes Roland Betts of Chelsea Piers, Deputy Mayor Daniel Doctoroff, Related's Steven Roth, and Vornado's Stephen Ross, all of whom are committed to the growth of Midtown and have a personal financial stake in it. Like the two mayors who preceded him, Bloomberg sees the West Side of Midtown Manhattan as the best hope for the expansion of Manhattan's central business district, finance capital's traditional neighborhood. Unlike his predecessors, however, he has a home-town business that stands to benefit.

Who Wins, Who Loses?

Who lost on 9/11? The majority of the some 2,800 people who were killed on that day lived outside New York City, and 20 percent were foreign born. Of the 125,000 people who lost their jobs, 80 percent came from outside Manhattan, and 60 percent of them earned less than the city's median income. There were undoubtedly thousands of undocumented immigrants who lost their jobs or suffered injuries but feared to seek help amid the avalanche of nativist sentiments in and out of government. About 6,000 people lost their homes or were forced to move. Some 14 million square feet of commercial space was destroyed, and another 20 million square feet was made vacant.

If the plans to rebuild after 9/11 were to be based on the needs of those who were directly and indirectly affected, the project might have turned out differently. If 9/11 was indeed an event of deep concern to everyone around the world, as the United States insisted in promoting its global antiterrorist campaign, then the participatory process would have engaged ideas from around the world and not just through an international competition to select an architectural team. But the planning process was American, and though the wounds of 9/11 were political, social, cultural, and psychological, the centerpiece of the planning process was a physical plan—how to arrange new office space in lower Manhattan.

Less than a year after 9/11, *Forbes* magazine predicted what would happen to the $21 billion that was allocated to rebuild lower Manhattan:

There will be windfall gains for large corporations, already powerful commercial property owners and residential landlords far from Ground Zero (to name a few). Losers will include countless small businesses and, perhaps, federal taxpayers.[41]

Forbes noted that all deals with businesses are individually negotiated, with little public visibility.

Understanding who benefited in the long run is complicated by unclear accounting by the federal government. It is impossible to know with any certainty how and where federal money was spent, and it is unlikely that all of the allocated funds were spent. Another problem is that while costs and losses were estimated at $80 to $100 billion, the federal commitment was only some $21 billion. With insurance payments totaling $30 to $40 billion, this means there was a net loss of at least $40 billion, and it is almost impossible to track these losses.[42]

It appears that about $7 billion of the federal money went to compensate some 5,500 people who are family members of victims and to settle some 2,675 injury claims, mostly by rescue workers. Although these people were the most directly affected, one can question whether direct compensation was the most appropriate strategy for dealing with the losses. The decision to allocate these funds may have been driven more by government's interest in preventing litigation that might have been more costly and could have opened up inquiries into the responsibility of federal, state, and local officials for the events of 9/11. Possibly another $1 billion went to clear the rubble from the WTC site. Emergency aid to small businesses and residents ran into bureaucratic roadblocks, and for many the money arrived too late—long after people were forced to move and had to find other sources of relief.

About $5 billion of rebuilding money was set aside for Liberty Bonds, which provide low-cost financing for downtown development through the use of tax-exempt bonds. Liberty Bonds are gifts to developers, and most Liberty Bond recipients are nowhere in sight of ground zero. Plans to use Liberty Bonds for the Bank of America headquarters and the *New York Times* headquarters raised a stir but have not changed government policy.[43] The bonds were used to finance a power plant in Queens and several buildings outside Manhattan. The requirement that 10 percent of units in residential buildings that were financed with Liberty Bonds must be reserved for affordable housing dwindles in importance when most of the subsidized properties are commercial and the definition of *affordable* is wide enough to exclude most people earning less than the median income in low-income neighborhoods.

About $2.7 billion in Community Development Block Grant (CDBG) funds went to the Empire State Development Corporation (ESDC) and the Lower Manhattan Development Corporation (LMDC). About 70 percent of these funds were given to businesses, and about 18 percent went to local residents.[44] CDBG, a program of federal subsidy originally set up to benefit low-income communities, became yet another conduit for aid to those who need it least. It allocated $1.7 billion to repair damage to the mass transit system and build a new transit hub in lower Manhattan. Some $2 to $5 billion more will be needed to build a transit link between lower Manhattan and JFK and Newark Airports, a gigantic controversial project that would serve almost exclusively the wealthy Wall Street crowd. There was no assistance to city and state governments for some $8.8 billion in revenues that were lost. This placed an additional burden on budgets already straining for balance. The cost for items of importance to the local residential community such as parks, community facilities, and services is less than half a billion.

Environmental Justice at Ground Zero

The full environmental and health impacts of 9/11 may not be known for many years to come, but a growing body of evidence suggests that these impacts were substantial. The response of government has gone from outright denial to cautious research but with a minimal commitment of resources. The most dramatic form of denial was the declaration by federal Environmental Protection Agency (EPA) head Christie Todd Whitman exactly one week after 9/11 that it was safe for people to live and work in lower Manhattan. Pictures of Mayor Giuliani and rescue workers without face masks flashed across TV screens for weeks and seemed to reassure everyone that health risks were minimal and temporary. The plume of smoke from the fires at ground zero drifted for weeks across the East River to Brooklyn and Queens and was not fully extinguished for months. It is now known that the EPA's testing was grossly inadequate, but even its limited testing showed alarming levels of toxic materials in the air, including asbestos, and was suppressed.[45]

A study by the Mount Sinai Medical Center showed that ten months after 9/11 over half of rescue workers had respiratory problems and almost three-fourths had ear, nose, and throat problems.[46] Two years after the disaster, the EPA's inspector general concluded that EPA had not gathered enough information to warrant its reassuring public statements and that the White House influenced the content of the EPA's press releases. Three years after 9/11, local residents, including LMDC member Madelyn Wils, continued to complain of respiratory problems. It took five years for government to begin monitoring local health conditions to determine the long-term effects of 9/11's toxic dust and fumes, and their effects on cancer rates will not be known for many years.

The tragedy that followed 9/11 was that both federal and local authorities rushed to move residents and businesses back into the World Trade Center neighborhood and spent billions of dollars to keep them there, while all along there were serious risks to human health. Some of the companies that could afford to have their buildings cleaned correctly before employees returned to work may have saved their workers from the worst effects of contaminants. But many companies employed unlicensed cleaning contractors whose workforce was almost entirely low-income immigrants, and there is no guarantee that the buildings were cleaned properly or that the workers will not suffer chronic illness or death as a result of their jobs. In a very different context, a new environmental justice issue emerged that was neglected by official planners just as the concentration of waste-transfer stations in communities of color had been overlooked.

The context for this negligence was the local drive to rebuild downtown real estate and the national security policy that sought to instill maximum confidence in the ability of federal, state, and local authorities to guarantee business as usual. This policy environment contributed to exclusionary urban planning in the post-9/11 era and built on fears raised by the 9/11 attack that instilled greater confidence in those holding power.

Rebuilding with Fear

In early discussions after 9/11, some argued that no skyscrapers should be built on the World Trade Center site because they would attract terrorist attacks. There were doomsday predictions about the end of cities on a global scale. Historic fears of New York City as too big, too dense, and too violent were called into play. Yet despite the powerful antiurban bias in the nation, these views had little resonance among business and government leaders in Washington and New York. Washington wanted to restore public confidence in its ability to repair the damage done, and New York's conservative leadership was in thrall to the REBNY rhetoric of patriotic defiance.[47]

As the plan for the WTC site evolved, however, fear emerged again as an ingredient of the design process. Indeed, since 9/11 fear of a terrorist attack has become a major factor in the design and management of all public spaces in the city, particularly in Manhattan. It is not difficult to understand the reasons for increasing concerns about risk and vulnerability to attacks. However, this is one area of planning and design in which decisions are being monopolized by the institutions of law enforcement and are made, unquestioned, behind closed doors. Whereas in the past, issues of public security could be addressed through an open, public dialogue, after 9/11 security was placed off-limits for public participation and instead relegated to private consultations with developers and their architects. The classic 1972 work of Oscar Newman, *Defensible Space: Crime Prevention through Urban Design*, long ago launched an open discussion among architects and planners about how (and indeed whether) physical design can reduce vulnerability to violence and crime, and this has generated many techniques that supposedly create safe urban environments.[48] Since 9/11, however, the public must accept on face value the assertions made by public authorities that the physical measures they mandate will improve security. This lack of critical public dialogue is contributing to an erosion of public control over the city's public places.

New York's thousands of miles of streets and sidewalks are its premiere public places, and they are supplemented by parks, both large and small. Since 9/11, the New York Civil Liberties Union has documented and legally challenged the city's draconian restrictions on the right to assembly on streets and sidewalks and the growing use of surveillance devices without an open planning process or public oversight.[49] New York may be losing some of its storied *urbanity*—the quality of urban life that maximizes the personal and cultural exchanges among diverse populations in public spaces.[50]

After 9/11, Manhattan's property owners went into action and took over public sidewalk and street space to carry out their own security plans. Around Manhattan office buildings, ugly concrete Jersey barriers, cheap metal fences, and gigantic planters (often with no plants in them) flourished. In response, the city's Art Commission issued guidelines for *Designing for Security: Using Art and Design to Improve Security*,[51] which only partially limited such abuses. Private owners and their police took over the public square outside the New York Stock Exchange for over two years until they were forced by a judge to give it up.[52] Opined Daniel Libeskind, "By responding brutally to a brutal event, you exacerbate the sense of danger."[53]

The fear of new attacks was a central element in the design of the new buildings at ground zero. The first 75 feet of the new Freedom Tower will be encased in steel and titanium to resist an attack with explosives. It will have an underground security screening area, an extra set of stairs for rescuers, and maximum-security safe zones on each floor. Special filters in the ventilation system will protect people against biological and chemical attacks. These measures were instituted with minimal review and public discussion. The Police Department has now become a senior partner in the design process, but its role is entirely behind closed doors. In June 2005, the New York Police Department forced David Childs to set back his new building 90 feet from West Street instead of the originally planned 25 feet.[54] The elimination of the unconventional twisted shape that Libeskind gave to the tower would help achieve this minimum setback.[55]

Manufacturing Consent and Broken Windows

New York City's law-and-order mayor Rudolph Giuliani set the stage for this shift before 9/11 by strengthening the role of the Police Department command and reversing the implementation of community-policing policies begun under his predecessor. Giuliani helped to popularize the "broken windows" philosophy, which was used to justify a crackdown on minor quality-of-life offenses (such as begging and unsolicited cleaning of car windows by homeless "squeegee men") occurring in public places.[56] This broken windows philosophy was essentially a public relations device behind a comprehensive approach to public security. Since the first terrorist attack on the WTC in 1993, Giuliani's public security policy had three components, all of which compromised urbanity—a military solution (more police, arrests, and restrictions on public gatherings and demonstrations), a technological solution (more video cameras, metal detectors, and ID cards), and an urban design solution (more gates, enclosed places, and defensible spaces, like the newly redesigned City Hall Park, once a wide-open public arena for free speech) (figure 7.2). These policies did not prevent the second attack on the WTC. Perhaps it was prophetic that the emergency bunker built in the WTC by Mayor Giuliani after 1993 was reduced to ashes on September 11.

The eight-year rule of Mayor Rudolph Giuliani was a stunningly successful effort to manufacture[57] consent for Giuliani's hard-line zero-tolerance security policies. Though he was elected by a minority of New Yorkers, he projected a global image as a popular mayor. He claimed credit for the drop in crime, economic growth, and improvements in the quality of life in New York City during his reign. Wayne Barrett's *Rudy! An Investigation of Rudolph Giuliani* is one of several studies to note

Figure 7.2
City Hall Park

that the drop in crime and economic growth were part of national trends that began at least four years before Giuliani took office.[58] Crime declined at the same rate under the prior mayor, David Dinkins, and in most major cities throughout the United States. The economic boom of the 1990s was national, not just local, and New York's share in the boom was not exceptional. In a recent article in *Harper's* that looks at Giuliani's record as mayor, Kevin Baker states, "A world in which the brand is more important than the facts was precisely the sort of world in which a Rudolph Giuliani could thrive."[59] Giuliani's run for president in the Republican primary relied heavily on his public security record and performance after 9/11, yet Wayne Barrett and New York firefighters who felt betrayed by Giuliani charge that this is also mass marketing.[60]

Property versus People

In sum, security measures, spending, and planning after 9/11 protected and enhanced both the power of the state and the value of property in lower Manhattan. The tragedy of 9/11 was also a commodified image reproduced on T-shirts and in media products. Ambulance-chasing investors, including local property owners, were anxious to cash in on new speculative opportunities and insurance windfalls. The rebuilding of lower Manhattan was good for business, as usual, and for business as usual. In a political environment in which discussion revolved mostly around the physical city, lost was any central focus on progressive community planning—the need to sustain individuals, families, and communities for future generations; improve the quality of urban life, public space, and the environment; and support the emotional, intellectual, cultural, and spiritual development of people as well as their material health and well-being. A spontaneous outburst of participatory planning was hijacked by the LMDC and diverted to narrow issues of physical form. Genuine concerns about security were translated into changes to the physical city without considering social and economic impacts. Measures taken by technocrats and police in isolation from the public evaded issues of basic human rights.

This is one of the disasters following 9/11. If planning to rebuild had been a democratic process founded on social justice, the silent victims of 9/11—thousands of immigrants who worked in lower Manhattan, lost their jobs, and who are suffering from the health effects of 9/11—would have had a say in determining the future of the city. Instead of a complex and extended dialogue recognizing the diversity and urbanity of the city, the discourse was dominated by the simplistic dualism of good versus evil. In the words of noted Latin American writer Eduardo Galeano, "In the struggle between good and evil, the people are always the ones to die."[61]

The Battle for Hell's Kitchen and the Plan for Midtown West

The battle for Hell's Kitchen, or the story of Midtown West, is currently the largest new real estate deal in the city. It illustrates the dynamic and complex relationships between global and local capital and the competition and cooperation that characterize the real estate world. Community planners need to understand these characteristics in developing strategies for community land. Midtown West is in the vortex of intense real estate development and at the very center of real estate's power, and it therefore is less vulnerable to community pressure than the more peripheral areas where community planning has emerged.

Out of the back streets of Hell's Kitchen on Manhattan's West Side, Mayor Michael Bloomberg is creating New York's first neighborhood enclave that will be developed and owned exclusively by the world of global finance. Midtown West is to be built on modern, neoliberal foundations, that is with large public subsidies to feed the development of a private enclave (see chapter 1 for discussion of the neoliberal city). It is to replace the gritty working-class Hell's Kitchen neighborhood, which was once filled with tenements, warehouses, and working-class people. Only minutes away from Times Square and with the renewed Hudson River waterfront as its backyard, Midtown West was originally to be centered around the existing Jacob Javits Convention Center, which would be expanded and crowned by a new stadium for the Jets football team built over the Metropolitan Transportation Authority's Hudson rail yards. After a lengthy community battle, the proposal for the Jets stadium was defeated. However, Midtown West will still see a massive expansion of office space and thousands of new apartments, most of them for the luxury market. All of this is part of Bloomberg's vision for the city's future, a plan that could have come out of any corporate-sponsored strategic planning session hosted in a Midtown office suite—and perhaps did.

The plan for Midtown West is shaped in the image of the neoliberal city, a collection of privately-built enclaves that monopolize public funding and compete with other cities for private wealth.[62] In conjunction with the plan for the 2012 Olympics, it would brand the city as the center of the world, the victor in the global competition among cities.

The crown jewel was to be the new stadium for the Jets football team, the site of opening ceremonies for the Olympics. But New York City came in fourth in the competition for the Olympics (London won). Local opposition to the stadium, including residents and businesses in the surrounding communities, built a successful campaign against the public subsidies that would have been needed to build the sports complex. But the real estate plan at the heart of Midtown West went forward along with a massive rezoning of the area.

The plan for Midtown West fused the interests of finance capital, media, entertainment, and sports with local politics. It included a zoning giveaway, new public infrastructure, and an innovative financing scheme that would keep future tax proceeds out of the city's budget and funnel them back into the financing stream for the new neighborhood. The total price tag for the public is likely to be upward of $8 billion. Although the details of funding are locked up in spreadsheets that may never be made public, Mayor Bloomberg has admitted that the city will have to sink some $5 billion into the whole deal; another $600 million in public funds would have gone to build the football stadium. The mayor designated Midtown West "the city's last frontier."

The City Planning Department produced *The Hudson Yards Plan*, a proposal to change the zoning to facilitate real estate development in the area.[63] This plan had no comprehensive analysis of economic, social, and physical conditions and needs. Its creators did not engage in dialogue with the people who live and work in the area. The plan did not mention the need for low-cost housing for working people, the lack of open space in Manhattan, or the chronic traffic mess, all conditions that would become worse with new market-rate development. Planning for Hudson Yards did not start with an assessment of citywide needs but instead treated the area as a separate enclave. This was not planning but the Department of City Planning's customary *zoning without a plan*. The upzoning from industrial to residential and commercial multiplied land prices overnight, amounting to a big welfare check to property owners and investors.

The rezoning of Midtown West in 2004 created the potential for 40 million square feet of office space and 13 million square feet of new housing. Questions about whether Manhattan could possibly absorb that amount of office space in the future were ignored, and the media seemed to forget that the trend over recent decades was the migration of office functions to places outside the city. Would a new mountain of office space in Midtown depress the office market in the rest of Manhattan and the city? Or is the gradual move away from Midtown inevitable and irreversible?[64] Deputy Mayor Daniel Doctoroff predicted it would take thirty-five to forty years for the office space to develop.

To the West Side property owners and developers, judging future demand is just part of the real estate crap shoot. What really matters to them is the *expectation* of growth so that their property values go up. The announcement of future zoning changes and public investments in Midtown West was enough to start a rash of speculation. Thus, Bloomberg kindled in Midtown West the same speculative fire that the Rockefellers lit in lower Manhattan thirty years ago with their plan for lower Manhattan.

Because the stakes are high, the office market in New York City can tolerate a good deal of overbuilding. A 10 to 15 percent vacancy rate for office space is considered normal, while the rate for the luxury apartment rental market is about half that amount. On the other hand, the overall vacancy rate for housing hasn't gone above 5 percent for almost a century. The local growth machine leads to overproduction of real estate at the top of the market, similar to the overproduction of commodities in the global growth machine.

The Midtown West rezoning created a mixed-use zoning district that incorporated some of the remaining low- to midrise residential, commercial, and industrial uses. In this district, property owners could chose industrial or residential uses. But with skyrocketing land prices, property owners would not choose to maintain an industrial use when they could convert to residential or commercial uses and charge much higher rents. (The mixed-use zone was also used against industry in Greenpoint/Williamsburg; see chapter 6.) Despite protests from the garment industry and unions, new development was allowed in the adjacent garment special district, chipping into the strict limits that had previously been placed on new residential development. The rezoning also nibbled away at a piece of the Clinton Special District to the north, an innovative regulatory haven for low-cost housing that had been forged decades ago by housing advocates who battled Midtown developers.

To hoist the potential value of the new real estate, the Bloomberg administration proposed a one-mile extension of the 7 subway line that was likely to cost some $3 billion, which would make it the most expensive piece of urban mass transit in the world. Brushed aside were proposals for above-ground light rail and a bus shuttle service that would cost one-tenth as much. The new subway would also give a boost to the expanded Jacob Javits Convention Center, which for decades has managed to move its clients in and out with taxis and plenty of parking. Running through Midtown West and lining the Hudson River waterfront would be an open-space network that would function more as a mall for area businesses and residents than a public park. These expensive pieces of public infrastructure made private development more attractive, and together they made a plan of sorts—to create more valuable real estate.

According to the *New York Times* and civic elites, Michael Bloomberg—mostly in the persona of his dynamic deputy mayor, Daniel Doctoroff—had grand visions for the future of the city and was therefore making planning respectable again.[65] They compared Doctoroff to Robert Moses, and several major exhibitions on Moses fed a revisionist effort to rehabilitate the master builder.[66] Some pointed to Moses's giant Midtown urban renewal project over forty years earlier that created Lincoln Center, the city's premiere cultural complex that houses world-famous cultural institutions like the Metropolitan Opera and New York Symphony. Lost in the new versions of history were the tens of thousands of working-class black and Latino people who were displaced with little ceremony or compensation to build the elite performing arts center. What a relief, they seemed to say. Not since the fiscal crisis and demise of Moses has New York seen such powerful visions. The city has found a way to make places for the rich again.

Most of the public was left in the dark about Bloomberg's unique financing scheme that would make the new Midtown West an exclusive privatized ghetto. The Hudson Yards Infrastructure Corporation would float bonds to fund the scheme, and they would be paid back from revenues generated by new office and luxury development in the area. The revenues would come from payments in lieu of taxes (PILOTs) by property owners and go to the Corporation, not into the city budget, to pay off the bondholders. This would be the city's first use of this scheme, known as *tax increment financing* (TIF), and it would likely be the largest TIF in the nation. The innovative financing arrangement would allow Midtown West to function like an independent corporate entity. It would depend on getting maximum revenues from real estate development, and therefore officials would want to maximize development to pay for basic infrastructure and services, regardless of the impact on the environment and the rest of the city. TIFs can also be risky because they depend on future real estate growth that may not materialize and could eventually lead to bailouts by the city and state long after everyone has forgotten that the projects were supposed to be self-sufficient.[67] TIFs are a distortion of Henry George's principle of recapturing land-value increases for public benefit. The recapture is usually minimal, and it is used exclusively to benefit the segregated enclave rather than to meet needs and rectify inequalities throughout the city.

Behind the city's financial shell game was the Jets stadium. There has never been a downtown stadium that did not require an enormous public subsidy, and the Jets stadium would not have been an exception. Although its financing was wrapped up in the TIF and funds for the Javits Convention Center, it would probably have been the most expensive stadium ever built in the world—which is perhaps one way to get recognition as a world city.[68]

The people who live and work in Hell's Kitchen and the surrounding neighborhoods put up roadblocks to the global dreams of Bloomberg and Company. The area targeted for new development is a mixture of low-rise residential, commercial, and industrial uses, huge swaths of concrete making up the access ramps to the Lincoln Tunnel, and truck and bus parking. Residents and businesses formed the Hell's Kitchen Neighborhood Association (HKNA), which held numerous community workshops and developed its own plan for the area. The HKNA plan favored more modest office development and a greater mix of small industrial and commercial uses. Its design alternatives eliminated the wall of towers that would form a barrier between the neighborhood and the waterfront. HKNA's main focus has been fighting the stadium. Both the office of Manhattan Borough President C. Virginia Fields and the HKNA developed alternative plans that would position housing and related uses over the Hudson rail yards where the Jets stadium was planned (figure 7.3). The central focus of these alternative plans was to create a viable and diverse West Side community that has many connections to the waterfront and public open spaces and a mixture of uses and is not just another downtown business complex.[69]

Community activists developed a sophisticated campaign to organize elected officials and public opinion. They made alliances with Midtown business interests who opposed the Jets stadium, including the family that owned Cablevision and the nearby Madison Square Garden and owners in the theater district to the north. They also filed a lawsuit challenging the environmental impact statement for the stadium. Ever since Mayor Rudolph Giuliani had first proposed building a stadium for the New York Yankees over the Hudson MTA rail yards, fears of unbearable traffic in this already congested area drove Manhattan residents to oppose any stadium. After the Olympics, the stadium would have hosted

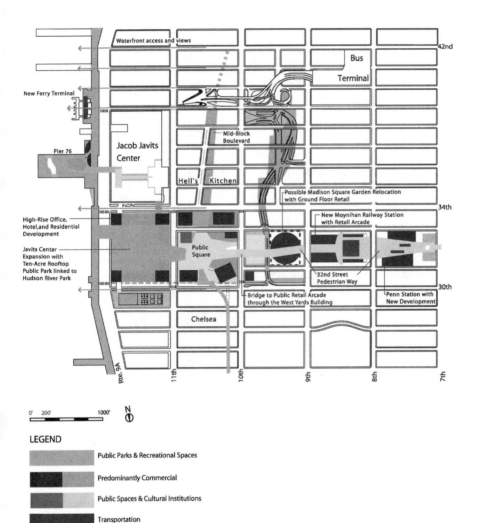

Figure 7.3
Hell's Kitchen Neighborhood Association concept plan

only eight regular-season Jets home games during the year, and the environmental analysis stated that most Jets fans would take mass transit. This claim was based on a survey in which the Jets asked their season ticketholders (most of whom live in car-dependent suburbs) if they were accustomed to using mass transit. Most said that they were. Based on this response, the people who created the environmental analysis took a big leap in logic and concluded that most fans who drove to see the Jets play in New Jersey's Meadowlands would take mass transit to see them in Manhattan. The plaintiffs questioned this conclusion, citing slower weekend subway schedules and decreased congestion on bridges entering Manhattan. Also, the total number of parking spaces in Midtown West was projected to expand, creating a greater incentive for fans to drive. In an effort to justify the costly stadium, the city and state had changed the proposed project from a stadium to a multiuse facility that would be used by the Javits Convention Center when the Jets were away. But this would have brought in more traffic than Jets games, and it was unclear whether the Javits Center really needed that much space.

In the end, the community coalition was able to kill the stadium plan because they out-organized the mayor and his coalition. The final blow was a vote by the state's Public Authority Control Board that failed to approve needed funding. The city is now moving ahead with options to build a mixed-use project over the rail yards, though initial proposals appear to bear little resemblance to the alternative community plan. Local housing activists were able to extract concessions from the city in the form of inclusionary zoning that could make up to 25 percent of new housing units affordable to low- and middle-income households. However, in the end, the upzoning approved by the City Planning Commission and City Council set in motion the wheels of speculative development, and City Hall moved forward with its new taxing authority. These measures would ultimately make Hell's Kitchen little more than a symbolic place name. In the end, when the economic stakes are as high as they are in Midtown and community-based organizations are forced into alliances with high-stakes players, it is difficult to exercise enough leverage to guarantee an inclusive, equitable, and just plan.

Olympics 2012: The World City Meets Local Real Estate

The tactics used to sell the Midtown West rezoning combined the ideology of globalization with local boosterism and dealmaking. The ideology of globalization was crystallized in the promotion of the city's bid for the 2012 Olympics. Resurrecting classical assimilationist ideology, the

bid announced that New York was the most global of all global cities—
"the melting pot of immigrant countries."[70] The local Olympics committee painted a romantic, rosy-eyed picture of ethnic groups from around
the world "living peacefully side by side . . . despite our differences, we
are bound together by a common humanity." New York, they said, "is
an Olympic Village every day."[71] Most of the city's new immigrants
would probably find a ticket to the games unaffordable, as they would
an apartment in Midtown West.

The city's Olympics 2012 plan revolved around the creation of two
giant axes that cross each other to form the Olympic X (figure 7.4). The
Olympic X adopts the classical morphology of monumental city planning
advocated by monarchs and military strategists. It emulates the north/
south *cardo* and the east/west *decumanus*, the imperial crossroads that
intersected at the center of ancient Roman cities; the baroque axis at the
heart of Georges-Eugène Haussman's urban renewal plan for nineteenth-
century Paris; and Pierre L'Enfant's plan for Washington, DC. At the
center of the Olympic X would be the globalized Midtown West, the
Colosseum of the Jets football team, and the Olympic Village in Hunters
Point (Queens) (a residential enclave for the athletes).[72]

The Olympics proposal projected the urban ideal of global capital—to
combine tourism, media, information technology, and sports to brand
centers of power in a way that makes them competitive.[73] But behind
the glossy propaganda that was designed to make New York City into
a hot commodity in the global marketplace there were also banal local
real estate interests. For example, the Olympics would jump-start
depressed land values in Midtown West. It would rescue the troubled
Queens West waterfront development in Hunters Point by fronting
Olympics money to build residential towers that have been stuck on the
drawing boards for two decades, thanks to faltering public-private partnerships. Several Bloomberg confidants had local real estate investments
and stood to benefit. Deputy Mayor Doctoroff, founder and head of the
local Olympics committee, is an investor in Midtown property. Roland
Betts, owner of the Chelsea Piers, a giant recreational facility on the
waterfront just south of Midtown, is a close associate of Bloomberg,
member of the local Olympics committee, and a Bloomberg appointee
to the Lower Manhattan Development Corporation. The creation of a
major tourist and recreational center in Midtown West would likely
bring more customers to the Chelsea Piers. Also, Midtown is coming
more and more under the control of finance capital's most powerful
weapon for controlling local real estate, the real estate investment trust

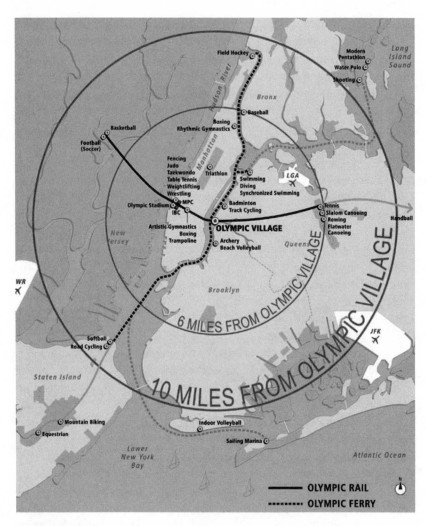

Figure 7.4
Map showing the Olympics 2012 plan

(see chapter 2). Midtown West may mark the most recent remarriage of global finance and real estate, but it also represents the triumph of zoning over planning and of privately controlled public finance (through tax increment financing) over the public budget and the difficulty of advancing inclusive community planning while in the very shadows of global capital.

Atlantic Yards: Urban Renewal All Over Again

Atlantic Yards is a proposal to build the largest and densest private development in Brooklyn by using the state government's powers of eminent domain and substantial public subsidies. The struggle over Atlantic Yards is a recent replay of the struggles against urban renewal by community residents and business owners who declare "We won't move" when the power of eminent domain is used to remove them. In this case, however, community organizers are facing an unusually powerful and skillful private development group that has persuaded top elected officials to support a business plan and sell it to the public as an irreversible fact. The elaborate marketing campaign uses images and symbols that are associated with the sports and entertainment world. It includes contractual agreements for jobs and affordable housing that are made between the developer and selected community-based organizations and that aim to legitimize the project in the eyes of low-income people of color. The developer has been skillful at using race and class to divide the community opposition to the multibillion-dollar project. This has not prevented the development of alternative plans, three court cases, and a popular documentary, *Brooklyn Matters*,[74] that illustrates how key the manipulation of race is to the project's future. After four years of opposition, however, the multiclass, multiethnic community coalition that opposes the plan continues to press for a more inclusive, community-based alternative.

In 2003, Forest City Ratner (FCR), a national real estate giant and real estate investment trust (REIT) that has virtually monopolized office development in downtown Brooklyn, proposed to build over a million square feet of office space, 4,500 apartments, and an arena for the Nets, a basketball team owned by FCR principles, above the Vanderbilt rail yards, which are owned by the Metropolitan Transportation Authority. The rail yards separate the residential neighborhoods of Prospect Heights and Fort Greene, east of downtown Brooklyn. FCR was already known among Brooklynites for its Metrotech complex in downtown Brooklyn, a 1980s suburban-style office enclave that absorbed generous public subsidies, turned its back on the adjacent African American neighborhood, and did little to boost local businesses. FCR also built the Atlantic Center, another forbidding mall that earned unanimous opprobium for a fortresslike design that seemed to keep the neighbors away. To ease the way for its triumph at the Vanderbilt rail yards, FCR persuaded the governor and mayor to back its plan before it was announced and convinced the state and city to throw in at least $229 million in direct subsidies (now over $300 million). The governor placed at FCR's disposal the Empire State Development Corporation (ESDC), an independent authority with a board of directors appointed by the governor. With ESDC involvement, the plan would not have to undergo ULURP review by the three affected community boards, the borough president, the City Planning Commission, or the City Council. The ESDC believed that it would be justified in condemning private owners and displacing almost a thousand residents and businesses, since the U.S. Supreme Court's 2005 decision in *Kelo v. New London* allowed local government wide latitude if it wished to condemn property solely for the vaguely defined purpose of economic development. Tenants and owners on the project site later filed a lawsuit challenging ESDC on the grounds that condemnation was being used to transfer property from one set of owners to a single hand-picked developer and that this was contrary to principles stated in *Kelo* and state law.

Like Alice in Wonderland in her looking-glass world, the planning for Atlantic Yards was all backwards.[75] In planning without the mirrors, government creates a plan for the area, looks at the potential environmental impacts of the plan, decides what to do, and then either takes action by itself or puts the plan out to private developers to bid on. In Atlantic Yards and increasingly in other megaprojects throughout the neoliberal city, the reverse is happening: the private developer does the plan, persuades government officials to back it, and then announces a done deal. This ideology of the fait accompli becomes a key instrument for moving through all stages of the planning and public approval process. It poses a serious challenge to community organizers because even those who find the project to be unacceptable are led to believe that nothing can be done to change or stop it.

This looking-glass world also has the environmental review process backwards. The purpose of the environmental impact analysis is to inform decision makers about the potential negative impacts of the project before they make their decisions. Project proponents are required to disclose these impacts, using a worst-case scenario that will alert decision makers to all possible consequences of their decisions. In this case, however, the decisions to approve the project were made in advance. The complex process of environmental review moved from a scope of work to a draft and a final statement but did not substantially change the contours of the project.

As community groups get more skilled at stopping megadevelopments like FCR's, developers are also getting more skilled at picking and choosing community-based partners. Shortly after announcing his grand plan for downtown Brooklyn, FCR's Bruce Ratner faced an outpouring of opposition from residents and business owners who did not want to move, objected to the scale of the project, and were deeply concerned about traffic and environmental impacts. They formed Develop Don't Destroy Brooklyn to oppose the project[76] and started preparing their own plan. The UNITY Plan workshop was convened by City Council member Leticia James under the direction of architect Marshall Brown (figure 7.5). The UNITY plan (UNderstanding, Imagining and Transforming the Yards) assumes no condemnation of property and a similar residential density but on a smaller footprint and in a more contextual scale and

Figure 7.5
Model of the UNITY proposal for Vanderbilt Yards, Brooklyn. *Credit:* Marshall Brown

configuration. There is no basketball arena in the UNITY plan. The principles for responsible development that emerged from the planning process stressed the need for integration of new development with the existing neighborhoods and included an affordable housing component.[77]

Before FCR announced its plan and in anticipation of neighborhood opposition, it lined up a community partner that would back its project. FCR owner Bruce Ratner made a deal with the Association of Community Organizations for Reform Now (ACORN), perhaps the largest nationwide grassroots advocacy group with a presence in low-income communities, including communities of color. The deal, sealed in an unprecedented written community benefits agreement (CBA), promised that 50 percent of all rental units would be affordable for people with low or moderate incomes. Ratner also signed an accord with BUILD, a group representing minority construction workers and unions, that would guarantee some local jobs and job training. These CBAs were developed in exclusive negotiations and included a gag order that prevented participants from criticizing the project.

Shortly after the execution of the ACORN CBA, FCR sidestepped the requirement of 50 percent affordable housing by cutting the amount of office space and adding market-rate condominium units to the project, which reduced the proportion of affordable housing to around 31 percent, with less than half of that going to low-income tenants (the program was structured in such a way that only 14 percent of all units would be affordable to those making less than the median income for Brooklyn). It was later revealed that BUILD had been only recently created, its leadership had no track record in job training or development, and it secretly received funding from FCR.

Community opposition to the FCR project included tenants and owners who refused to be bought out and vowed to fight eminent domain (figure 7.6). Judging from testimony that was presented in the environmental review process, many residents also objected to the location of an arena on a site bordered by low- to midrise residential communities. Others were worried about the high density (this would be one the densest projects in the city), existing traffic and transit deficiencies and the likelihood that they would worsen since no improvements were planned (the site is at the juncture of three major thoroughfares and one of the borough's most dangerous intersections), the lack of public open space, secondary displacement of affordable housing and local businesses, and a tower-in-the-park design that required the closing of local

Figure 7.6
Protesters from Develop Don't Destroy Brooklyn. *Credit:* Amy Greer

streets and would effectively isolate the new development from the surrounding neighborhoods. Even those who might be inclined to accept some version of the proposed project protested the lack of local input. However, by making a deal in advance with the governor and mayor and going through the ESDC, FCR effectively evaded the city's land-use review process and avoided having to answer to local neighborhood groups. A single public hearing on the scope of work for the environmental review and another on the draft environmental impact statement were the only forums for community input. FCR, ACORN, and the construction trades financed busloads of supporters to disrupt the forums. The environmental review process is strictly a forum for disclosure of potential environmental impacts. It is not geared toward planning, and in these forums ESDC officials never responded to concerns or allowed a dialogue or shared decision making.[78]

Deal Making and Race Baiting
Whatever the merits or problems of the FCR project, it has brought out some of the most controversial and difficult issues for both community organizing and planning strategy. The first critical question is whether community-based organizations should partner with developers in developer-driven deals and, if so, when. ACORN and elected officials who

supported the project have argued that the CBA is a victory because it guarantees affordable housing at a time when public funding is drying up, because the CBA redistributes wealth, and because it will help keep at least some local residents from being forced out by new development. But ACORN overlooked deep community opposition to the project and never sought community consensus; signed an exclusive CBA with a clause that required ACORN to publicly support the project, thereby taking away their ability to work together with other community groups opposing the project; and ACORN signed an agreement with no legal guarantees that the affordable housing would be built or within the reach of low-income people or people displaced by FCR. Experts commenting in the environmental review on housing impacts also charged that the giant luxury project would likely displace more low-income people than the new affordable units, and more local retailers. The Atlantic Yards CBA is the first developer-initiated CBA, unlike CBAs in other parts of the nation that were the result of a negotiated settlement followed by a struggle between community and developer.[79] It set a precedent of developer-initiated CBAs that was soon followed by the Yankees to advance their proposal for a new stadium and Columbia University to advance its proposal to expand into West Harlem. As these CBAs proliferate, it raises a question about whether they are legitimate instruments for community involvement or developer tactics that undermine the legitimacy of the public land use review process.

Race is a fundamental but largely unspoken issue in the Atlantic Yards development. In initiatives like Atlantic Yards (and IKEA in Red Hook; see chapter 6), developers driving the planning process have been skillful in using race to divide communities, taking advantage of deep racial divisions that exist within communities. Since ACORN and BUILD have largely African American members, FCR supporters are quick to pose as champions of civil rights and low-income housing for people of color. They have tagged the opposition as upper-income—white brownstoners who were looking to protect their quiet blocks and exclude poor people. But a careful look at the lineup for and against the project reveals no such facile division. According to Nicholas Confessore of the *New York Times*, "Atlantic Yards has drawn no true color line in Brooklyn, but only a blur of intersecting agendas, and constituencies, both black and white."[80] Those lined up in favor of the project include white and black elected officials, community-based organizations, and religious leaders. Against the project are white and black elected officials, community-based organizations, and religious leaders. City Councilman Charles

Barron, a former Black Panther, is one of a few elected officials who have decried race baiting by developers (he also did so in the IKEA case) and at the same time spoken out against institutional racism in government. Barron called the project "instant gentrification." Bob Law, another former Black Panther who owns a local business, says he thinks that Bruce Ratner "gives out a little money here and there to whoever he chooses, he makes some billions, and what we get in return are some temporary jobs on a construction site and those jobs are dead-end jobs. . . . It's a con game."[81]

Developer-driven planning is growing and is taking its toll on the integrity of community-based organizations. In the pursuit of public-private partnerships, community groups may mimic the deal making that occurs in the real estate sector. In the case of Atlantic Yards, community organizations whose main focus has been to extract concessions from the developer seem to have copied the short-term approach of real estate developers and corporate strategic planning. As soon as organizations put deal making ahead of organizing, they leave little space for democratic planning. ACORN, a prominent nonprofit housing developer, chose to act independently without the involvement of a sizeable number of community groups—block and neighborhood associations, environmental and transportation advocacy groups, and community boards—including those who were troubled by the project as well as those who supported or opposed it. As with all community coalitions, a broad community effort would invariably include people and organizations that do not share ACORN's passion for social justice, but such is the nature of coalitions (and FCR has not been known as an advocate of social justice). As the struggle over Atlantic Yards continues, ACORN has maintained an exclusive dialogue with FCR, with which it has a contractual relation, and has had no significant dialogue with the majority of community-based organizations seeking to influence, modify, or overthrow the megaproject. As a result, ACORN relinquished its ability to build unity in the community and strengthen its own leverage in dealing with FCR.

FCR has used to its advantage the public debate over the size of the project. In response to concerns in the community about the large scale of the project, FCR twice cut the size of the project in small increments but ended up with more or less the same size it started with because it had also increased the project size at one point. In another megaproject, community advocates on Manhattan's West Side were successful in getting Donald Trump to cut his Riverside South project in half, but the question will always remain whether Trump doubled the size of his original plan in anticipation of community opposition and the need for a negotiated deal. Although cutting megaprojects down to size can be an important goal of local organizing, such a pattern results in a perverse syndrome in which developers start with a high bid, look good by making concessions, but always remain in the driver's seat.

The basic problem with developer-driven planning is that the entire policy debate revolves around the developer's proposals, not around a plan that is based on what is best for the neighborhood and city. Community organizations are diverted away from pursuing plans that will meet their needs and instead toward negotiating over a developer's plan. They can end up mimicking the real estate industry and become local power brokers instead of community advocates. Community meetings and the press focus on potential impacts and appropriate concessions by the developer, but few people project a different sort of process in which plans can start with the problems, needs, and proposals of people who live and work in communities. Should not communities come up with their own plans through an open democratic process and then let developers compete for the right to implement them?

And More Urban Renewal?

Following the Atlantic Yards scenario, developers are becoming more aggressive in holding the threat of eminent domain over the heads of small businesses and residents. For example, Columbia University has stated publicly that if necessary it would resort to ESDC sponsorship and the use of eminent domain to accomplish its expansion plan in West Harlem. The city is also proposing condemnation in Willets Point, Queens, a thriving auto service district with 225 businesses and some 1,800 jobs that the city would like to relocate to create a giant commercial center.[82] The city also displaced twenty-three small ethnic businesses from the Bronx Terminal Market in favor of the Related Corporation and chain superstores, a project financed by tax incentives and Liberty Bonds.[83] And the city has moved hundreds of street vendors off 125th Street in Harlem and Fulton Street in Brooklyn to make way for established national chains.

The next chapter looks at the relationship between community planning and broader progressive politics, the ways that community planning can consolidate democratic control over community land, and the challenges ahead.

III

The Future of Progressive Community Planning

8

Progressive Directions for Community Planners

The essence of planning advocacy is local community planning. . . . We do it because the city doesn't. The City doesn't care about its local communities. It is too interested in helping the real estate industry and its commercial interests make a dollar. It is beholden to expressway developers, suburban sprawl profiteers, big real estate interests and bankers, all of whom reap the profits from zoning manipulation and land development.
—Walter Thabit, "Planning and Advocacy"[1]

Where is progressive community planning going, what are its prospects, and what kind of strategy is needed to advance progressive planning in New York City and other global cities? This chapter is for the community planners and organizers who are asking these questions and for the students and professionals who ought to be asking them.

The stories of New York City's community plans illustrate the strategic importance of strengthening *community land*. Long-term planning should inventory community land and outline strategies to preserve and expand it. Community land can include a wide variety of land-tenure systems but should be subject to democratic control and respect principles of economic, social, and environmental justice at citywide, regional, national, and global levels. Methods for strengthening community land include ownership and control by nonprofits, community land trusts, and public agencies; public land banking; rent and eviction controls; limits on equity gains from real estate; land-use and zoning regulations; and participation in budget making.

Community planners need to understand and operate in the middle of *conflict*, *contradictions*, and *complexity*. Community and real estate are not homogeneous, and each is characterized by complex internal relations, conflicts, and moments of consensus. Community organizers and planners need to distinguish tactical and strategic allies, know how and when to advance and retreat, negotiate agreements, and change position.

In the end, community planning can be part of multiple struggles for political power that take place at local, regional, national, and global levels.

Community planners are in a unique position to demonstrate in concrete terms how community land can be used to *prevent displacement and gentrification and to eliminate environmental injustices.* There is no simple method or formula for balancing the struggle against noxious facilities and the struggle for development without gentrification. But community land is of strategic importance, and community planning can be one of the most powerful tools for identifying specific strategies and tactics to preserve, improve, and sustain healthy neighborhoods.

Progressive community planning—planning that seeks to achieve local and global equality, social inclusion, and environmental justice—is not a set of values that every community planner necessarily shares or propagates. Those of us who are committed to progressive planning, however, need to have a better understanding of how it plays out in the real world of community planning. We need to look critically at the ways that our professional work, individually and collectively, contributes to our objectives of social justice.[2]

The Challenges Ahead

It would be naïve to think that the rising tide of community-based planning, as impressive as it may be, will necessarily continue to grow or even survive. Government leaders have yet to display the political will needed to help community planning grow beyond this insurgent stage. Mayor Bloomberg's West Side stadium and Olympics 2012 bombs were defused, but there are likely to be many more explosive devices, like Brooklyn's Atlantic Yards, that will erode established neighborhoods, use public funding to expand private fortunes, and undermine community plans. In early 2007, Mayor Bloomberg announced a set of principles to guide long-term planning for the city, PlaNYC2030, but omitted any significant role in decision making for communities.[3] Borough presidents and City Council members have little incentive to promote community-based planning because it can dilute their powers in a system in which they have to fight for every bit of it.

Megaprojects, new luxury enclaves, and big-box stores are still on the horizon. For example, after losing a first round to neighborhoods and organized labor, Wal-Mart is determined to make a breakthrough in favor of giant, suburban-style, auto-dependent commercial development in the outer boroughs that will further erode the cohesiveness of neighborhoods.[4] Real estate values continue to go through the ceiling (even if the boom has begun to slow), legal protections for tenants are under siege, more affordable housing is being lost than created, and the future for displacement and gentrification appears bright.[5] When the real estate bubble bursts, the neighborhoods with people of modest incomes will pay the heaviest price relative to their assets, as was seen in the wholesale abandonment of buildings in the 1960s and 1970s. All of this may or may not spur more protest and activism, and it will not necessarily strengthen community planning. It really depends on us.

In the long run, structural divisions of race and class will continue to separate neighborhoods, the city, and the region and undermine democratic planning until people from urban social movements with the courage to confront inequalities rise to positions of leadership. And until there is an end to imperial and neocolonial thinking that demonizes the other, new immigrant communities will continue to remain outside the realm of political power where land-use controls are guarded as tools of nativist privilege. New Yorkers can help loosen real estate's control over neighborhoods by continuing to fill the city's public places in protest, and local successes will be strengthened by solidarity with the urban and rural social movements throughout the world that are declaring "We won't move" and "Another world is possible." Democratic community planning cannot be accomplished in New York without linking up with others who are confronting unbridled global capital.

The obstacles facing community planning are enormous, and its most reliable advocates and allies are part of the broader movements for progressive social change in the city—including movements for environmental justice, affordable and low-income housing, sustainable development, accessible and quality health care and child care, multicultural education, living wages, gender equality, and transportation justice. The city's progressive movements, however, tend to be fragmented and oriented around single issues. They came together in 1990 to win City Hall for David Dinkins, but were then unable to implement a progressive, alternative policy agenda for the city. The permanent government, lobbyists, technocrats, and professional insiders never yielded the reins of power, and community planners did not know how to grasp them. And when they did get a little piece of power, they were often overwhelmed with both the day-to-day minutiae of government operations and the complex institutional obstacle course through which any new initiative must navigate. Progressives must learn to be both good managers and strong advocates for equality and justice, demonstrating in practice that indeed another world is possible.

The city's progressive movements will need to end the tyranny of angry white men like Rudolph Giuliani over local politics. But to do so will require an extraordinary coming together of the beautiful mosaic of diverse communities that David Dinkins hypothesized. Such a task is too important, however, to be left to elected officials who have been trained in a political culture that rewards timidity, behind-the-scenes deal making, and ethnic politics instead of advocacy for economic and social justice. Looking back on the extraordinary role played by progressive women in defending the city's neighborhoods—Bella Abzug, Jane Benedict, Hortense Gabel, Yolanda García, Frances Goldin, Jane Jacobs, Margarita López, Ruth Messinger, Marie Runyon, Beverly Moss Spatt, Jane Woods, and many more—it might be that women will finally have a chance to do what generations of male leadership have been unable to.

A Ten-Point Strategy for Community-Based Planning

Strategies for land
1. Expand the public trust, and consolidate community land.
2. Connect land and people.
3. Consolidate the urban commons.
4. Create a land bank for the commons.
5. Regulate the commons.
6. Create more community land trusts.

Strategies for people
7. Promote quality of life instead of the growth machine.
8. Think locally, regionally, and globally.
9. Take comprehensive planning back to the future.
10. Think of the seventh generation.

1. Expand the public trust, and consolidate community land. Community land is a powerful instrument for securing affordable housing and fighting displacement and gentrification. It can be a key element in securing long-term benefits for neighborhoods that are successful in reducing and eliminating the concentration of noxious facilities. It can be a powerful tool for environmental justice.

By helping to expand the commons, community planning will confront the global practices of privatization and budgetary austerity that have become the hallmarks of neoliberalism. If planning starts with the assumption that nothing can be implemented without a big private partner (who usually turns out to be the senior partner), it has relinquished the most powerful tools for controlling the use of land—public and nonprofit entities that operate in the public domain. Let the experience with New York City parks be a warning: a handful of well-endowed park conservancies like the Central Park Convervancy raise funds for well-maintained playgrounds in and near wealthy neighborhoods and host profitable concessions, while the city's Department of Parks has a budget under siege that cannot adequately maintain parks in most neighborhoods. Park improvements everywhere increasingly depend on revenues from these public-private partnerships. Payments in lieu of taxes and tax increment financing must be stopped. They are financial bonanzas for private developers and will impoverish public services throughout the city. It is time to revitalize the public sector so that it serves the public.

2. Connect land and people. Using a definition of *land* as a set of relations and not a thing (see chapter 1), land-use planning needs to be redefined in theory and practice. The city's planning bureaucracy has been unable to make the connections between land and people. Environmental concerns are referred to the Department of Environmental Protection, sanitation concerns to the Department of Sanitation, and transportation to the Department of Transportation. In the real world of neighborhoods and urban living, these are indivisible, but there is no Department of Neighborhoods that looks at the whole and not just the parts. Community boards might serve this function but they have neither the resources nor the mandate. The transportation network needs to be planned for cleaner air and safer streets, not just to move traffic. We need to plan to reduce waste and its impacts on public health, not just take out the garbage. Daily decisions in government should be informed by an understanding of environmental impacts on people and not just relegated to developer-sponsored environmental impact statements.

While in some ways New York City government has been ahead of the nation's other big cities—in mass transit and affordable housing, for example—it is far behind when it comes to planning for our air, water, and food, three basic elements for sustaining life in the city. A city's airshed is tied to its land. The federal government's strict clean air rules for fuel and vehicles have helped clean the air significantly since the 1970s, but the city itself has done little to improve the air by limiting traffic and energy use. The high density and mass transit that make New York City a pioneer in the fight against urban sprawl are not the result of progressive environmental policy but rather unintended consequences of a dynamic real estate industry, and the city lags when it comes to maximizing the environmental benefits of high density because real estate exerts an inordinate influence on local environmental policy.

The city's watersheds are tied to its land. Federal policy and funding plus industrial flight have had more to do with securing clean surface water than city policy. The federal government forced the city to build fourteen waste-water plants and put up the money for them. The federal government forced the city to stop ocean dumping. Entirely off the radar screen of planners are the polluted underground aquifers in the city—its many natural streams that are covered with concrete and asphalt. Stewardship of the land should value the water under the streets, in the bay, and in local rivers and not just around the upstate reservoirs that supply drinking water or value-enhancing, odorless waterfront views.[6]

The city's foodshed is tied to its land. Land in the city is treated as alien to the production and quality of food, as if it were external to urban life and instead the sole responsibility of food conglomerates and supermarkets. Community-assisted agriculture, community gardens, farmers' markets, and urban agriculture strengthen our connection with land in and around the city. Foodshed planning is a public health priority because obesity and diabetes, especially among children, have reached epidemic proportions.[7] Foodshed planning plus planning for transportation, recreational, and educational systems can also encourage exercise and help make a healthy and active city.[8]

The quality of buildings is connected to the land and the well-being of people. Poor Indoor air quality is as significant a contributor to poor health as is outdoor air quality. Beyond reforming the outmoded building code so that new buildings will not be sick buildings, we need to find ways that all of the buildings in our neighborhoods are healthy. The most practical way to make every building and neighborhood energy-efficient and healthy for its occupants is to break down the barriers between private and public spaces, promoting the improvement of both environments. We have to plan for green neighborhoods, cities, and regions, not just for new green buildings that sell at a premium on the luxury market.[9]

Reestablishing the link between land, air, water, food, and buildings also helps reestablish the severed ties between urban planning and public health that linked these two professions at their birth.[10] We may need to introduce health impact statements for every new project to help us be mindful of health, but these will be useless if they are based on the narrow approach now followed with environmental impact statements, which are merely disclosure documents and not planning tools. In the end, we should work toward transforming the relationship between people, land, and the environment through holistic, health-based approaches to community planning that take into account the complexity of urban life, including the psychological, symbolic, cultural, and spiritual functions of land.

Reestablishing a connection between land and people is increasingly a global question as more of the world's population becomes urbanized in ways that break the historic ties of people with land. Urban land in the largest global cities is increasingly monopolized by financial conglomerates for whom urban places are fundamentally the same as microchips or movies and other commodities traded in the global marketplace. Pulled into the vortex of globalized commodity production are land and its mineral components, crops, buildings, landscapes, water, and people. Antiglobal social movements like the Anti-Coke Campaign and the movement against genetically modified foods are organizing to reclaim their connections with the land.[11]

3.   Consolidate the urban commons.   Given the wealth and power of the Trumps and Vornados, isn't the idea of building an urban commons a quixotic dream? In fact, if we take an inventory of the commons today, much urban land is already in the commons. What remains is to acknowledge it, guarantee its stewardship, and make it better. First, a substantial portion of land in the city is already under some form of public ownership or control and outside the circuit of commodity exchange. About 30 percent of all land in the city is publicly owned streets and sidewalks. We can put the public on public streets and end the monopoly of private cars, and we can plan our stoops and sidewalks so that they are high-quality public spaces. Of the remaining 70 percent of land, about half is used for infrastructure, public institutions, community facilities, and open space. The other half is already developed, and 5 percent of that is used for public or nonprofit housing. Over half of the city's developable vacant land is in peripheral areas, especially on Staten Island, where land prices are not yet high enough to produce pressures for significant numbers of new private housing units. Some of this land can be put in the public trust (and not just as backyard green space for Staten Islanders). About 30 percent of the city's developable land is tax-exempt, and though the institutions (like universities and hospitals) that own much of this land do not necessarily operate in the public interest and some are worse than private developers when it comes to addressing the public interest, a lot of this land will be kept off the market for a long time to come.

4. Create a land bank for the commons.   The good news is that a sizeable urban commons already exists. The bad news is that there is little space left to expand it. With so little land that is privately owned and zoned for development, the pressures remain intense to develop in these central locations and keep them out of the commons. This also increases pressures to shrink the commons by converting low-cost housing to market-rate housing and upzoning selected outlying areas. The solution that has yet to be tried is for the city to plan in partnership with neighborhoods for a more sustainable, long-range growth strategy that meets local as well as regional needs and at the same time expands the commons.

In the long-term future, however, there is one instrument that could help expand the commons—land banking. The proportion of land owned by the city could have been higher if government had not foolishly divested itself of so many vacant lots over the last forty years. The city could have retained ownership and leased its land to private or nonprofit owners for public purposes, such as low-income housing. The city could have sold the land with deed restrictions that incorporated community objectives—for example, stipulations that housing remain affordable to people with modest incomes in perpetuity. Instead, the city sold much of the land without any serious land-use planning. Good land in areas served by subways was given away so that low-density, low-quality housing could be built following the Charlotte Gardens model (see chapter 4). Individual lots in many neighborhoods were auctioned off to the highest bidder with no restrictions.

All of this was done because of an ideological rigidity that was promoted by the real estate industry for its own financial reasons and that saw land banking by the city as practically un-American. The next time around, community planners will have to fight harder against the myth that the city should not land bank because it is bad for development or because government cannot possibly plan. In the city of Stockholm, almost all land was at one time land-banked. This was not a policy dreamed up by socialists. The city was built on land ceded by the crown, and planned high-density neighborhoods in the suburbs were built around mass transit stops in one of the world's best examples of orderly planned growth. If land is simply given away to the highest bidder, the future of the city will be controlled by the bidders and not by the people who live and work there and must live with the consequences. Community planners in New York City have already demonstrated that when challenged they have lots of good ideas about how to plan for growth in their neighborhoods and beyond. Publicly assembled land could and should be subject to democratically developed community planning.

Land banking makes sense everywhere in the world because it is a precondition for social control over new development. If developable land is in the hands of multiple private owners, the owners retain the greatest power in the planning process. Competition among them may sometimes make any sensible land development impossible. Ironically, this is the very contradiction that leads governments to undertake urban renewal programs to assemble private land for redevelopment. But land banking with community involvement and planning can guarantee that new development does not have to rely on the urban renewal bulldozer and displace existing residents and businesses.

5. Regulate the commons. Zoning and land-use regulation can ensure that privately owned land is used and developed in ways that meet community needs, effectively placing it in the commons. Too often, however, local activists have to spend their time fighting against zoning changes to prevent the worst from happening instead of using land-use regulations to make the best happen. In other words, land-use regulation is too often reactive, not proactive.

A fundamental principle is worth restating here: private ownership of land *by itself* is not the obstacle, just as public ownership is not necessarily the solution. More generally, *the failure to control the use of land through an open democratic process* is the central problem. The problem is not development but the lack of democratic control over development through community planning. While current zoning could theoretically triple the size of the city, in reality zoning restrictions in large parts of the city seriously limit the amount and type of development, and the costs of land and development make growth prohibitive in other places.

Zoning devices like special districts, special permits, contextual zones, natural districts, mixed-use districts, and inclusionary zoning can be used to implement planning objectives, but they are more often set up as defensive measures in reaction to proposed development. The

Department of City Planning (DCP) is forever pressing for more as-of-right zoning because it follows the myth of market magic and gives greater freedom to developers. But as-of-right regulations only postpone the resolution of disputes over land use and fail to resolve them. Other tools for community planning that are already in place include landmark preservation districts, city tax policies that now encourage conversions and new construction but could be used to stimulate other types of development or land preservation, and tax benefits for elderly homeowners.

As this book's case studies on waterfront neighborhoods demonstrate, DCP today is aggressively upzoning in areas of recent interest to real estate developers following a three-prong approach founded on the neoliberal principle that social benefits must be tied to private development. The strategy involves (1) *mixed-use zoning*, which is applied in a way that instead encourages single-use residential development and produces a de facto residential zone; (2) *waterfront zoning*, which links the development of waterfront public access to private residential and commercial development and effectively privatizes the waterfront; and (3) *inclusionary zoning*, which in New York City is optional and not mandatory and in practice provides a small number of affordable housing units along with a large number of luxury units while effectively displacing many more affordable units from neighborhoods. Community planners need to confront this three-headed monster and propose progressive alternatives that preserve and encourage mixed use, create public parks on the waterfront, and mandate new affordable housing while preserving existing affordable units.

New York City has one of the most complex arrays of land-use tools. They were put in place because people demanded that their legislators take action to limit the market. But what is needed throughout the city is not just a giant toolkit of techniques but conscious and comprehensive strategies, neighborhood by neighborhood, that combine and integrate all of these mechanisms in a way that allows communities to control their markets and their destinies for generations to come. In the long run, this will help communities gain control of land.

New York's developed system of land-use controls offers many lessons for other global cities, even as they are under pressure to reduce regulations. One of the greatest paradoxes is that this giant center of private real estate has one of the most complex and developed systems of land-use control in the world. Those who are struggling elsewhere to impose greater public control on land use should appreciate the New York City lesson.

6. Create more community land trusts. The community land trust is one of the most underutilized instruments for community planning in the nation's cities. Land trusts in the United States are mostly located in rural areas to preserve farmland and wilderness.[12] These rural trusts tend to be financed by philanthropy. For example, in the area north of San Francisco, the Marin Agricultural Land Trust has helped keep the majority of land in northern Marin County free from runaway subdivisions. This has been a huge benefit to residents of this wealthy area, but the question for those of us hunkered down on the New York City waterfront is how can we achieve this kind of control in a huge city that has hundreds of neighborhoods and faces intense development pressures? Efforts to bring the rural land trust to the cities tend to deal with open space, not housing. The nationwide Trust for the Public Land, along with other groups, is working in New York and other cities and has helped preserve community gardens and parkland in the five boroughs. However, some of this land is in neighborhoods where land preservation and social exclusion go hand in hand.

The community land trust is a potential model for cities like New York because it is used to preserve affordable housing. There are some 160 community land trusts in the United States, many of which provide low-cost housing in cities.[13] As described in chapter 3, two land trusts in the city protect low-income housing by providing low-cost long-term leases to tenant-run mutual housing associations.[14] In neighborhoods struggling to stop displacement and the homogeneity of gentrification, land trusts can be a powerful tool. Land trusts can take land out of the speculative market and preserve it for affordable housing in perpetuity. When the housing is owned and managed by limited-equity cooperatives and government subsidies are used, the cost of the housing portion can also be written down drastically. The question now is how to get this for everyone who needs it.

In Boston's Roxbury neighborhood, the Dudley Street Neighborhood Initiative started a community land trust. But it also achieved something that every neighborhood should have in its tool kit of land-use controls. It got the City of Boston's powerful Redevelopment Authority to delegate its power of eminent domain. This enabled the Initiative to assemble the vacant lots it needed to build new housing and stop dumping in the neighborhood and ensure that development met the priorities set out in the neighborhood plan.[15] Unlike its government sponsor, the Dudley Street Neighborhood Initiative used eminent domain without displacing people. New York City's Department of Housing Preservation and

Development, on the other hand, keeps a tight fist on its urban renewal powers and has given away too much to developers who contribute more to the mayors' campaigns than the neighborhoods they build in. Although in many neighborhoods, the department acknowledges the priorities of community development corporations, community-based organizations should not have to beg for the land that should be theirs and waste precious resources navigating the arcane land-disposition process. The city should cede full control over city-owned vacant land to organizations that will use it in accordance with democratic, community-initiated 197a plans. Gus Newport, formerly executive director of the Institute for Community Economics in Springfield, Massachusetts, an advocate for community land trusts, became aware of land trusts during his tenure as director of the Dudley Street Neighborhood Initiative and understood their value in preserving affordable housing:

Insufficient affordable housing is being developed to fulfill the need, and most that is developed remains affordable only during the terms of the initial financing, due to relatively short-term subsidies, after which time it reverts to market rates. As a result, over the longer term, public affordable housing resources actually aid gentrification, eventually displacing the very people they were meant to assist.[16]

7. Promote quality of life instead of a growth machine.   Community planners need to develop alternatives to the growth machine orthodoxy that makes the number of new jobs and housing units the sole criterion for evaluating plans. We need to reinvent the concept of quality of life and define it very concretely and specifically in our own terms, not according to the slogans of angry politicians who try to sweep homeless people off the streets. Quality of life has to do with the health and well-being of all individuals regardless of where they live and work. As Andre Gorz once noted, economic growth has stopped improving living conditions, and higher wages alone will not improve the quality of life: "Living better depends less and less on individual consumer goods the worker can buy on the market, and more and more on social investments to fight dirt, noise, inadequate housing, crowding on public transportation, and the oppressive and repressive nature of working life."[17]

The community planning movement has at times followed the lead of grassroots organizations that believed that government's main development objective is a quantitative increase in jobs and housing. In the 2005 mayoral elections, the leading candidates dueled over who could produce the most jobs and housing, and many community and civic groups encouraged the bidding war without demanding a debate about the quality of community life beyond the numbers. What good are more jobs and higher salaries if rents go up, people are forced to move and commute longer distances, and the poorest neighborhoods get all the local unwanted land uses? What good are more affordable housing units if they are overwhelmed by luxury units and force people out of existing affordable units when they neither need nor want to move? If new jobs include low-wage, dead-end jobs without benefits and require moving from one part of the region to another, how is that desirable development? And if more jobs and housing do not also mean meeting neighborhood needs for schools, health care, transportation, and other services, they could instead result in greater burdens on an already stressed infrastructure.

8. Think locally, regionally, and globally.   The strongest local strategy is a global one. Nothing that is done in the city will have any durable value unless it is linked to the world beyond. The administrative boundaries of the City of New York contain less than a third of the population in the New York region, even though the city captures much of the region's financial resources. Its greatest regional resource is people, not financial markets. Regional coalitions for affordable housing, public transportation, and environmental protection need to grow and challenge the fragmented governmental framework that is unable to plan in the public interest because local elected officials are wedded to narrow local property interests. New York City's housing crisis is exacerbated by exclusionary zoning in the suburbs. There can be no resolution of the city's traffic congestion as long as the suburbs continue to add lanes to the expressways that lead into the city. And as long as state legislatures cannot be persuaded to increase financing for the central cities, state expenditures will continue to reinforce local economic inequalities.

There is no neat divide between New York City and the suburbs. The dualistic central city/suburban, black/white contradictions of the 1960s no longer have much meaning. The majority of New York City's working-class neighborhoods have less in common with the city's Silk Stocking districts than they do with the scores of smaller cities in the region and the growing numbers of ethnically diverse working-class suburbs. The community-planning movement can help create the conditions that will break the institutional stagnation of local government planning and cross the artificial lines of political jurisdiction that keep people from organizing for progressive change.

Urban planners have been looking in the wrong places for solutions to the fragmentation and lack of planning in the New York City region. For all of its efforts and corporate support, the Regional Planning Association, working at the regional level, has been unable to unlock the key to regional planning after some eighty years of trying. As demonstrated by the Organization of Waterfront Neighborhoods plan and the Tri-State Transportation Campaign, for example, progressive community-based planning needs to engage with regional organizing efforts, and some of the strongest support for regional planning comes from community-based organizations. The race and class divisions in the region, however, are perhaps the most significant obstacle, and progressive community planning has done a better job of confronting these divisions than the professional planners. They are the best hope for regional planning.

The city's community-based movements have historically played an important role in changing national urban policies and must continue to do so. Scores of local community groups join national advocacy networks, such as the National Low Income Housing Coalition, because it is virtually impossible to sustain neighborhood-based development without direct or indirect government support. Although direct federal government spending on poverty reduction and urban development continues to decline, indirect subsidies through tax incentives and abatements continue to mushroom. Despite the promotion of public-private partnerships, privatization, and the neoliberal city since the 1970s, the urban infrastructure could not survive today without federal aid. This will be limited for many years to come by the federal government's huge debt resulting from the Iraq war and military budget but for cities there is clearly no private alternative to an expanded public commitment.

9. Take comprehensive planning back to the future.   Putting all these elements together is still not enough because the whole is greater than the sum of its parts. Community planning forces dialogues within neighborhoods that look at all aspects of life in the city, region, and world. Community planning is resurrecting and transforming the discredited, orthodox rational-comprehensive planning approaches (see chapter 1) by making comprehensiveness an open, democratic and participatory process that is no longer the privileged domain for technocrats. I learned about the value of holistic approaches to planning in my decades of work as a community planner, mostly from community activists whose own daily lives force them to experience the many interrelated aspects of community life. To maximize their political effectiveness, they are also compelled to understand the relationships between their neighborhood and the urban region, national urban policies, and globalized trends. I have often found them more capable of thinking comprehensively and globally than the technocratic urban planners whose sterile world views of cities are formed by looking at aerial photographs and color-coded maps. This is not the rational-comprehensive planning advanced by Baron Haussmann in his nineteenth-century plan to wipe out the working-class neighborhoods of central Paris. It is a new holistic, progressive community planning.[18]

10. Think of the seventh generation.   Community planning needs to break away from the narrow paradigms of strategic planning that migrated to it from a business model that is incapable of thinking past the next investment cycle. There are other ways to look at the future. The Great Law of the Iroquois Confederacy, for example, states that "In our every deliberation, we must consider the impact of our decisions on the next seven generations."

Planning by corporations, City Hall, and communities rarely looks beyond five or ten years, which is a very short-term horizon in a city where major projects take at least that long from the time they are proposed to the time they are built. The bogus practice of environmental impact assessment, which at most looks ten years into the future, is thoroughly inadequate as a tool except for the planning firms and law firms that earn large fees for preparing those assessments. With global climate changes, diminishing energy sources, disappearing natural species, and escalating global inequalities, it is time to change the way that decisions about our living environment are made.

True, seven generations is a long time—nearly two centuries—and no one, including highly trained professional planners and futurists, can predict how conditions will change or guarantee that plans will remain valid over long periods of time. But planning for the seventh generation should not be understood as yet another prosaic, modernist tool for rational planning based on simplistic linear cause-effect relations. It is a way of thinking that should govern deliberation and decision making. It means asking the question, "Will our plans meet the needs of the next seven generations?" even if our answers cannot be quantified and verified with any degree of certainty. Right now, no one bothers to ask the question. Had that question been posed before the launch of the oil economy and private automobile almost a hundred years ago, we might not be facing global warming or urban environmental and health crises today.

Some cultures may well challenge the whole notion of planning because they do not share the view that the world is divided between past, present, and future. If the world is timeless, what fundamental difference is there among human actions in all three periods? While modern Western philosophy interprets such thinking as an invitation to paralysis, it could also be an entrée to a new, more humane approach to planning. It calls into question our traditional focus on land, which fetishizes its future value and devalues its past and present.

The Campaign and Task Force for Community-Based Planning

Some concrete steps are being taken toward progressive community-based planning in New York City. By the end of the 1990s, community planners in New York became frustrated with the lack of interest and support by government for community plans. City agencies did not help much with 197a plans, and once the plans were finished and approved, they were ignored (see chapter 6). In 2001, a group of community planners formed the Campaign for Community-based Planning, which brought the issue before candidates in the 2001 city election. The Campaign created a Community-Based Plannning Task Force that imported from other cities elected officials who supported relatively successful community planning, held a forum with them and the mayoral candidates, and met with City Council candidates. In 2004, it organized a summit that developed detailed recommendations on how to improve community planning in New York.[19] The Task Force includes twenty-two community-based organizations, civic, and professional groups and twelve community boards and receives staff support from the Municipal Art Society Planning Center.

The Task Force has three main objectives. First, community boards and community-based organizations should have the resources that they need to plan. Community boards should have professional planners, and their members and staff should receive training so they can assume greater responsibilities in the land-use review and planning processes. The average community board in New York has a population of 135,000, larger than the capital of New York State, yet their budgets are only about $200,000 each. City Hall should not continue to complain about the way community boards operate unless it is prepared to equip them to do better.

Second, community boards need to be more representative of their diverse populations. Too often, the only criterion for community board membership is loyalty to the borough president or City Council member, and some boards have been run by the same small group of people for decades. The city's new immigrants, youth, and minorities should be represented, as should all neighborhoods within the community district. Many community-based organizations are reluctant to have community boards receive more resources unless they become more inclusive and democratic, and giving community boards more power and resources without opening them up would only make things worse for community planning. All community boards should work closely with community-based organizations, and no board should be able to declare that it alone represents the community.

Third, community plans need to be implemented. This requires a political commitment from the mayor, borough presidents, and City Council members. Although elected officials often act as if community planning means ceding some of their own powers, they need to be shown how it can ultimately give greater power and protection to those elected officials who stand behind a united community-planning process. Perhaps most important for implementation is the need to link community planning with the budget process. The plans should have budgets, which ought to be coordinated with the city's capital and expense budget process. Government agencies should assume responsibility for implementing plan elements and monitor the implementation process. Lessons can be learned from the participatory budgeting process that is used in many Brazilian cities as a tool of community planning. For example, every year in the city of Porto Alegre, which is about the size of Queens, some 40,000 people take part in the process of shaping the city's budget.[20] In New York, there is only one public budget consultation a year in each of the five boroughs.

Community planning should not just stake out a bigger space in the city's planning world but must completely change the way that the city plans. The building blocks for citywide planning policy—which itself ought to be a part of regional policy and the basic framework within which community planning takes place—should be 197a plans. The only hope for the Regional Plan Association agenda, in fact, is the expansion of inclusionary community planning in New York City and the inner suburbs, which have more in common with the city than the exurban periphery. The city and region are too large and complex for a single master plan, but a process of integrated, multilevel planning is feasible and has been working in places like Holland, Germany, and Sweden for decades.[21]

They Did It in Rochester!

None of the recommendations of the Community-Based Planning Task Force are particularly radical, and most have been implemented in other U.S. cities where community planning has received significant government support. In almost all of these cities, neighborhood-based protest movements that were conscious about issues of racial justice helped to generate this support. For example, after directing the local Urban League for twenty-one years, William A. Johnson Jr. was elected mayor of Rochester, New York. Johnson, who spoke on two occasions at events hosted by the Community-Based Planning Task Force, understood how difficult it was for African American neighborhoods like his own to get their priorities dealt with by City Hall. So in 1994, he organized a program called Neighbors Building Neighborhoods and gave neighborhood groups authority to plan and set their budget priorities—as part of a partnership with City Hall, not as a downloading of responsibilities or a miraculous abdication of the mayor's power.[22]

In Seattle, Mayor Norman Rice, an African American with local neighborhood roots, felt so strongly about the need for community planning that he created the Neighborhood Planning Office to do it, sidestepping the official planning agency, which had proven itself to be an obstacle in the past. The mayor's team of eleven community organizers and planners was given the mandate to help the city's neighborhood organizations develop their plans and connect local activists with information and experts from city agencies. Each community received funds to hire its own planner. The mayor's office organized local planning committees and also worked with Seattle's equivalent of New York's community boards. In the space of four intense years (1994 to 1998), thirty-eight community plans were completed. Richard Conlin, chair of the City Council's Committee on Neighborhoods, Sustainability, and Community Development, took responsibility for coordinating implementation of the plan recommendations, including specific projects as well as changes in overall city policy and practice that were proposed by more than one neighborhood plan. Some 1,200 of these changes were implemented in the two years after the plans were completed. Seattle's Department of Neighborhoods, with an annual budget of around $4.5 million in 2001, also implemented specific plan recommendations. The Seattle neighborhood plans were done in the context of the already approved Seattle Comprehensive Plan, which is mandated by the state of Washington. Contrary to the assertion often made by skeptics who believe community-based planning is equivalent to not-in-my-backyard opposition to undesirable projects, every one of the thirty-eight community plans accepted the growth targets proposed by the city administration.[23]

Under African American mayors, the cities of Baltimore and Houston also embarked on community-planning initiatives. In Minneapolis, Milwaukee, and many other cities, government has financed community-planning efforts. So it can be done in big, diverse cities if there is a political will. Throughout the United States, a different kind of community planning, by and for the elite in suburbs and small towns, has excluded instead of included and is still as American as apple pie. We don't need more of that kind of planning.

What Kind of Planning Process?

If New York City's mayor suddenly announced that he would fully support community-based planning in the city's five boroughs, fifty-nine community districts, and hundreds of neighborhoods, he might mark the end of a long struggle to legitimize community planning. But this move would also be the beginning of another long struggle to guarantee the integrity of the process and ensure that it becomes inclusionary, democratic, and progressive, not exclusionary. How can this change happen? Unfortunately, there are no blueprints, and change will not happen smoothly in the real estate capital of the world, where neighborhoods are sharply divided by race and class and the political culture is arguably weak when it comes to democratic power sharing.

Not only are there no blueprints for democratic community planning, but blueprints are usually used to frustrate democracy in planning. A planning process that depends on recipes pulled from a cookbook will produce meaningless plans that might look good on a shelf but will never help change the world. There will be foundations, planning consultants, and professors of urban planning who will try to sell the city on their blueprints for churning out community plans. This would be an easy way out for city bosses (especially if they can give the contracts to their friends), and if these plans failed, the bosses would have someone else to blame. It would delight the city's in-house planners because they would feel vindicated and be absolved forever from having to do any community planning.

As discussed first in chapter 1, strategic planning usually entails establishing goals and objectives, assessing opportunities and constraints, and setting out priorities. Its ultimate objective is to establish consensus. Consensus is not bad, and all plans require some consensus, but how and when to reach consensus are tactical questions and not strategic ones. When consensus becomes the main objective, it has the effect of submerging and obscuring the most important problems and issues that need to be addressed, particularly differences of race and class. The rush to consensus is often driven by the length of a consultant's contract or an elected official's term, not by the demands of long-term political strategy. Consensus is also used as a façade to conceal the differences and inequalities that are inevitably at the heart of every community's life. Under the strategic planning mantra, the visioning process proceeds on the assumption that everyone's vision has equal weight, but that is simply not the case, and there is often little discussion of how the imbalance can be rectified.

The Role of Professional Planners

Throughout most of the world, urban planning emerged from within architecture, engineering, and the building professions. It remains focused on the physical form of cities and the built environment but is still not able to make connections with the everyday economic and social life of cities. City planning in the United States, though linked with the building professions in its early years, is on the whole better able to address these connections. The critiques of Jane Jacobs and Paul Davidoff helped turn the profession away from physical determinism. However, there is now a strong revisionist drift back toward narrow physical planning.

Today students in graduate urban planning programs are eager to learn geographic information systems (GIS) technology, which has now become the basic tool of land-use analysis. GIS can be a powerful tool for physical planning and for revealing social and economic inequalities, patterns of land ownership, and ways to control land use. It can help people visualize alternative futures. Yet the tendency to rely on technological fixes that enhance the role of the professional is a powerful one. Also, GIS is often used the way that planners used hand-colored maps in the past—to mystify the planning process. It can fixate the planning process on the detached aerial view of neighborhoods from above and leave out the view from below at street level and in the everyday lives of people who live and work in communities.

Brightly colored GIS maps are often at the core of Power Point presentations made to silent audiences in darkened rooms. In these circumstances, discussions of land use often skip over the question of the relationship between land and people. The mapping of space fails to deal with places or displacement, which are the core elements of community planning. This does not mean that planners should turn away from GIS or physical planning. On the contrary, progressive planners who would focus on issues of social equity should become experts in physical planning and not cede this arena of expertise to a new technocratic elite. They should see neighborhoods both from below and from above.

Organizing Community Planners

Progressive community planners need to seek out each other and build stronger ties of mutual support. Planners Network was founded in 1975. It is an organization of progressive urban planners, activists, and academics based in North America, and its statement of principles best outlines the framework for progressive planning today:

We believe that planning should be a tool for allocating resources and developing the environment to eliminate the great inequalities of wealth and power in our society, rather than to maintain and justify the status quo. This includes opposition to racial, economic, and environmental injustice, and discrimination by gender and sexual orientation. We believe that planning should be used to assure adequate food, clothing, shelter, medical care, jobs, safe working conditions, and a healthful environment. We advocate public responsibility for meeting these needs, because the private market has proven incapable of doing so.[24]

Planners Network members include professionals, activists, students, and academics from throughout North America who are working on a broad array of local, regional, and national issues related to community planning. These issues include environmental justice, sustainable transportation, the preservation and development of low-income housing, worker-owned enterprises, indigenous planning, planning the healthy and active city, food security, and so forth. This diverse array of activities by urban planners reflects both the maturation and fragmentation of community-based movements: as they grow and begin to tackle issues in more comprehensive and holistic ways, these movements are also driven to specialize to implement their ideas. Many have established alternative community-based institutions based on cooperation instead of competition, and these require professionalism, if not professionals, to ensure their survival.[25] These community-based organizations are the local institutional foundation and testing ground for a new society, though they are also David facing Goliath. Severely limited in a political economy ruled by corporate greed, they can be corrupted and coopted. If they become a conscious part of the historic struggles to stop displacement and to control community land, they can help build the momentum needed to create a better and more just urban environment.

Since *community* is an abstraction, professional planners have to learn how to talk not with abstractions but real people. They must deal with individuals in all their diversity and complexity to begin to understand the communities they are part of. That means young and old, Latino and Indian, janitor and lab technician, tenant and homeowner, gay and straight. Our rich and diverse neighborhoods will not sit down and agree on what's best for the community. Dialogue, debate, and discussion will lead to disagreements about what is most important. Thus, ongoing dialogue, which includes conflict, is as important as consensus. The challenge for community planners is how to manage this dialogue in a way that produces political unity in areas where that is possible, allows creative alternatives space to emerge in other areas, and builds the capacity in the long run for communities, in all their diversity, to control the use of their land. For this, there can be no rigid timetable. The most successful community planning takes generations. While the plan should look ahead seven generations, so should the planning process.

New York City's community planning is insignificant if it is not understood as part of a long history of community organizing to gain control over land—both its production and reproduction—and everyday life. The current struggles in post-Katrina New Orleans are an important signal of the resiliency of those who declare, "We won't move." Working people and small business owners in New Orleans are organizing to prevent powerful real estate interests from evicting them permanently from their communities. They are attempting to build a process of democratic planning in which economic and racial justice are not compromised.[26] To keep these uphill battles in perspective, perhaps we need to think seven generations ahead and ask this question: if the empire fails, as all empires have, then who will control the land?

Notes

Chapter 1

1. Manuel Castells, *The City and the Grassroots* (Berkeley: University of California Press, 1983); Anders Corr, *No Trespassing: Squatting, Rent Strikes and Land Struggles Worldwide* (Cambridge, MA: South End Press, 1999).

2. <http://www.hic-net.org>.

3. <http://www.icahd.org>.

4. <http://www.cohre.org>.

5. Rachel G. Bratt, Michael E. Stone, and Chester Hartman, eds., *A Right to Housing: Foundation for a New Social Agenda* (Philadelphia: Temple University Press, 2006).

6. Chester Hartman, Dennis Keating, Richard LeGates, with Steve Turner, *Displacement: How to Fight It* (San Francisco: Legal Services Anti-Displacement Project, 1981), 3.

7. Community-Based Planning Task Force, *Livable Neighborhoods for a Livable City: Policy Recommendations to Strengthen Community-Based Planning in New York City* (New York: Municipal Art Society Planning Center, 2005).

8. Perhaps the only existing comparable book about community planning is William Peterman, *Neighborhood Planning and Community-Based Development* (Thousand Oaks, CA: Sage, 2000), which is about Chicago neighborhoods. It is also based on the author's participation in community planning.

9. For example, Janet Abu-Loghod, *From Urban Village to East Village* (Oxford: Blackwell, 1994); Jill Jonnes, *South Bronx Rising* (New York: Fordham University Press, 2002); Jan Lin, *Reconstructing Chinatown: Ethnic Enclave, Global Change* (Minneapolis: University of Minnesota Press, 1998); Milagros Ricourt and Ruby Danta, *Hispanas de Queens: Latino Panethnicity in a New York City Neighborhood* (Ithaca, NY: Cornell University Press, 2003); Walter Thabit, *How East New York Became a Ghetto* (New York: New York University Press, 2003).

10. Some of the existing work that deals with the city is in Todd Bressi, ed., *Planning and Zoning in New York City* (New Brunswick, NJ: Rutgers University

Center for Urban Policy Research, 1993); Robert Caro, *The Power Broker: Robert Moses and the Fall of New York* (New York: Vintage, 1975); Robert Fitch, *The Assassination of New York* (New York: Routledge, 1993); Matthew Gandy, *Concrete and Clay: Reworking Nature in New York City* (Cambridge, MA: MIT Press, 2003); and Jane Jacobs, *The Death and Life of Great American Cities* (New York: Vintage, 1961). Existing work on the region includes Michael N. Danielson and Jameson W. Doig, *New York: The Politics of Urban Regional Development* (Berkeley: University of California Press, 1982); Michael K. Heiman, *The Quiet Evolution: Power, Planning, and Profits in New York State* (New York: Praeger, 1988); Robert D. Yaro and Tony Hiss, *A Region at Risk* (Washington, DC: Island Press, 1996).

11. John H. Mollenkopf and Manuel Castells, eds., *Dual City: Restructuring New York* (New York: Russell Sage Foundation, 1992); Susan S. Fainstein, *The City Builders: Property Development in New York and London, 1980–2000* (Lawrence: University of Kansas Press, 2001); Jewel Bellush and Dick Netzer, eds., *Urban Politics New York Style* (Armonk, NY: Sharpe, 1990).

12. This includes, for example, Wayne Barrett, *Rudy! An Investigative Biography of Rudolph Giuliani* (New York: Basic Books, 2000); John Hull Mollenkopf, *Phoenix in the Ashes: The Rise and Fall of the Koch Coalition in New York City* (Princeton, NJ: Princeton University Press, 1992).

13. Tyler Anbinder, *Five Points* (New York: Plume, 2001); Edwin Borroughs and Mike Wallace, *Gotham: The History of New York City to 1898* (Oxford: Oxford University Press, 1999); Kenneth T. Jackson, ed., *The Encyclopedia of New York* (New Haven, CT: Yale University Press, 1995); James Waldon Johnson, *Black Manhattan* (New York: Da Capo Press, 1958); Thomas Kessner, *Capital City: New York City and the Men behind America's Rise to Economic Dominance, 1860–1900* (New York: Simon & Schuster, 2003); Roy Rosenzweig and Betsy Blackmar, *A History of Central Park: The Park and the People* (New York: Holt, 1994).

14. Tom Angotti, "Confronting Globalization: The Role of Progressive Planners," in Tom Angotti and Ann Forsyth, eds., *Progressive Planning Reader* (New York: Planners Network, 2004), 78–80.

15. The work of Andy Merrifield, *Dialectical Urbanism: Social Struggles in the Capitalist City* (New York: Monthly Review Press, 2002); William Sites, *Remaking New York: Primitive Globalization and the Politics of Urban Community* (Minneapolis: University of Minnesota Press, 2003); and Neil Smith, *Gentrification and the Revanchist City* (London: Routledge, 1996), make important contributions in this direction.

16. Or as V. I. Lenin put it in his noted work, "What Is to Be Done?," in *Selected Works* (Moscow: Progress Publishers, 1975), 1: 92–241.

17. Fitch, *Assassination of New York*.

18. In *New State Spaces: Urban Governance and the Rescaling of Statehood* (Oxford: Oxford University Press, 2004), Neil Brenner traces the complex rescaling of state power as a result of the growth of metropolitan regions. According to Brenner, "The long-entrenched primacy of the national scale of political-

economic regulation has been destabilized as new scalar hierarchies of state institutional organization and state regulatory activity have been forged" (3).

19. One such example is Bernie Jones, *Neighborhood Planning: A Guide for Citizens and Planners* (Chicago: American Planning Association, 1990).

20. David Harvey, "The Urban Process under Capitalism: A Framework for Analysis," in Michael Dear and Allen J. Scott, eds., *Urbanization and Urban Planning in Capitalist Society* (London: Methuen, 1981), 91–121.

21. A classical approach to comprehensive planning in the public interest is that of Alan Altschuler, "The Goals of Comprehensive Planning," *Journal of the American Institute of Planners* 31:33 (1965), 186–197. See also Eric Damian Kelly and Barbara Becker, *Community Planning: An Introduction to the Comprehensive Plan* (Washington, DC: Island Press, 2000). The classical critique is in Paul Davidoff, "Advocacy and Pluralism in Planning," *Journal of the American Institute of Planners* 31:4 (November 1965): 331–338, discussed later in this chapter.

22. Stephen Burghardt, ed., *Tenants and the Housing Crisis* (Dexter, MI: New Press, 1971); Joshua B. Freeman, *Working Class New York* (New York: New Press, 2000); Ira Katznelson, *City Trenches: Urban Politics and the Patterning of Class in the United States* (New York: Pantheon, 1981); Ronald Lawson, *The Tenant Movement in New York City* (New Brunswick, NJ: Rutgers University Press, 1986); Richard B. Stoftt, *Workers in the Metropolis: Class, Ethnicity, and Youth in Antebellum New York City* (Ithaca, NY: Cornell University Press, 1990); W. Dennis Keating, Michael B. Teitz, and Andrejs Skaburskis, *Rent Control: Regulation and the Rental Housing Market* (New Brunswick, NJ: Rutgers Center for Urban Policy Research, 1998).

23. Eugene Reps, "Requiem for Zoning," in H. Wentworth Eldridge, ed., *Taming Megalopolis* (Garden City, NY: Anchor, 1964), 746–759.

24. Jamie L. Delemos, "Community-Based Participatory Research: Changing Scientific Practice from Research *on* Communities to Research *with* and *for* Communities," *Local Environment* 11:3 (June 2006): 329–338.

25. Thomas L. Harper and Stanley M. Stein, *Dialogical Planning in a Fragmented Society* (New Brunswick, NJ: Rutgers Center for Urban Policy Research, 2006); John Forester, *Planning in the Face of Power* (Berkeley: University of California Press, 1989). For an example of participatory action research, see Keith Pezzoli, *Human Settlements and Planning for Ecological Sustainability: The Case of Mexico City* (Cambridge, MA: MIT Press, 1998).

26. Leonardo Benevolo, *The Origins of Modern Town Planning* (Cambridge, MA: MIT Press, 1967).

27. Chapter 2 discusses how Garden City ideas influenced the Regional Plan Association in New York. For a review of the major planning theories, see Susan Fainstein and Scott Campbell, eds., *Readings in Planning Theory* (London: Blackwell, 1996).

28. Jacobs, *Death and Life of Great American Cities*. See also Roberta Grandes Gratz, *The Living City* (New York: Simon & Schuster, 1989), a work about New York City that was inspired by Jacobs.

29. Caro, *Power Broker.*

30. Charles Hostovsky, "The Paradox of the Rational Comprehensive Model of Planning," *Journal of Planning Education and Research* 25 (2006): 382–395.

31. Jason Hackworth, *The Neoliberal City* (Ithaca, NY: Cornell University Press, 2007).

32. Ibid., 10.

33. Ibid., 11.

34. Peter Marcuse, "Planners Network at the U.S. Social Forum: Other Cities Are Possible," *Progressive Planning* (Planners Network) 171 (Spring 2007): 33–34.

35. See Peter Hall, *Great Planning Disasters* (Berkeley: University of California Press, 1980).

36. Portions of this section were previously published in Thomas Angotti, "Advocacy and Community Planning: The Legacy," *Progressive Planning* 171 (Spring 2007): 21–24.

37. Davidoff, "Advocacy and Pluralism."

38. See also Paul Davidoff and Thomas Reiner, "A Choice Theory of Planning," *Journal of the American Institute of Planners* 28 (May 1962): 103–115.

39. Norman Krumholz and John Forester, *Making Equity Planning Work* (Philadelphia: Temple University Press, 1990), 256–257.

40. Charles Lindblom, "The Science of Muddling Through," *Public Administration Review* 30 (Spring 1959): 79–88.

41. Dolores Hayden, *Redesigning the American Dream* (New York: Norton, 1984); Dolores Hayden, *The Power of Place: Urban Landscapes as Public History* (Cambridge, MA: MIT Press, 1996); Leonie Sandercock, ed., *Making the Invisible Visible: A Multicultural Planning History* (Berkeley: University of California Press, 1998); and Leonie Sandercock, *Towards Cosmopolis: Planning for Multicultural Cities* (Chichester: Wiley, 1998). Also Leonie Sandercock and Ann Forsyth, "Feminist Theory and Planning Theory: The Epistemological Linkages," in Scott Campbell and Susan Fainstein, eds., *Readings in Planning Theory* (Oxford: Blackwell, 1996), 471–474.

42. Reggie Modlich, Letter to the Editor, *Progressive Planning* 169 (Fall 2006): 39.

43. Ted Jojola, "Indigenous Planning and Tribal Community Development," in Tom Angotti and Ann Forsyth, eds., *Progressive Planning Reader* (New York: Planners Network, 2004), 36–38; Nicholas Christos Zaferatos, "Planning the Native American Tribal Community," *Journal of the American Planning Association* 64:4 (Autumn 1998): 395–410.

44. Julian Agyeman, Robert D. Bullard, and Bob Evans, eds., *Just Sustainabilities: Development in an Unequal World* (Cambridge, MA: MIT Press, 2003); Timothy Beatley and Kristy Manning, *The Ecology of Place: Planning for Environment, Economy, and Community* (Washington, DC: Island Press, 1997); Kent E. Portney, *Taking Sustainable Cities Seriously: Economic Development,*

the Environment, and Quality of Life in American Cities (Cambridge, MA: MIT Press, 2003).

45. Robert D. Bullard, *Dumping in Dixie: Race, Class and Environmental Quality* (Boulder, CO: Westview, 1990); Richard Hofrichter, ed., *Toxic Struggles: The Theory and Practice of Environmental Justice* (Philadelphia: New Society, 1993); Lawrence D. Frank, Peter O. Engelke, and Thomas L. Schmid, *Health and Community Design: The Impact of the Built Environment on Physical Activity* (Washington, DC: Island Press, 2003); Nicholas Freudenberg, Sandro Galea, and David Vlahov, eds., *Cities and the Health of the Public* (Nashville, TN: Vanderbilt University Press, 2006).

46. Marie Kennedy, "From Advocacy Planning to Transformative Community Planning," *Progressive Planning* 171 (Spring 2007): 24–27.

47. Paulo Freire, *Pedagogy of the Oppressed* (New York: Continuum, 2002).

48. There is a rich literature about *communicative planning* that explores how professionals can advance equity issues by sharing information, stories, and knowledge. While communicative theory suggests that planners can play a progressive role and help legitimize progressive ideas and practices, it also gives rise to practices in which the planner is mostly a mediator of conflicts or a professional negotiator, not an advocate. It can lead to the reification of consensus, which often results in outcomes in which the most powerful force the least powerful to come to an agreement. For a strong argument in favor of communicative planning, see Patsy Healey, "Planning through Debate: The Communicative Turn in Planning Theory," in Campbell and Fainstein, *Readings in Planning Theory*, 234–257.

49. Rosabeth Moss Kanter, *Community and Commitment: Communes and Utopias in Sociological Perspective* (Cambridge, MA: Harvard University Press, 1972).

50. Benevolo, *Origins of Modern Town Planning*.

51. Joan Roelofs, "Socialists and Cities," *Progressive Planning* 156 (Summer 2003): 16–20.

52. Karl Marx and Friedrich Engels, *Selected Works* (New York: International, 1968), 97.

53. Friedrich Engels, *The Condition of the Working Class in England* (Moscow: Progress, 1973); Friedrich Engels, *The Housing Question* (Moscow: Progress, 1975); Friedrich Engels, *Socialism: Utopian and Scientific* (New York: International Publishers, 1969).

54. Tom Angotti, "The Socialist City, Still," in Tom Angotti and Ann Forsyth, eds., *Progressive Planning Reader* , (New York: Planners Network, 2003): 11–13; Thomas Angotti, *Metropolis 2000: Planning, Poverty and Politics* (New York: Routledge, 1993), 110–141.

55. Morris Zeitlin, "Soviet Urbanization and Urban Planning," *Political Affairs* 64:4 (April 1985): 27–34; Robert J. Osborne, "How the Russians Plan Their Cities," *Trans-Action* 3:6 (September–October 1966): 25–30.

56. David Harvey, *Spaces of Hope* (Berkeley: University of California Press, 2000), 196.

57. The war of position and biding time are concepts that were used by Italian Communist Antonio Gramsci in formulating a strategy for working-class rule in Italy at a time when the power of the ruling classes was hegemonic. See John M. Cammett, *Antonio Gramsci and the Origins of Italian Communism* (Stanford, CA: Stanford University Press, 1967), 201–212; Anne Showstack Sassoon, *Gramsci's Politics* (Minneapolis: University of Minnesota Press, 1987).

58. Edward J. Kaiser, David R. Godschalk, and F. Stuart Chapin Jr., *Urban Land Use Planning* (Urbana: University of Illinois Press, 1995), 5.

59. Ibid., 8.

60. Sidney Plotkin, *Keep Out: The Struggle for Land Use Control* (Berkeley: University of California Press, 1987).

61. Michael E. Stone, "Social Ownership," in Rachel G. Bratt, Michael E. Stone, and Chester Hartman, eds., *A Right to Housing: Foundation for a New Social Agenda* (Philadelphia: Temple University Press, 2006), 240–260; John Emmeus Davis, *Shared Equity Homeownership: The Changing Landscape of Resale-Restricted, Owner-Occupied Housing* (West Orange, NJ: National Housing Institute, 2006). An early approximation to this concept of social ownership emerged in New York City's housing movement. See Peter K. Hawley, *Housing in the Public Domain: The Only Solution* (New York: Metropolitan Council on Housing, 1978).

62. Tony Hiss, *The Experience of Place* (New York: Vintage, 1990); Dolores Hayden, *The Power of Place: Urban Landscapes as Public History* (Cambridge, MA: MIT Press, 1996).

63. Henri Lefebvre, *The Production of Space* (Cambridge, MA: Blackwell, 1991).

64. Hayden, *Power of Place*, 2–43.

65. Mudrooroo, *Us Mob* (Sydney, Australia: Angus & Robertson, 1995), 200–201.

66. Stephen Hendricks, "Promised Land," *Orion* (July–August 2005): 65.

67. Ibid.

68. Shepard Krech, *The Ecological Indian: Myth and History* (New York: Norton, 1999).

69. The story of Collasai was told to me by villagers during a 1990 visit.

70. Friends of the Commons, *The State of the Commons: 2003/04* (Minneapolis, MN: Tomales Bay Institute, 2003), 3. See also <http://www.onthecommons.org>.

71. Merrifield, *Dialectical Urbanism*, 17.

72. Harvey, *Spaces of Hope*, 58, 59.

73. Engels, *Housing Question*, 20.

74. David Harvey, *The Limits to Capital* (Oxford: Oxford University Press, 1982). The classic work on surplus absorption is Paul A. Baran and Paul Sweezy, *Monopoly Capital* (New York: Monthly Review Press, 1966).

75. Manning Marable, *Black Liberation in Conservative America* (Boston: South End Press, 1997), 9.

76. Frances Fox Piven and Richard A. Cloward, *Regulating the Poor: The Functions of Social Welfare* (New York: Random House, 1971).

77. Merrifield, *Dialectical Urbanism*; Georges Politzer, *Elementary Principles of Philosophy* (New York: International Publishers, 1976).

78. Harvey, *Spaces of Hope*, 170–171.

79. Actually, the concept of strategic planning originated in the Pentagon and migrated to the corporate world, where it became a management tool and then an alternative to the traditional rational-comprehensive planning model as it came under increasing criticism. For a developed view of strategic planning, see Lewis D. Hopkins and Marisa A. Zapata, eds., *Engaging the Future: Forecasts, Scenarios, Plans and Projects* (Cambridge, MA: Lincoln Institute of Land Policy, 2007).

80. Kennedy, "From Advocacy Planning."

81. Sherry Arnstein, "A Ladder of Citizen Participation," *Journal of the American Institute of Planners* 8:3 (July 1969): 216–224. This points to a fundamental difference between representative and participatory democracy. For a discussion of participatory democracy, see Peter Bachrach and Aryeh Botwinick, *Power and Empowerment: A Radical Theory of Participatory Democracy* (Philadelphia: Temple University Press, 1992).

82. Julie Sze, *Noxious New York: The Racial Politics of Urban Health and Environmental Justice*, (Cambridge, MA: MIT Press 2006).

83. There are multiple meanings and interpretations of *gentrification*. See Neil Smith and Peter Williams, eds., *Gentrification of the City* (Boston: Allen & Unwin, 1986); Neil Smith, *The New Urban Frontier: Gentrification and the Revanchist City* (London: Routledge, 1996).

84. See Andrew Grant-Thomas and John A. Powell, "Toward a Structural Racism Framework," *Poverty and Race* 15: 6 (November–December 2006): 3–5.

85. Sze, *Noxious New York*.

86. Howard Zinn, *A People's History of the United States, 1492–Present* (New York: HarperCollins, 1999).

Chapter 2

1. Kenneth T. Jackson, ed, *The Encyclopedia of New York* (New Haven, CT: Yale University Press, 1995), 989–990.

2. Troy Palma, "Home Builders Developing Commercial Characteristics," *Washington Business Journal*, September 15, 2003, <http://washington .bizjournals.com/Washington/stories/2003/09/15/focus11.html>.

3. For more on the concept of the growth machine, see John R. Logan and Harvey L. Molotch, *Urban Fortunes: The Political Economy of Place* (Berkeley:

University of California Press, 1987). See also John Mollenkopf, *The Contested City* (Princeton, NJ: Princeton University Press, 1983).

4. See New York City Partnership, Inc., *The Partnership Blueprint: Strengthening New York as a World City* (New York: New York City Partnership, Inc., 1984).

5. *Crain's New York Business*, April 21, 2003, 34.

6. Donald Trump with Dave Shiflett, *Trump: The America We Deserve* (Los Angeles: Renaissance Books, 2000), 22–25. See also Timothy L. O'Brien and Eric Dash, "Trump's Billionaire Persona Belies Troubles with His Empire," *New York Times*, September 8, 2004, C1, C2.

7. Susan S. Fainstein, *The City Builders: Property Development in New York and London, 1980–2000* (Lawrence: University of Kansas Press, 2001).

8. Centrality is a *use-value*. It serves a purpose independently of any additional value it acquires in a land market—that is, in addition to its *exchange-value*.

9. As noted elsewhere, there are many physical and social barriers to the ripples, which may cause leapfrogging and other variations in the concentric pattern. Temporary troughs in land values can be due to things like wetlands that can't be easily built on or municipal regulations that are unchanging. In the long run, the pattern smooths out.

10. See chapter 1.

11. Kenneth Jackson, *Crabgrass Frontier: The Suburbanization of the United States* (New York: Oxford University Press, 1985).

12. Manuel Castells, *The Rise of the Network Society* (Cambridge, MA: Blackwell, 1996); Manuel Castells, *The Informational City* (Cambridge, MA: Blackwell, 1989).

13. Naomi Klein, *The Shock Doctrine: The Rise of Disaster Capitalism* (New York: Metropolitan Books, 2007).

14. Peter Marcuse, "Housing Policy and the Myth of the Benevolent State," in Rachel G. Bratt, Chester Hartman, and Ann Meyerson, eds., *Critical Perspectives on Housing* (Philadelphia: Temple University Press, 1986), 248–263.

15. See Homefront, *Housing Abandonment in New York City* (New York: Homefront, 1977).

16. See Nadine Brozan, "The Price of 'Wow!' Keeps On Rising," *New York Times*, September 7, 2003, Real Estate 1, 6.

17. Rent controls do not apply to luxury units or new unsubsidized apartments.

18. Peter Marcuse, *Housing Abandonment: Does Rent Control Make a Difference?* (Washington, DC: Conference on Alternative State and Local Policies, 1982).

19. See John H. Mollenkopf and Manuel Castells, eds., *Dual City: Restructuring New York* (New York: Russell Sage Foundation, 1992).

20. Lewis Mumford Center, "Separate and Unequal: Racial and Ethnic Neighborhoods in the Twenty-first Century," <http://mumford1.dyndns.org/cen2000/

SepUneq/ PublicSepDataPages/MonitorPages/5600Monitor.htm>, accessed April 26, 2005. See also Douglas S. Massey and Nancy A. Denton, *American Apartheid: Segregation and the Making of the Underclass* (Cambridge, MA: Harvard University Press, 1993); Norman Fainstein, "Black Ghettoization and Social Mobility," in Michael Peter Smith and Joe R. Feagin, eds., *The Bubbling Cauldron: Race, Ethnicity and the Urban Crisis* (Minneapolis: University of Minnesota Press, 1995), 123–141.

21. On transnational trends in immigration, see Saskia Sassen, *Globalization and Its Discontents* (New York: New Press, 1998); Héctor Cordero-Guzmán, Robert C. Smith, and Ramón Grosfoguel, *Migration, Transnationalization, and Race in a Changing New York* (Philadelphia: Temple University Press, 2001); Andrés Torres, *Between Melting Pot and Mosaic: African Americans and Puerto Ricans in the New York Political Economy* (Philadelphia: Temple University Press, 1995); Frank Bonilla, Edwin Meléndez, Rebecca Morales, and María de los Angeles Torres, *Borderless Borders: U.S. Latinos, Latin Americans, and the Paradox of Interdependence* (Philadelphia: Temple University Press, 1998); Nancy Foner, *From Ellis Island to JFK: New York's Two Great Waves of Immigration* (New Haven, CT: Yale University Press, 2000).

22. For an outline of urban inequalities in the United States, see Peter Dreier, John Mollenkopf, and Todd Swanstrom, *Place Matters: Metropolitics for the Twenty-first Century* (Lawrence: University Press of Kansas, 2001).

23. See Bennett Harrison, *Lean and Mean: Why Large Corporations Will Continue to Dominate the Economy* (New York: Guilford Press, 1994).

24. New York City Department of City Planning, *Citywide Industry Study* (New York: Department of City Planning, 1993).

25. New York City Department of City Planning, *Citywide Industry Study* (New York: Department of City Planning, 1993); New York City Department of City Planning, *Comprehensive Waterfront Plan* (New York: Department of City Planning, 1992).

26. Joshua B. Freeman, *Working Class New York* (New York: New Press, 2000).

27. Because New York City has never been a one-factory town, its diverse manufacturing base helped it avoid being crippled by a single factory closing, in the way that Youngstown, Ohio, was affected when its steel plant shut down. In fact, small industries should do quite well in a densely populated city like New York during this age of flexible production. But because real estate drives the city's land-use policy, industrial areas remain under siege by land developers.

28. For a thorough discussion of the political economy of tourism and urban marketing, see Dennis R. Judd and Susan S. Fainstein, eds., *The Tourist City* (New Haven, CT: Yale University Press, 1999). See also Sharon Zukin, *Landscapes of Power* (Berkeley: University of California Press, 1991).

29. Alexander Reichl, *Reconstructing Times Square: Politics and Culture in Urban Development* (Lawrence: University of Kansas Press, 1999); William R. Taylor, ed., *Inventing Times Square: Commerce and Culture at the Crossroads of the World* (Baltimore: Johns Hopkins University Press, 1999).

30. Daniel Rose, "Real Estate: Evolution of an Industry," *Real Estate Issues* (Fall 2003): 48.

31. Jason Hackworth, "Local Autonomy, Bond Rating Agencies and Neoliberal Urbanism in the United States," *International Journal of Urban and Regional Research* 26:4 (2002): 707–725.

32. Alex Frangos, "Affordable-Housing Empire Fuels Developer's Upscale Aims: Master of Tax-Credit Deals, Stephen Ross Sets Sights on Pennsylvania Station, Buying Apartments in Queens," *Wall Street Journal*, August 22, 2006, A1.

33. Barbara Jarvie, "Vornado Plays Waiting Game," <http://www.globest .com/news/582_582/newyork/146417-1.html>.

34. David Lombino, "'Grand' Profits in Garden Deal Is Vornado's Boast to Investors," *The Sun*, June 8, 2006, 1.

35. Pratt Center for Community Development and Habitat for Humanity NYC, *Reforming New York City's 421-a Property Tax Exemption Program: Subsidize Affordable Homes, Not Luxury Development* (New York: Pratt Center, April 2006); Pratt Center for Community Development and Policy Link, *Increasing Housing Opportunity in New York City: The Case for Inclusionary Zoning* (New York: Pratt Center, October 2004); Tom Angotti, "Inclusionary Zoning," September 2006, <http://www.gothamgazette.com/article/landuse/20060905/12/ 1962>.

36. Lecture at Hunter College, New York City, May 9, 2003.

37. William Sites, *Remaking New York: Primitive Globalization and the Politics of Urban Community* (Minneapolis: University of Minnesota Press, 2003), 25.

38. Tom Angotti and Ron Shiffman, "Megastores Mean Lost New York Jobs," *New York Times*, April 18, 1995, OpEd page. See also Tom Angotti, "Not Ready for Wal-Mart," *Gotham Gazette*, February 2005, <http://www .gothamgazette.com/article/landuse/20050215/12/1321>; Jane Holtz Kay, "The Suburbanization of New York: Home Town, No Town or New Town?," *Progressive Planning* 161 (Fall 2004): 31–33.

39. Karl Polanyi, *The Great Transformation* (Boston: Beacon Press, 1957). Although the U.S. empire's expansion leaped ahead around the end of the nineteenth century, it actually began with the arrival of European settlers, whose first conquest was the appropriation of Indian territories. See Roxanne Dunbar-Ortiz, "The Grid of History: Cowboys and Indians," *Monthly Review* 55:3 (July–August 2003): 83–92. Because Indian tribes had no concept of private property, land to them could never be real estate. The European invasion turned communal land into real estate.

40. Hans Blumenfeld, *The Modern Metropolis* (Cambridge, MA: MIT Press, 1971); Tom Angotti, *Metropolis 2000: Planning, Poverty and Politics* (New York: Routledge, 1993).

41. Angotti, *Metropolis 2000*, ch. 1.

42. Real Estate Board of New York, "REBNY: Resolute in Commitment to the Big Apple's Growth," advertisement, *New York Times*, January 16, 2003, C17.

43. Clifton Hood, *722 Miles: The Building of the Subways and How They Transformed New York* (Baltimore: Johns Hopkins University Press, 1993).

44. See the discussion in chapter 1 and David Harvey, *Spaces of Hope* (Berkeley: University of California Press, 2000), 24–31.

45. Edwin Borroughs and Mike Wallace, *Gotham: The History of New York City to 1898* (Oxford: Oxford University Press, 1999), 55–56.

46. Christine Boyer, *Dreaming the Rational City* (Cambridge, MA: MIT Press, 1987).

47. Roy Rosenzweig and Betsy Blackmar, *A History of Central Park: The Park and the People* (New York: Holt, 1994).

48. Andrew Haswell Green, leader of the Central Park Commission, diverged from Olmstead's vision of a park for passive recreation. Instead, he implemented a vision of the park as a center for cultural activities that would educate and dignify the working masses. Thus, the Metropolitan Museum of Art and Central Park Zoo were among the earliest institutions to punctuate Olmstead and Vaux's rolling country landscape.

49. Richard Plunz, *A History of Housing in New York City* (New York: Columbia University Press, 1990).

50. Roy Lubove, *Progressives and the Slums* (Pittsburgh: University of Pittsburgh Press, 1963).

51. Dennis R. Judd and Todd Swanstrom, *City Politics: Private Power and Public Policy* (New York: HarperCollins, 1994), 98.

52. Julian F. Jaffe, *Crusade against Radicalism: New York during the Red Scare, 1914–1924* (Port Washington, NY: Kennikat Press, 1972).

53. Jacob Riis, *How the Other Half Lives Studies Among the Tenements of New York* (New York: Scribner, 1890). Available at <http://tenant.net/Community/Riis/chap13.html>, accessed February 18, 2005.

54. Some settlement houses were what might be called early examples of faith-based urban programs. Catholic and Protestant churches supported settlement work as part of a missionary paternalism aimed at recruiting souls.

55. Ebenezer Howard, *Garden Cities of Tomorrow* (London: Faber & Faber, 1965).

56. Town and Country Planning Association, *New Towns: The British Experience* (London: Charles Knight, 1972).

57. Michael K. Heiman, *The Quiet Evolution: Power, Planning, and Profits in New York State* (New York: Praeger, 1988).

58. This is the image portrayed by Robert Fitch in *The Assassination of New York* (New York: Routledge, 1993).

59. Tony Schuman and Elliott Sclar, "Race, Class and Space: A Historical Comparison of the Three Regional Plans for New York," *Planners Network* 128 (March–April 1998): 6–11.

60. See John A. Powell, "Addressing Regional Dilemmas for Minority Communities," in Bruce Katz, ed., *Reflections on Regionalism* (Washington, DC: Brookings Institution Press, 2000), 218–246.

61. For example, RPA has supported a community-based planning effort to create a Brooklyn waterfront greenway.

62. Schuman and Sclar, "Race, Class and Space."

63. Kenneth Jackson, *Crabgrass Frontier: The Suburbanization of the United States* (New York: Oxford University Press, 1985).

64. I use the terms *urbanity* and *urbanism* interchangeably to mean the quality of urban life that maximizes the personal and cultural exchange among people in public spaces.

65. The folly of this premise is obvious today, but at that time most urban planners and policy makers went along with it. Walter Thabit, then a planner in the Lower East Side, was a lone voice of sanity in his "Planning and Civil Defense," *Journal of the American Institute of Planners* 24:1 (February 1959): 35–39.

66. June Manning Thomas and Marsha Ritzdorf, eds., *Urban Planning and the African American Community* (Thousand Oaks, CA: Sage, 1997).

67. This may be another example of nondecision making. Peter Bachrach and Morton Baratz, "Two Faces of Power," *American Political Science Review* 52 (December 1962): 947–952.

68. Gwendolyn Wright, *Building the Dream: A Social History of Housing in America* (Cambridge, MA: MIT Press, 1981).

69. Freeman, *Working Class*. With the launching of the cold war, the Truman administration targeted the Soviet Union externally and labor internally. Since New York City was still a strong labor city, it continued to be a target for the anticommunist, antiurban, and anti-immigrant fears of conservatives and nativists. Popularly elected socialists and communists like Congressman Vito Marcantonio, founder of the American Labor Party, were isolated and unable to hold their offices. In 1945, LaGuardia, a close ally of Marcantonio, decided not to run for another term as mayor. In 1946, he was appointed director general of the United Nations Relief and Rehabilitation Administration but resigned in disgust at Washington's withdrawal of financial support for the agency as it embarked on a global anticommunist crusade. Yet even as the city's left and organized labor came under attack during the McCarthy period, labor's base of power was shifting rapidly from big cities to suburbs. Gerald Meyer, *Vito Marcantonio: Radical Politician 1902–1954* (Albany: State University of New York Press, 1989).

70. Robert Caro, *The Power Broker: Robert Moses and the Fall of New York* (New York: Vintage, 1975).

71. Susan S. Fainstein, *The City Builders: Property, Politics, and Planning in London and New York* (Oxford: Blackwell, 1994), 169.

72. Senator McNeil Mitchell and Assemblyman Alfred A. Lama sponsored New York State legislation in 1955 that guaranteed mortgages for middle-income housing development. A smaller city program followed the state model. See also chapter 3.

73. The Swiss-born French architect LeCorbusier (1887–1965) proposed the "tower in the park" model, which combined high-rise buildings with ground-level open space. But LeCorbusier did not conceive of the ground-level open space as public space. Indeed, he urged architects to "kill the street."

74. Beverly Moss Spatt, "A Report on the New York Plan," Report to the New York City Planning Commission, reprinted in *AIP Journal* 36:6 (November 1970): 438–444.

75. Beverly Moss Spatt, *A Proposal to Change the Structure of City Planning* (New York: Praeger, 1971).

76. Interview with Beverly Moss Spatt, March 25, 2005.

77. *Blockbusting* is defined on p. 49 of this chapter.

78. *Redlining* is a practice in which banks and insurance companies refuse to approve financing in certain (usually nonwhite) neighborhoods, effectively by drawing a red line around those areas. Redlining makes it difficult for existing property owners to refinance, get home improvement loans, and sell their properties.

79. David E. Rosenbaum, "Nixon Tapes at Key Time Now Drawing Scant Interest," *New York Times*, December 14, 2003, 43.

80. Roger E. Alcaly and David Mermelstein, *The Fiscal Crisis of American Cities* (New York: Vintage, 1977).

81. Peter D. Salins, "Reviving New York City's Housing Market," in Michael H. Schill, ed., *Housing and Community Development in New York City* (Albany: State Universtiy of New York Press, 1999), 53–71.

82. Dennis W. Keating, Michael B. Teitz, and Andrejs Skaburskis, *Rent Control: Regulation and the Rental Housing Market* (New Brunswick, NJ: Rutgers Center for Urban Policy Research, 1998).

83. Elliott D. Sclar and Richard C. Leone, *You Don't Always Get What You Pay For: The Economics of Privatization* (New York: Century Foundation, 2001).

84. Timothy Williams, "On Randalls Island, Deal with Elite Schools Means New Ball Fields," *New York Times*, February 10, 2007, B3.

85. New York City Department of City Planning, *Comprehensive Waterfront Plan* (New York: Department of City Planning, 1992).

86. Homefront, *Housing Abandonment in New York City*.

87. Marshall Berman, *All That Is Solid Melts into Air* (New York: Penguin, 1988).

88. Chester Hartman and Gregory D. Squires, eds., *There Is No Such Thing as a Natural Disaster* (New York: Routledge, 2006).

Chapter 3

1. The African Burial Ground in lower Manhattan, which was uncovered during the construction of a federal office building in the 1990s, is now a memorial site.

It is interesting to contrast the way that this site was dealt with and the planned memorials at the World Trade Center site. Most of the African Burial Ground was built over, but a tiny plot of adjacent land was reserved as a memorial where some excavated remains were eventually reburied. By contrast, the entire footprints of the two World Trade Center towers will not be built on.

2. James Waldon Johnson, *Black Manhattan* (New York: Da Capo Press, 1958).

3. Ibid., 147.

4. Ibid., 127. See also Howard Zinn, *A Peoples History of the United States* (New York: HarperCollins, 1999), 235–236.

5. Tyler Anbinder, *Five Points* (New York: Plume, 2001), 431–433.

6. See Gwendolyn Wright, *Building the Dream: A Social History of Housing in America* (Cambridge, MA: MIT Press, 1981), 247.

7. Henry George, *Progress and Poverty* (New York: Shalkenbach Foundation, 1956).

8. The Lincoln Institute of Land Policy (<http://www.lincolninst.edu>) and E. F. Schumacher Society (<http://www.smallisbeautiful.org>) draw from aspects of Henry George's philosophy and promote socially responsible land policy.

9. See Ronald Lawson, *The Tenant Movement in New York City* (New Brunswick, NJ: Ruters Universtiy Press, 1986), and Stephen Burghardt, ed., *Tenants and the Housing Crisis* (Dexter, MI: New Press, 1972).

10. W. Dennis Keating, "Rent Regulation in New York City: A Protracted Saga," in W. Dennis Keating, Michael B. Teitz, and Andrejs Skaburskis, *Rent Control: Regulation and the Rental Housing Market* (New Brunswick, NJ: Rutgers Center for Urban Policy Research, 1988), 151–168.

11. Richard Plunz, *A History of Housing in New York City* (New York: Columbia University Press, 1990), 151–163.

12. See Mark Naison, "Tenant Activism in the Great Depression," in Lawson, *Tenant Movement*, 94–133.

13. As an Italian with a Jewish wife, LaGuardia advanced the interests of the newly ascendant European immigrant groups that had been locked out of power by Tammany Hall. But LaGuardia at times lent himself to anti-immigrant measures (such as removing street vendors) that were compatible with the reformers' notions of cleaning up the city.

14. LaGuardia was a founding member of the American Labor Party and a powerful New Deal liberal who was committed to social equality. He enjoyed strong union and working-class support. The first fusion candidate, he joined forces with the conservative Republican Party to get elected but throughout his tenure maintained strong ties with radical Congressman Vito Marcantonio and the American Labor Party. LaGuardia was an energetic and early opponent of fascism at home and abroad.

15. Mike Wallace, "Gotham in World War II" paper presented at the Gotham Center seminar on Postwar New York City, November 19, 2003.

16. Coop City drew many working-class and middle-class residents, mostly white, from Manhattan's Upper West Side and from the South Bronx. In this sense, it helped contribute to neighborhood abandonment and the resegregation of the city. See Lawson, *Tenant Movement.*

17. Bill Price, "Tipping Point: Racism in City Planning," in *Profits Are Destroying Our Homes* (New York: Homefront, 1975), 14.

18. *Berman v. Parker*, 348 U.S. 26 (1954).

19. Robert Caro, *The Power Broker: Robert Moses and the Fall of New York* (New York: Vintage, 1975), 968.

20. Peter Marcuse, "Housing Policy and the Myth of the Benevolent State," in Rachel G. Bratt, Chester Hartman, and Ann Meyerson, eds., *Critical Perspectives on Housing* (Philadelphia: Temple University Press, 1986), 248–263.

21. Mark Naison, *Rent Strikes in New York* (Somerville, MA: New England Free Press, 1967).

22. William Sites, *Remaking New York: Primitive Globalization and the Politicis of Urban Community* (Minneapolis: University of Minnesota Press, 2003).

23. Jane Jacobs, *The Death and Life of Great American Cities* (New York: Vintage, 1961).

24. Tom Angotti, "Jane Jacobs, New York Rebel," *Progressive Planning* 168 (Summer 2006): 28–29.

25. Paul Davidoff, "Advocacy and Pluralism in Planning," *Journal of the American Institute of Planners* 31:3 (November 1965): 331–338. Planners Network publishes the quarterly *Progressive Planning Magazine.* For information, see <http://www.plannersnetwork.org>.

26. Matthew Gandy, *Concrete and Clay: Reworking Nature in New York City* (Cambridge, MA: MIT Press, 2002), 162–177.

27. Saul Alinsky, *Reveille for Radicals* (New York: Vintage, 1946).

28. For an account of community opposition to institutional expansion, see William Worthy, *The Rape of Our Neighborhoods* (New York: Morrow, 1976).

29. Stephen D. Mittenthal and Hans B. C. Spiegel, *Urban Confrontation: City versus Neighborhood in the Model Cities Planning Process* (New York: Columbia University School of Architecture, Institute of Urban Environment, 1970).

30. Derek Edgell, *The Movement for Community Control of New York City's Schools 1966–1970: Class Wars* (Lewiston, NY: Mellen Press, 1998); Marilyn Gittel, *School Boards and School Policy: An Evaluation of Decentralization in New York City* (New York: Praeger, 1973); Diane Ravitch, *The Great School Wars: A History of the New York City Public Schools* (New York: Basic Books, 1988).

31. Neil Smith, *Gentrification and the Revanchist City* (London: Routledge, 1996).

32. A *squatter* is someone who occupies property without a lease or deed. Some squatters may perceive themselves as renters without leases. When the city's

housing agency wants to evict tenants who do not pay rent, it may brand them as squatters even though the tenants think of themselves as tenants who are being harassed by an irresponsible landlord. See Anders Corr, *No Trespassing: Squatting, Rent Strikes and Land Struggles Worldwide* (Cambridge, MA: South End Press, 1999).

33. *Homesteaders* occupy housing, with or without a legal contract, for the purpose of improving the property and securing a stable form of tenure, usually ownership.

34. Anne Brotherton, "Conflict of Interests, Law Enforcement and Social Change: A Case Study of Squatters on Morningside Heights," Ph.D. dissertation, Fordham University, New York, 1974.

35. Jennifer Steinhauer, "Coming Full Circle, City to Sell Blighted Lots," *New York Times*, August 19, 2005, B1, B6.

36. Walter Thabit, *How East New York Became a Ghetto* (New York: New York University Press, 2003), 205–214.

37. Smith, *Gentrification*, 210–232; Janet Abu-Lughod, *From Urban Village to East Village* (Oxford: Blackwell, 1994).

38. Rachel Bratt, "Community Development Corporations: Challenges in Supporting a Right to Housing," in Rachel G. Bratt, Michael E. Stone, and Chester Hartman, *A Right to Housing: Foundation for a New Social Agenda* (Philadelphia: Temple University Press, 2006), 340–363.

39. See <http://www.anhd.org>.

40. Randy Stoecker, "Community Development and Community Organizing: Apples and Oranges? Chicken and Egg?," 2001, <http://comm.-org.wisc.edu/drafts/orgdevppr2c.htm>, accessed October 26, 2005.

41. Peter Marcuse, "Neighborhood Policy and the Distribution of Power: New York City's Community Boards," *Policy Studies Journal* 16:2, Winter (1987), 277–289.

42. Downzoning reduces the size of potential development; upzoning increases it.

43. Tom Angotti and Eva Hanhardt (2001) "Problems and Prospects for Healthy Mixed-Use Communities in New York City," *Planning Practice and Research.* 16:2 (2001): 145–154. See also Jacobs, *Death and Life.*

44. Thomas Angotti, <http://www.gothamgazette.com/article/landuse/2004072 0/12/1042>, accessed October 26, 2005. The Manhattan Institute, a leading neoliberal think tank in New York City, reflecting discontent with the environmental impact statement among developers and policy makers, has proposed a major overhaul. Hope Cohen, *Rethinking Environmental Review: A Handbook on What Can Be Done* (New York: Center for Rethinking Development, Manhattan Institute, May 2007), <http://www.manhattan-institute.org/html/rethinking_environmental_review.htm>.

45. Saskia Sassen, *Globalization and Its Discontents* (New York: New Press, 1998).

46. Community-based organizations are often considered part of the amorphous category of *civil society*, part of a third force between the state and private sectors. The role of civil society is critical to any understanding of social and political life, but in the real world, the social and political differences within civil society are so great that the general category is often not helpful. The relationships of different elements in civil society to the state also differ dramatically.

Chapter 4

1. The full name of the original group was Cooper Square Community Development Committee and Businessmen's Association, Inc. It was always commonly known as The Cooper Square Committee. At some point, most likely in the 1970s or early 1980s, it just became the Cooper Square Committee. Throughout the text both names are used; however, when the context is the 1970s and beyond, the shorter name is used.

2. These and the following quotations are from Frances Goldin, interview with Marci Reaven and Tom Angotti, December 1, 2003.

3. The approach used by Christopher Mele in *Selling the Lower East Side: Culture, Real Estate, and Resistance in New York City* (Minneapolis: University of Minnesota Press, 2000), looks at culture and not politics or economics as the most significant factor in neighborhood transformation and thus misses the significance of Cooper Square. Janet Abu-Lughod, *From Urban Vaillage to East Village* (Oxford: Blackwell, 1994), seems to place the criterion for success by community activists so high that only a complete end to gentrification would appear to reach it.

4. Many of the details for this story come from Walter Thabit, "Cooper Square Chronology," unpublished paper, June 1, 2004.

5. Marci Reaven, interview with Walter Thabit, June 27, 2003.

6. Frances Goldin, interview with Marci Reaven and Tom Angotti, December 1, 2003.

7. Cooper Square Community Development Committee and Businessmen's Association, *An Alternate Plan for Cooper Square* (New York: Cooper Square Community Developmoent Committee and Businessmen's Association, 1961).

8. This basic principle of progressive planning may be undermined by current terminology that subverts the progressive focus on human values. Terminology that emphasizes "building assets" or "human capital" in communities suggests that the only way to value humans is to treat them as capital, thereby facilitating the transformation of everything dead and alive into a commodity.

9. An excerpt from an internal staff memorandum reveals the City Planning Department's solidarity with Robert Moses's philosophy of displacement: "The theory that a tenant has an indisputable right to be relocated in new housing within the area from which he has been displaced at prices he can afford is not to be found in the law nor has the city ever implicitly or explicitly committed itself to such a course of action. It is not even good planning." Thabit, *How East*

New York Became a Ghetto. Unfortunately, DCP's approach has not changed much since Moses.

10. Abeles, Schwartz & Associates and Walter Thabit, *Early Action Plan: An Alternate Plan for Cooper Square* (New York: New York City Housing and Development Administration and the Cooper Square Development Committee and Businessmen's Association, 1969).

11. Lower East Side Joint Planning Council, *This Land Is Ours* (New York: Lower East Side Joint Planning Council, March 1984).

12. Today, after several privatization pushes and the Giuliani administration's initiative requiring prompt sales of tax-deliquent properties, the alternative management programs are mostly history.

13. Community Service Society, *Balancing Acts: The Experience of Mutual Housing Associations and Community Land Trusts in Urban Neighborhoods* (New York: Community Service Society, 1996).

14. Tom Angotti with Cecilia Jagu, *Community Land Trusts and Low-Income Multifamily Rental Housing* (Cambridge, MA: Lincoln Institute of Land Policy, 2006).

15. Goldin ran for office on the same ticket with DuBois.

16. We Stay! ¡Nos Quedamos¡ is located at 811 Courtlandt Avenue, Bronx, NY 10451, telephone 718 585 2323, fax 718 585 8628, e-mail quedamos@aol .com.

17. The new development will be a pilot project in the recently initiated program by the United States Green Building Council (http://www.usgbc.org) to provide LEED certification for neighborhood development and not just individual buildings. LEED stands for Leadership in Energy and Environmental Design. Information on the We Stay! project is at http://www.sustainable.org/ casestudies/newyork/NY_af_melrose.

18. See Jill Jonnes, *South Bronx Rising* (New York: Fordham University P:ress, 2002).

19. Ibid.

20. Jocelyne Chait, Margeret E. Seip, and Petr Stand, *Achieving a Balance: Housing and Open Space in Bronx Community District 3* (New York: Design Trust for Public Space, 2000).

Chapter 5

1. Locally unwanted land uses (LULUs) include waste-transfer stations, bus depots, highways, and waste-treatment plants.

2. Juliana Maantay, "Race and Waste: Options for Equity Planning in New York City," *Planners Network* 145 (January–February 2001): 1, 6–10.

3. See Peter Bachrach and Morton Baratz, "Two Faces of Power," *American Political Science Review* 52 (December 1962): 947–952.

4. A leading urban planning text makes this facile equation. See Edward J. Kaiser, David R. Godschalk, and F. Stuart Chapin Jr., *Urban Land Use Planning* (Urbana: University of Illinois Press, 1995), 26.

5. Jason Corburn, *Street Science* (Cambridge, MA: MIT Press, 2005).

6. United Church of Christ Commission for Racial Justice, *Toxic Wastes and Race in the United States* (New York: United Church of Christ, 1987).

7. See Robert W. Collin, Timothy Beatley, and William Harris, "Environmental Racism: A Challenge to Community Development," *Journal of Black Studies* 25:3 (January 1995): 354–376; Michael K. Heiman, ed., "Race, Waste, and Class: New Perspectives on Environmental Justice," *Antipode* (special issue) 28:2 (1996).

8. Julian Agyeman, Robert D. Bullard, and Bob Evans, *Just Sustainabilities: Development in an Unequal World* (Cambridge, MA: MIT Press, 2003), 1–80.

9. This overview of the environmental justice movement in New York City benefits substantially from the excellent analysis by Julie Sze in *Noxious New York: The Racial Politics of Urban Health and Environmental Justice* (Cambridge, MA: MIT Press, 2006).

10. Robert Caro, *The Power Broker: Robert Moses and the Fall of New York* (New York: Vintage, 1975), 510–513.

11. Anthony DePalma, "State Leads in Ill Effects from Diesels, Report Says," *New York Times.* February 23, 2005, <http://www.nytimes.com/2005/02/23/nyregion/23diesel.html?ex=1132722000&en=4985b8b42545503f&ei=5070>, accessed November 12, 2005.

12. <http://www.weact.org>.

13. West Harlem Environmental Action, *Harlem on the River*, report prepared by Mitchell J. Silver of Abeles Phillips Preiss & Shapiro, December 4, 1999.

14. Tom Angotti, "The Filtration Plant Deal in the Bronx: Flawed Planning, Environmental Injustice," *Gotham Gazette* (November 2004), <http://www.gothamgazette.com/article/landuse/20041115/12/1179>.

15. <http://222.thepoint.org>, <http://www.ssbx.org>.

16. See Douglas Gillison, "The Other Black Sea," *Village Voice,* March 31–April 6, 2004, 22; Nicholas Confessore, "Cuomo Moves toward Lawsuit over a Fifty-Year-Old Oil Spill in Greenpoint," *New York Times.* February 9, 2007, B1, B8.

17. Benjamin Miller, *Fat of the Land* (New York: Four Walls Eight Windows, 2000), 200, 262–278.

18. A similar struggle was successfully waged in Los Angeles. See Louis Blumberg and Robert Gottlieb, *War on Waste* (Washington, DC: Island Press, 1989).

19. Matthew Gandy, *Concrete and Clay: Reworking Nature in New York City* (Cambridge, MA: MIT Press, 2002), 193–210.

20. Corburn, *Street Science.*

21. This was in keeping with a long tradition of the city's evasion of environmental laws and forced compliance by the courts. In 1888, a court forced the city to stop dumping garbage in the ocean.

22. For an analysis of how the public relations industry soft-sells environmental hazards, see John C. Stauber and Sheldon Rampton, *Toxic Sludge Is Good for You* (Monroe, ME: Common Courage Press, 1995), 99–122.

23. Miller, *Fat of the Land*.

24. Sam Williams, "Sludge and Scandal," *Gotham Gazette* (February 2004, <http://www.gothamgazette.com/article/environment/20040212/7/869>.

25. Kemba Johnson, "Green with Envy," *City Limits* (January 2000):16.

26. See Lis Harris, *Tilting at Mills: Green Dreams, Dirty Dealings, and the Corporate Squeeze* (Boston: Houghton Mifflin, 2003), and Allen Hershkowitz, *Bronx Ecology: Blueprint for a New Environmentalism* (Washington, DC: Island Press, 2003).

27. I was also an OWN member, representing Planners Network, the organization of progressive urban planners.

28. Susan Strasser, *Waste and Want* (New York: Holt, 1999).

29. See <http://www.waterwire.net/News/fullstory.cfm?ContID=1356>.

30. Eddie Bautista, *Taking Out the Garbage* (New York: New York Lawyers for the Public Interest, n.d.). This document provides an excellent synthesis of information and analysis of events, which I have relied on here, in addition to my direct involvement as a member of OWN.

31. As quoted in David Naguib Pellow, *Garbage Wars: The Struggle for Environmental Justice in Chicago* (Cambridge, MA: MIT Press, 2002), 135.

32. OWN/Consumers Union, *Taking Out the Trash*, <http://www.consumersunion.org/other/trash/about.htm>.

33. Winne Hu, "City Council Backs Mayor's Trash Disposal Plan," *New York Times*, July 20, 2006, B1, B5.

34. Bautista, *Taking Out the Garbage*.

35. Independent Budget Office, "Closing Fresh Kills Means Mounting Costs to Dispose of New York City's Garbage," February 5, 2001; Independent Budget Office, "Under New Plan Cost of Disposing Curbside Waste Grows, for Now," June 2, 2005.

36. Eric Lipton, "City Seeks Ideas as Trash Costs Dwarf Estimate," *New York Times*, December 2, 2003, B1, B7.

37. Richard Perez-Peña, "State Admits Plants Headed to Poor Areas," *New York Times*, March 15, 2001, B1.

38. Sze, *Noxious New York*, 163.

39. Omar Freilla, "Burying Robert Moses' Legacy in New York City," in Robert D. Bullard, Glenn S. Johnson, and Angel O.Torres, eds., *Highway Robbery: Transportation Racism and New Routes to Equity* (Cambridge, MA: South End Press, 2004), 75–96. See also Robert D. Bullard and Glenn S. Johnson, eds., *Just*

Transportation: Dismantling Race and Class Barriers to Mobility (Gabriola Island, BC: New Society, 1997).

40. Aaron Naparstek, "Traffic against the People: New York City's Transportation Planners Move Cars at All Costs," *Progressive Planning* 160 (Summer 2004): 18–20.

41. <http://www.tstc.org>.

42. Asthma is a complex respiratory syndrome with many potential causes. Indoor air quality is also a likely trigger for asthma. In tightly sealed apartments and work environments, cockroaches and vermin can degrade air quality and make people's respiratory systems vulnerable to disease.

43. Jason Corburn, "Confronting the Challenges in Reconnecting Urban Planning and Public Health," *American Journal of Public Health* 94:4 (2004): 541–546.

Chapter 6

1. For a review of community planning in the 1980s, see Municipal Art Society, *The Will to Plan: Community-Initiated Planning in New York City* (New York: Municipal Art Society, n.d.).

2. Beverly Moss Spatt, *A Proposal to Change the Structure of City Planning* (New York: Praeger, 1971).

3. From the day David Dinkins took office, the media fixated on details of his personal life as they had done with no other mayor. They would later overlook Rudolph Giuliani's marital problems, weird habits (like dressing in drag and imitating a Mafia don), and personal discomfort in the presence of black people (as commented on by, among others, Giuliani's ally Calvin Butts, minister of the Abysinnian Baptist Church in Harlem). See Wayne Barrett, *Rudy! An Investigative Biography of Rudolph Giuliani* (New York: Basic Books, 2000).

4. City of New York City Planning Commission, *Rules for the Processing of Plans Pursuant to Charter Section 197-a* (New York: City of New York, 1991).

5. All quotes from ibid.

6. Borough of the Bronx Community Board 3, *Partnership for the Future: A 197-a Plan for the Revitalization of Bronx Community District #3* (New York: City of New York, 1993).

7. A review of the earliest 197a plans may be found in the report by the Municipal Art Society Planning Center, *The State of 197-a Planning in New York City* (New York: Municipal Art Society Planning Center, 1998), and Thomas Angotti, "New York City's '197-a' Community Planning Experience: Power to the People or Less Work for Planners?," *Planning Practice and Research* 12:1 (1997): 59–67.

8. Interview with Eugenia Flatow, November 12, 2004.

9. Phone interview with John Dudley, August 26, 2004.

10. The Planning Center Briefing Book on community plans is at <http://www. mas.org>. See also the fall 2002 issue of *The Livable City* by the Municipal Art Society. It is significant that it took the nonprofit MAS to assemble the first collection of community plans, a task that would be expected to be a priorty for the agency that is responsible for planning in the city. While the Department of City Planning's Web site allows for the retrieval of up-to-date information on zoning and land use, it does not list community plans in one place, and approved 197a plans are not accessible on-line.

11. Municipal Art Society, *The Will to Plan*, 11–13; Susan Saegert et al., "The Promise and Challenges of Co-ops in a Hot Real Estate Market," *Shelterforce* 142 (July–August 2005): 16–18.

12. "A Fight for Ethnic Survival," *Street: Magazine of the Environment*, Summer-Fall 1973, reprinted in Tom Angotti, ed., *Lessons in Community-Based Planning: The Case of Red Hook* (New York: Pratt Institute Graduate Center for Planning and the Environment, 1999), 17–19.

13. I was a senior planner in the Brooklyn office of the Department of City Planning, worked on the waterfront plan, and later helped in the preparation of the community plan.

14. Community Board 6, *Red Hook: A Plan for Community Regeneration* (Brooklyn: Community Board 6, 1994).

15. Joe Sexton, "Residents of a Brooklyn Enclave Create Own Urban Renewal Plan," *New York Times*, January 29, 1995, 1.

16. *Coalition to Revitalize Our Waterfront Now v. City of New York*, 101955 N.Y. Supreme Court (2005); Tom Angotti, "Ikea and Red Hook's Racial Divide," *Gotham Gazette* (June 2004), <http://www.gothamgazette.com/article/landuse/2 0040615/12/1008>.

17. Joseph Berger and Charles V. Bagli, "For Whom Will the Foghorn Blow?," *New York Times*. January 19, 2006, B1, B7.

18. <http://www.nyc.gov/planyc2030>.

19. Eddie Bautista, "An Organizer's Story," in Angotti, *Lessons in Community-Based Planning*, 9–15.

20. Leah Kreger, "Affordable Housing: A Community United?," *Brooklyn Rail* (March 2007, 1. See also North Brooklyn Alliance, <http://www.northbrook-lynalliance.org>.

21. Tom Angotti and Eva Hanhardt, "Problems and Prospects for Health Mixed-Use Communities in New York City," *Planning Practice and Research* 16:2 (2001): 145–154.

22. For example, a vocal group of white Greenpoint residents prevented the renovation and reopening of a public recreation area based on racially charged concerns about unruly children who would use the facilities. See Vojislava Filipcevic, *Participatory Planning and Community Conflict in a New York City Neighborhood: An Analysis of the Greenpoint 197-a Planning Process* (New York: Pratt Institute Graduate Center for Planning and the Environment, Demonstration of Professional Competence, 1999).

23. "Manhattanville Special," *West Harlem Herald* (Fall 2006).

24. Lewis D. Hopkins and Marisa A. Zapata, eds., *Engaging the Future: Forecasts, Scenarios, Plans, and Projects* (Cambridge, MA: Lincoln Institute of Land Policy, 2007). For a critique of strategic planning, see Otília Arantes, Carlos Vainer, and Ermínia Maricato, *A Cidade do Pensamento Único* (Petrópolis: Editora Vozes, 2000).

25. *The Livable City* (2002): 5.

26. New York City Economic Development Corporation, *Sherman Creek: Planning Workshop Synopsis/Sinopsis del Taller de Planificación* (New York: Economic Development Corporation, n.d.).

27. Community Board 2 197a Working Group, *A Community-based Plan for the Old Brooklyn District*, Draft (November 1996).

28. <http://www.izny.org>.

29. Robert F. Worth, "Agency Adopts Park Plan for Brooklyn Waterfront," *New York Times*, July 27, 2005, B3.

30. In 2007, Janette Sadik-Kahn, a TA supporter and bicyclist, was appointed DOT Commissioner and began to introduce changes in staff and city transportation policies.

31. Paul S. White, "The Politics of Fear and the Specter of Traffic Gridlock," *Transportation Alternatives Magazine* 10:4 (Fall 2004): 3.

32. Tom Angotti, "Long Commutes and Lost Opportunities for Planning," *Gotham Gazette* (March 2004), <http://www.gothamgazette.com/article/landus e/20040317/12/916>. See <http://www.vision42.org> on the 42nd Street light rail proposal.

Chapter 7

1. Today, when many of the excluded are not United States citizens and some are not legal residents, the term can be used in a negative way to exclude people from power. A more inclusive use of the term, however, is common among human rights advocates. To avoid confusion, I avoid use of the term *citizen*.

2. Daniel Patrick Moynihan, *Maximim Feasible Misunderstanding: Community Action in the War on Poverty* (New York: Free Press, 1970).

3. Alexis De Tocqueville, *Democracy in America* (New York: Mentor, 1956); Robert D. Putnam, *Bowling Alone: The Collapse and Revival of American Community* (New York: Simon & Schuster, 2001); Robert D. Putnam with Robert Leonardi and Rafaella Nanetti, *Making Democracy Work* (Princeton: Princeton University Press, 1994).

4. Michael Parenti, *Democracy for the Few* (Boston: Bedford/St. Martin's, 2002); Greg Palast, *The Best Democracy Money Can Buy* (New York: Plume, 2003).

5. See my articles "Zoning Instead of Planning in Greenpoint/Williamsburg," *Gotham Gazette* (May 2005), <htgtp://www.gothamgazette.com/article/landuse

/20050517/12/1419>, and "Rezoning Proposals Squeeze Out Affordable Housing from Both Ends," *Gotham Gazette* (October 2004), <http://www.gothamgazette .com/article/landuse/20041007/12/1140>, accessed August 10, 2005.

6. Angotti, "Rezoning Proposals Squeeze Out Affordable Housing."

7. Interview with Bernard Haber, October 15, 2005.

8. Arnstein's ladder is really more like a pyramid. Sherry Arnstein, "A Ladder of Citizen Participation," *Journal of American Institute of Planners* 8:4 (1969): 216–224.

9. Tom Angotti, *Metropolis 2000: Planning, Poverty and Politics* (New York: Routledge, 1993), 36–71; Jane Jacobs, *The Death and Life of Great American Cities* (New York : Vintage, 1961), introduction.

10. A third building collapsed and other buildings were so damaged or contaminated they had to be demolished.

11. Real Estate Board of New York, *Key Principles in Rebuilding Lower Manhattan* (New York: REBNY, n.d.).

12. Real Estate Board of New York, "REBNY: Celebrating Signs of Renewal," *New York Times*, advertisement, January 15, 2004, C15.

13. As quoted in Deborah Solomon, "From the Rubble, Ideas for Rebirth," *New York Times*, September 30, 2001, E37.

14. Neil Smith, "Scales of Terror: The Manufacturing of Nationalism and the War for U.S. Globalism," in Michael Sorkin and Sharon Zukin, eds., *After the World Trade Center: Rethinking New York City* (New York: Routledge, 2002), 97–108.

15. Margarita Gutman provides an excellent summary of the early opinions, particularly those expressed through coverage in the *New York Times*, in "El Futuro urbano en la arena pública," *New York: El Futur de Manhattan*: Forum Universal de les Cultures Barcelona 2004, Collegi Oficial d'Arquitectes de Cata-lunya, 25 de Juny de 2002 (Barcelona, Spain), 1–22. See also Arielle Goldberg, "Civic Engagement in the Rebuilding of the World Trade Center," in John Mollenkopf, ed., *Contentious City: The Politics of Recovery in New York City* (New York: Russell Sage Foundation, 2005), 112–139.

16. Municipal Art Society, *Imagine New York: The People's Visions. Summary Report* (New York: Municipal Art Society, 2002).

17. Sascha Brodsky, "Chinatown Still Hurting after 9/11, Report Says," *Downtown Express*, April 10, 2002.

18. See <http://www.voicesofsept11.org>, <http://www.peacesfultomorrow .org>, and <http://www.coalitionof911families.org>.

19. Tom Angotti, "The Make-up of the Lower Manhattan Redevelopment Corporation," *Gotham Gazette* (December 2001), <http://www.gothamgazette.com/ landuse/dec.01.shtml>, accessed August 10, 2005.

20. Ada Louise Huxtable, " 'Downtown' Is More Than Ground Zero," *Wall Street Journal*, August 7, 2002, <http://online.wsj.com/article/ 0,,SB1028674214132736120.djm,00.html>, accessed August 15, 2002.

21. Civic Alliance to Rebuild Downtown, *Listening to the City: Report of the Proceedings* New York: Civic Alliance to Rebuild Downtown, 2002).

22. Ibid., 11.

23. Ibid., 21.

24. "A Living Memorial," *Wall Street Journal*, September 11, 2002, A14.

25. Civic Alliance to Rebuild Downtown, *Listening to the City*, 13.

26. Herbert Muschamp, "Don't Rebuild, Reimagine," *New York Times Magazine*, September 8, 2002, 46–60, 63.

27. David W. Dunlap, "Unheard Voices on Planning New Trade Center," *New York Times*, October 16, 2003, B3.

28. Peter Marcuse, "Designing without a Plan," *Progressive Planning* 154 (Winter 2003): 1, 10–13.

29. Charles V. Bagli and Edward Wyatt, "At Helm of Trade Center Site, as He Always Planned to Be," *New York Times*, July 21, 2003, <http://www.nytimes.com/2003/07/21nyregion/21SILV.html>, accessed July 21, 2003.

30. Edward Wyatt, "Design Team for Trade Center Reveals a Revised Master Plan," *New York Times*, September 18, 2003, B1.

31. Mike Kelly, "Dissent at Ground Zero," 2005, <http://www.voicesofsept11.org/groundzero/080205.htm>, accessed August 8, 2005.

32. <http://www.coalitionof911families.org>.

33. Erin Chan, "Grief Aside, Some Memorials Are More Equal Than Others," *New York Times*, September 28, 2003, B5. In November 2006, a small permanent memorial opened at a waterfront location near the crash site.

34. Jennifer Steinhauer, "Mayor's Proposal Envisions Lower Manhattan as an Urban Hamlet," *New York Times*, December 13, 2002, B3.

35. Edward Wyatt, "City Is Seeking Bigger Role in Rebuilding," *New York Times*, March ·*, 2003, B1.

36. Bagli and Wyatt, "At Helm of Trade Center Site."

37. Jack Newfield and Paul DuBrul, *The Abuse of Power: The Permanent Government and the Fall of New York* (New York: Viking Press, 1977), 88.

38. Carol Willis, ed., *The Lower Manhattan Plan: The 1966 Vision for Downtown New York* (New York: Princeton Architectural Press, 2002). See also Eric Darnton, *Divided We Stand* (New York: Basic Books, 1999); Angus Kress Gillespie, *Twin Towers: The Life of New York City's World Trade Center* (New York: New American Library, 2002); and the fine collection of essays in Sorkin and Zukin, *After the World Trade Center*.

39. Robert D. Yaro and Tony Hiss, *A Region at Risk* (Washington, DC: Island Press,1996).

40. Charles V. Bagli, "As Companies Scatter, Doubts on Return of Financial District," *New York Times*. September 16, 2002, B1, B6.

41. Tomas Kellner and Brett Nelson, "A Tempest over $21 Billion," *Forbes*, May 27, 2002, 113–114, 116, 121–122.

42. Carolyn Maloney, "Where's Our $21 Billion?," *Gotham Gazette* (June 2004), <http://www.gothamgazette.com/article/20040628/202/1017>.

43. Charles V. Bagli, (2003) "Plans to Use Tax-Free Bonds for Midtown Tower Cause a Stir," *New York Times.* September 5, 2003, B3.

44. Good Jobs New York and Fiscal Policy Institute, *Breakdown of the Community Development Block Grant Funds Allocated as of March 16, 2004* (New York: Good Jobs New York and Fiscal Policy Institute, 2004).

45. See Juan González, *Fallout* (New York: New Press, 2002).

46. Kirk Johnson, "Federal Study Shows High Number of Ground Zero Workers Had Health Problems Last Year," *New York Times.* January 28, 2003, B4.

47. Fear has always been an element in U.S. urban planning, a reflection of militarism in national policy and a lengthy history of slavery and racial apartheid. The interstate highway system, arguably the country's largest public works project, is the backbone of the U.S. metropolis. It was first called the *Defense Highway System* because it was to disperse industry and the population to minimize the impact of a nuclear attack on the United States. White fears of blacks and new immigrants accompanied suburban sprawl and locked people in their cars and private homes away from urban spaces. Fear was also used to rationalize the concentration and isolation of high-density central cities, both in upscale enclaves and low-income communities of color.

48. Oscar Newman, *Defensible Space: Crime Prevention through Urban Design* (New York: Macmillan, 1972). See also John R. Aiello and Andrew Baum, eds., *Residential Crowding and Design* (New York: Plenum, 1979).

49. New York Civil Liberties Union, *Arresting Protest* (New York: NYCLU, 2003); New York Civil Liberaties Union, *Who's Watching: Video Camera Surveillance in New York City and the Need for Public Oversight.* (New York: NYCLU, 2006).

50. Setha M. Low, "Spaces of Reflection, Recovery, and Resistance: Reimagining the Postindustrial Plaza," in Sorkin and Zukin, *After the World Trade Center*, 163–172; and Neil Smith, *Gentrification and the Revanchist City* (London: Routledge, 1996).

51. Art Commission of the City of New York, *Designing for Security: Using Art and Design to Improve Security* (New York: Art Commission of the City of New York, 2002).

52. David W. Dunlap, (2004), "The Streets (around Wall Street) Belong to the People," *New York Times* , April 1, 2004, B3.

53. As quoted in David W. Dunlap, "Envisioning a Safer City without Turning It into Slab City," *New York Times.* April 17, 2003, D3.

54. One of the Police Department's midtown Manhattan precincts has also begun to play a central role in the design and management of the traffic network. It persuaded the city to erect iron barriers to prevent pedestrians from jaywalking in areas with maximum pedestrian density. Advocacy groups like Transportation Alternatives instead called for traffic reduction, widening of sidewalks, and traffic-calming measures.

55. Patrick D. Healy and Charles V. Bagli, "Pataki and Bloomberg Endorse Changes in Ground Zero Tower," *New York Times*. May 5, 2005, A1, B8.

56. For an analysis and critique of "broken windows," see Bernard E. Harcourt, *Illusion of Order: The False Promise of Broken Windows* (Cambridge, MA: Harvard University Press, 2001).

57. The inventors of this concept are Noam Chomsky and Edward S. Herman in their *Manufacturing Consent: The Political Economy of the Mass Media* (New York: Pantheon, 2002).

58. Wayne Barrett, *Rudy! An Investigative Biography of Rudolph Giuliani* (New York: Basic Books, 2000).

59. Baker also notes: "Giuliani's two terms as mayor are the only elective office he has ever held, and true to the postideological politics of the 1990s, he achieved almost nothing of significance in that time." Kevin Baker, "A Fate Worse Than Bush: Rudolph Giuliani and the Politics of Personality," *Harper's* 315 (August 2007): 31–39.

60. Wayne Barrett, "Five Big Lies about 9/11," *Village Voice* 52:32, August 8, 2007, 23 ff.

61. Eduardo Galeano, *El Teatro del Bien y el Mal* (Montevideo, Uruguay: Brecha, 2001), published in English as *The Theater of Good and Evil*, <http: www.zmag.org>, September 21, 2001.

62. See Jason Hackworth, *The Neoliberal City: Governance, Ideology and Development in American Urbanism* (Ithaca, NY: Cornell University Press, 2007).

63. See <http://www.nyc.gov/html/dcp/html/hyards>, For analysis of Midtown West and the Hell's Kitchen area, see Steven L. Newman Real Estate Institute, "West Side Story," *Properties* (Winter 2002).

64. Jonathan Bowles and Joel Kotkin, "Engine Failure," Center for an Urban Future, September 8, 2003, <http://www.nycfuture.org/content/reports/report_view.cfm?repkey+118>.

65. Charles Bagli, "Grand Vision for Remaking the West Side," *New York Times*. February 10, 2003, B1.

66. Phillip Lopate, "A Town Revived, a Villain Redeemed," *New York Times*, City Section, February 11, 2007, 3.

67. The city's Independent Budget Office has called into question whether this would be either feasible or equitable. Independent Budget Office, "Learning from Experience: A Primer on Tax Increment Financing," New York, September 2002. See also National Education Association, *Protecting Public Education from Tax Giveaways to Corporations* , January 2003. Joyce Purnick put her finger on the political issue with PILOTs: they evade City Council involvement. Joyce Purnick, "Pilots That Fly under Radar of the Council," *New York Times*. March 10, 2005.

68. Joanna Cagan and Neil de Mause, *Field of Schemes* (Monroe, ME: Common Courage Press, 1998); Neil de Mause, "If They Build It, You'll Pay," *Village Voice*, March 2–8, 2005, 18–19.

69. See <http://www.helskitchen.net>.

70. The concept of immigrant countries in the city propaganda is revealing. It projects on other countries around the world the way that native New Yorkers see the rest of the world—as sources of immigrants, not as countries with distinct histories, cultures, economies, and livelihoods whether or not their people immigrate. The immigrant country is a truly imperial concept.

71. Quotations from <http://www.nyc2012.com>. There is no mention of the problems of discrimination faced by immigrant communities or violations of basic human rights experienced. The recent case of Amadou Diallo, a West African immigrant who was murdered by police in a hail of bullets while entering his home in the Bronx, is certainly familiar to many black New Yorkers.

72. For more on the Olympics 2012 plan, see New York City, *NYC 2012: The Plan for a New York Olympics Games* (2001), and <http://www.nyc2012.com>. See also Duff Wilson, "City Unveils Its Last and Best Bid to Gain 2012 Summer Olympics," *New York Times*, November 18, 2004, A1, D2.

73. See chapter 2 and Dennis R. Judd and Susan S. Fainstein, eds., *The Tourist City* (New Haven, CT: Yale University Press, 1999).

74. See <http://www.brooklynmatters.com>.

75. Alice is caught up in a giant chess game of powerful players over which she has no control, and the characters she meets talk nonsense. Tom Angotti, "Atlantic Yards: Through the Looking Glass," *Gotham Gazette* (November 2005), <http://www.gothamgazette.com/article/landuse/20051115/12/1654>.

76. See Develop Don't Destroy Brooklyn's website at <http://www.developdontdestroy.org>.

77. The UNITY Plan can be found at <http://www.unityplan.org>. The updated plan was released in September 2007.

78. See the comments by the Council of Brooklyn Neighborhoods on the Draft Scope of Work and the Draft Environmental Impact Statement at <http://www.cbneighborhoods.homestead.com> (prepared by a consultant team that I headed under the Hunter College Center for Community Planning and Development).

79. The first community benefits agreement was developed by the Figueroa Corridor Coalition in Los Angeles. See Jacqueline Leavitt, "Linking Housing to Community Economic Development with Community Benefits Agreements: The Case of the Figueroa Corridor Coalition for Economic Justice," in Paul Ong and Anastasia Loukaitou-Sideris, *Jobs and Economic Development in Minority Communities* (Philadelphia: Temple Universtiy Press, 2006), 257–276. See Good Jobs New York at <http://www.goodjobsny.org/cba.htm>.

80. Nicholas Confessore, "Perspectives on the Atlantic Yards Development through the Prism of Race," *New York Times* , November 12, 2006, 35–36.

81. Interview with Bob Law by Isabel Hill, November 2006.

82. Tom Angotti and Steven Romalewski, *Willets Point Land Use Study* (New York: Hunter College Center for Community Planning and Development, 2006).

83. See <http://www.gothamgazette.com/article/Land%20Use/200511213/12/1680>.

Chapter 8

1. Walter Thabit, "Planning and Advocacy," comments prepared for the Planners Network Conference, New York, 2004, where Thabit was recognized as a Pioneer of Advocacy Planning.

2. Some recent thinking on comprehensive liberal reform in New York City may be found in John Mollenkopf and Ken Emerson, eds., *Rethinking the Urban Agenda: Reinvigorating the Liberal Tradition in New York City and Urban America* (New York: Century Foundation Press, 2001); Mike Wallace, *A New Deal for New York* (New York: Bell & Weiland, 2002). More progressive approaches that address structural issues of race and class in a comprehensive way and across sectors of the economy and society have yet to be constructed.

3. See <http://www.nyc.gov/Planyc2030>; Tom Angotti, "Atlantic Yards and the Sustainability Test," *Gotham Gazette* (June 2007), <http://www.gothamgazette.com/article/landuse/20070605/12/2197>.

4. Steven Greenhouse, "Foes Dig In as Wal-Mart Aims for City," *New York Times*. February 10, 2005, A1. See <Wal-MartNoWay.org>.

5. Janny Scott, "Lower-Priced Housing Is Vanishing at a Faster Pace," *New York Times*. May 27, 2006, B3.

6. Matthew Gandy, *Concrete and Clay: Reworking Nature in New York City* (Cambridge, MA: MIT Press, 2002), 19–75.

7. Nearly half of New York City's elementary school students are overweight or obese, a higher rate than in the nation as a whole. The rate of school students who are obese is 24 percent, but the rate is 31 percent among Latino children. Richard Pérez-Peña, "Obesity on Rise in New York Public Schools," *New York Times*. July 9, 2003, B1, B6.

8. See the special issue on "Planning for the Active City," *Progressive Planning* 157 (Fall 2003).

9. Tom Angotti, "Setting Standards for Green Neighborhoods," *Gotham Gazette*, January 2008. <http://www.gothamgazette.com/article/landuse/200801 09/12/2397>.

GreenHome (<http://www.greenhomenyc.org>) is a group that advocates the greening of both individual buildings and the city.

10. Jason Corburn, "Confronting the Challenges in Reconnecting Urban Planning and Public Health," *American Journal of Public Health* 94 (2004): 541–546; Jason Corburn, "Urban Planning and Health Disparities: Implications for Research and Practice," *Planning Practice and Research* 20:2 (2005): 111–126.

11. The Campaign to Stop Killer Coke is at <http://www.killercoke.org>, and the Campaign to Label Genetically Engineered Foods is at <http://www.thecampaign.org>.

12. For a basic explanation of how a land trust works, see Robert Swann, "The Community Land Trust," in Peter Barnes, ed., *The People's Land: A Reader on Land Reform in the United States* (Emmaus, PA: Rodale Press, 1975), 215–217.

13. Rosalind Greenstein and Yesim Suyngu-Eryilmaz, "Community Land Trusts: Leasing Land for Affordable Housing," *Land Lines* (April 2005): 8–10.

14. Tom Angotti with Cecilia Jagu, *Community Land Trusts and Low-Income Multifamily Rental Housing* (Cambridge, MA: Lincoln Institute of Land Policy, 2006).

15. See Peter Medoff and Holy Sklar, *Streets of Hope* (Boston: South End Press, 1994).

16. Gus Newport, "The CLT Model: A Tool for Permanently Affordable Housing and Wealth Generation," *Poverty and Race* 14:1 (January–February 2005): 11–13.

17. Andre Gorz, *Ecology as Politics* (Boston: South End Press, 1980), 133.

18. Tom Angotti and Julie Sze, "Environmental Justice and Transdisciplinary Urban Health Research and Policy in the United States," forthcoming, in Nicholas Freudenberg, Susan Klitzman, and Susan Saegert, eds., *Urban Health: Interdisciplinary Approaches to Research and Practice* (San Francisco: Jossey-Bass Publishers).

19. Municipal Art Society Planning Center, *Livable Neighborhoods for a Livable City: Policy Recommendations to Strengthen Community-Based Planning in New York City* (New York: Municipal Art Society Planning Center, 2005).

20. See Boaventura de Sousa Santos, "Participatory Budgeting in Porto Alegre: Toward a Redistributive Democracy," *Politics and Society* 26:4 (December 1998): 461–510.

21. Peter Newman and Andy Thornley, *Urban Planning in Europe: International Competition, National Systems and Planning Projects* (London: Routledge, 1996).

22. William A. Johnson Jr., "Rochester: The Path Less Traveled," *Planners Network* 148 (July–August 2001): 1, 14–15.

23. Personal interviews with City Council member Richard Conlin and Karma Ruder, director of the Seattle Neighborhood Planning Office in 1999. See also Jim Diers, *Neighbor Power: Building Community the Seattle Way* (Seattle: University of Washington Press, 2004).

24. See <http://www.plannersnetwork.org>.

25. For examples, see James L. DeFillipis, "Community-Based Participatory Research: Changing Scientific Practice from Research on Communities to Research with and for Communities," *Local Environment* 11:3 (June 2004): 329–338.

26. Chester Hartman and Gregory D. Squires, eds., *There Is No Such Thing as a Natural Disaster* (New York: Routledge, 2006).

Selected Bibliography

Abu-Lughod, Janet. *From Urban Village to East Village*. Oxford: Blackwell, 1994.

Agyeman, Julian, Robert D. Bullard, and Bob Evans, eds. *Just Sustainabilities: Development in an Unequal World*. Cambridge, MA: MIT Press, 2003.

Alcaly, Roger E., and David Mermelstein. *The Fiscal Crisis of American Cities*. New York: Vintage, 1977.

Anbinder, Tyler. *Five Points*. New York: Plume, 2001.

Angotti, Thomas. *Metropolis 2000: Planning, Poverty and Politics*. New York: Routledge, 1993.

Angotti, Tom, ed. *Lessons in Community-based Planning: The Case of Red Hook*. New York: Pratt Institute Graduate Center for Planning and the Environment, 1999.

Arnstein, Sherry. "A Ladder of Citizen Participation." *Journal of the American Institute of Planners* 8:4 (July 1969): 216–224.

Barrett, Wayne. *Rudy! An Investigative Biography of Rudolph Giuliani*. New York: Basic Books, 2000.

Bellush, Jewel, and Dick Netzer, eds. *Urban Politics New York Style*. Armonk, NY: Sharpe, 1990.

Berman, Marshall. *All That Is Solid Melts into Air*. New York: Penguin, 1988.

Blumberg, Louis, and Gottlieb, Robert. *War on Waste*. Washington, DC: Island Press, 1989.

Borroughs, Edwin, and Mike Wallace. *Gotham: The History of New York City to 1898*. Oxford: Oxford University Press, 1999.

Bratt, Rachel G., Michael E. Stone, and Chester Hartman, eds. *A Right to Housing: Foundation for a New Social Agenda*. Philadelphia: Temple University Press, 2006.

Bressi, Todd, ed. *Planning and Zoning in New York City*. New Brunswick, NJ: Rutgers University Center for Urban Policy Research, 1993.

Burghardt, Stephen, ed. *Tenants and the Housing Crisis*. Dexter, MI: New Press, 1972.

Cagan, Joanna, and Neil de Mause. *Field of Schemes*. Monroe, ME: Common Courage Press, 1998.

Caro, Robert. *The Power Broker: Robert Moses and the Fall of New York*. New York: Vintage, 1975.

Community-Based Planning Task Force. *Liveable Neighborhoods for a Livable City: Policy Recommendations to Strengthen Community-Based Planning in New York City*. New York: Municipal Art Society Planning Center, 2005.

Corburn, Jason. *Street Science*. Cambridge, MA: MIT Press, 2005.

Cordero-Guzmán, Héctor, Robert C. Smith, and Ramón Grosfoguel. *Migration, Transnationalization and Race in a Changing New York*. Philadelphia: Temple University Press, 2001.

Cox, Oliver C. *Caste, Class and Race*. New York: Monthly Review Press, 1948.

Danielson, Michael N., and Jameson W. Doig. *New York: The Politics of Urban Regional Development*. Berkeley: University of California Press, 1982.

Davidoff, Paul. "Advocacy and Pluralism in Planning." *Journal of the American Institute of Planners* 31:4 (November 1965): 331–338.

DeFilippis, James. *Unmaking Goliath: Community Control in the Face of Global Capital*. New York: Routledge, 2004.

Delemos, Jamie L. "Community-Based Participatory Research: Changing Scientific Practice from Research on Communities to Research with and for Communities." *Local Environment* 11:3 (June 2006): 329–338.

Diaz, David R. *Barrio Urbanism: Chicanos, Planning and American Cities*. New York: Routledge, 2005.

Douglass, Frederick. *Black Reconstruction in America, 1860–1880*. New York: Atheneum, 1975.

Fainstein, Susan S. *The City Builders: Property Development in New York and London, 1980–2000*. Lawrence: University of Kansas, 2001.

Fainstein, Susan S. *The City Builders: Property, Politics, and Planning in London and New York*. Oxford: Blackwell, 1994.

Fitch, Robert. *The Assassination of New York*. New York: Routledge, 1993.

Foner, Nancy. *From Ellis Island to JFK: New York's Two Great Waves of Immigration*. New Haven, CT: Yale University Press, 2000.

Freeman, Joshua B. *Working Class New York*. New York: New Press, 2000.

Gandy, Matthew. *Concrete and Clay: Reworking Nature in New York City*. Cambridge, MA: MIT Press, 2002.

George, Henry. *Progress and Poverty*. New York: Schalkenbach Foundation, 1956.

Gratz, Roberta Grandes. *The Living City*. New York: Simon & Schuster, 1989.

Hackworth, Jason. *The Neoliberal City: Governance, Ideology and Development in American Urbanism*. Ithaca: Cornell University Press, 2007.

Hall, Peter. *Great Planning Disasters*. Berkeley: University of California Press, 1980.

Harris, Lis. *Tilting at Mills: Green Dreams, Dirty Dealings, and the Corporate Squeeze*. Boston: Houghton Mifflin, 2003.

Harvey, David. *Spaces of Hope*. Berkeley: University of California Press, 2000.

Hawley, Peter K. *Housing in the Public Domain: The Only Solution*. New York: Metropolitan Council on Housing, 1978.

Hayden, Dolores. *Redesigning the American Dream: The Future of Housing, Work, and Family Life*. New York: W.W. Norton, 1984.

Heiman, Michael K. *The Quiet Evolution: Power, Planning, and Profits in New York State*. New York: Praeger, 1988.

Hershkowitz, Allen. *Bronx Ecology: Blueprint for a New Environmentalism*. Washington, DC: Island Press, 2003.

Hiss, Tony. *The Experience of Place*. New York: Vintage, 1990.

Homefront. *Housing Abandonment in New York City*. New York: Homefront, 1977.

Hood, Clifton. *722 Miles: The Building of the Subways and How They Transformed New York*. Baltimore, MD: Johns Hopkins University Press, 1993.

Jackson, Kenneth T., ed. *The Encyclopedia of New York*. New Haven, CT: Yale University Press, 1995.

Jacobs, Jane. *The Death and Life of Great American Cities*. New York: Vintage, 1961.

Johnson, James Waldon. *Black Manhattan*. New York: Da Capo Press, 1958.

Jonnes, Jill. *South Bronx Rising*. New York: Fordham University Press, 2002.

Judd, Dennis R., and Todd Swanstrom. *City Politics: Private Power and Public Policy*. New York: HarperCollins, 1994.

Judd, Dennis R., and Susan C. Fainstein, eds. *The Tourist City*. New Haven, CT: Yale University Press, 1999.

Katznelson, Ira. *City Trenches: Urban Politics and the Patterning of Class in the United States*. New York: Pantheon, 1981.

Keating, W. Dennis, Michael B. Teitz, and Andrejs Skaburskis. *Rent Control: Regulation and the Rental Housing Market*. New Brunswick, NJ: Rutgers Center for Urban Policy Research, 1998.

Kessner, Thomas. *Capital City: New York City and the Men behind America's Rise to Economic Dominance, 1860–1900*. New York: Simon & Schuster, 2003.

Krumholz, Norman, and John Forester. *Making Equity Planning Work*. Philadelphia: Temple University Press, 1990.

LaDuke, Winona. *All Our Relations*. Cambridge, MA: South End Press, 1999.

Lawson, Ronald. *The Tenant Movement in New York City*. New Brunswick, NJ: Rutgers University Press, 1986.

Lefebvre, Henri. *The Production of Space*. Cambridge, MA: Blackwell, 1991.

Logan, John R., and Harvey L. Molotch. *Urban Fortunes: The Political Economy of Place*. Berkeley: University of California Press, 1987.

Marcuse, Peter. *Housing Abandonment: Does Rent Control Make a Difference?* Washington, DC: Conference on Alternative State and Local Policies, 1982.

Marcuse, Peter. "Housing Policy and the Myth of the Benevolent State." In Rachel G. Bratt, Chester Hartman, and Ann Meyerson, eds., *Critical Perspectives on Housing* (248–263). Philadelphia: Temple University Press, 1986.

Merrifield, Andy. *Dialectical Urbanism: Social Struggles in the Capitalist City*. New York: Monthly Review Press, 2002.

Miller, Benjamin. *Fat of the Land*. New York: Four Walls Eight Windows, 2000.

Mills, C. Wright. *The Power Elite*. London: Oxford University Press, 1956.

Mollenkopf, John Hull. *Phoenix in the Ashes: The Rise and Fall of the Koch Coalition in New York City*. Princeton, NJ: Princeton University Press, 1992.

Mollenkopf, John H., and Manuel Castells, eds. *Dual City: Restructuring New York*. New York: Russell Sage Foundation, 1992.

Mollenkopf, John, and Ken Emerson, eds. *Rethinking the Urban Agenda*. New York: Century Foundation Press, 2001.

Mollenkopf, John, ed. (2005) *Contentious City: The Politics of Recovery in New York City*. New York: Russell Sage Foundation, 2005.

Ong, Paul, and Anastasia Loukaitou-Sideris. *Jobs and Economic Development in Minority Communities*. Philadelphia: Temple University Press, 2006.

Pellow, David Naguib. *Garbage Wars: The Struggle for Environmental Justice in Chicago*. Cambridge, MA: MIT Press, 2002.

Peterman, William. *Neighborhood Planning and Community-Based Development*. Thousand Oaks, CA: Sage, 2000.

Plotkin, Sidney. *Keep Out: The Struggle for Land Use Control*. Berkeley: University of California Press, 1987.

Plunz, Richard. *A History of Housing in New York City*. New York: Columbia University Press, 1990.

Reichl, Alexander. *Reconstructing Times Square: Politics and Culture in Urban Development*. Lawrence: University Press of Kansas, 1999.

Rosenzweig, Roy, and Betsy Blackmar. *A History of Central Park: The Park and the People*. New York: Holt, 1994.

Rubin, Herbert J. *Renewing Hope within Neighborhoods of Despair*. Albany: State University of New York Press, 2000.

Sandercock, Leonie, ed. *Making the Invisible Visible: A Multicultural Planning History*. Berkeley: University of California Press, 1998a.

Sandercock, Leonie. *Towards Cosmopolis: Planning for Multicultural Cities*. Chichester: Wiley, 1998b.

Schill, Michael H., ed. *Housing and Community Development in New York City.* Albany: State University of New York Press, 1999.

Sites, William. *Remaking New York: Primitive Globalization and the Politics of Urban Community.* Minneapolis: University of Minnesota Press, 2003.

Smith, Neil. *Gentrification and the Revanchist City.* London: Routledge, 1996.

Sorkin, Michael, and Sharon Zukin, eds. *After the World Trade Center: Rethinking New York City.* New York: Routledge, 2002.

Spatt, Beverly Moss. *A Proposal to Change the Structure of City Planning.* New York: Praeger, 1971.

Strasser, Susan. *Waste and Want.* New York: Holt, 1999.

Sze, Julie. *Noxious New York: The Racial Politics of Urban Health and Environmental Justice.* Cambridge, MA: MIT Press, 2006.

Thabit, Walter. "Planning and Civil Defense." *Journal of the American Institute of Planners* 24:1 (February 1959): 35–39.

Thabit, Walter. *How East New York Became a Ghetto.* New York: New York University Press, 2003.

Torres, Andrés. *Between Melting Pot and Mosaic: African Americans and Puerto Ricans in the New York Political Economy.* Philadephia: Temple University Press, 1995.

Worthy, William. *The Rape of Our Neighborhoods.* New York: Morrow, 1976.

Wright, Gwendolyn. *Building the Dream: A Social History of Housing in America.* Cambridge, MA: MIT Press, 1981.

Yaro, Robert D., and Tony Hiss. *A Region at Risk.* Washington, DC: Island Press, 1996.

Zukin, Sharon. *Landscapes of Power.* Berkeley: University of California Press, 1991.

Index

Urban and Industrial Environments

Series editor: Robert Gottlieb, Henry R. Luce Professor of Urban and Environmental Policy, Occidental College

Steve Lerner, *Diamond: A Struggle for Environmental Justice in Louisiana's Chemical Corridor*

Jason Corburn, *Street Science: Community Knowledge and Environmental Health Justice*

Peggy F. Barlett, ed., *Urban Place: Reconnecting with the Natural World*

David Naguib Pellow and Robert J. Brulle, eds., *Power, Justice, and the Environment: A Critical Appraisal of the Environmental Justice Movement*

Eran Ben-Joseph, *The Code of the City: Standards and the Hidden Language of Place Making*

Nancy J. Myers and Carolyn Raffensperger, eds., *Precautionary Tools for Reshaping Environmental Policy*

Kelly Sims Gallagher, *China Shifts Gears: Automakers, Oil, Pollution, and Development*

Kerry H. Whiteside, *Precautionary Politics: Principle and Practice in Confronting Environmental Risk*

Ronald Sandler and Phaedra C. Pezzullo, eds., *Environmental Justice and Environmentalism: The Social Justice Challenge to the Environmental Movement*

Julie Sze, *Noxious New York: The Racial Politics of Urban Health and Environmental Justice*

Robert D. Bullard, ed., *Growing Smarter: Achieving Livable Communities, Environmental Justice, and Regional Equity*

Ann Rappaport and Sarah Hammond Creighton, *Degrees That Matter: Climate Change and the University*

Michael Egan, *Barry Commoner and the Science of Survival: The Remaking of American Environmentalism*

David J. Hess, *Alternative Pathways in Science and Industry: Activism, Innovation, and the Environment in an Era of Globalization*

Peter F. Cannavò, *The Working Landscape: Founding, Preservation, and the Politics of Place*

Paul Stanton Kibel, ed., *Rivertown: Rethinking Urban Rivers*

Kevin P. Gallagher and Lyuba Zarsky, *The Enclave Economy: Foreign Investment and Sustainable Development in Mexico's Silicon Valley*

David N. Pellow, *Resisting Global Toxics: Transnational Movements for Environmental Justice*

Robert Gottlieb, *Reinventing Los Angeles: Nature and Community in the Global City*

David V. Carruthers, ed., *Environmental Justice in Latin America: Problems, Promise, and Practice*

Tom Angotti, *New York for Sale: Community Planning Confronts Global Real Estate*